Y0-BQN-136

Castles & KINGS

Ontario's Forgotten Palaces

RON BROWN

Polar Bear Press, Toronto

CASTLES & KINGS © 2001 by Ron Brown. All rights reserved. No part of this book may be used or reproduced in any manner whatsoever without prior written permission except in the case of brief quotations embodied in reviews. For information, contact Polar Bear Press, 35 Prince Andrew Place, Toronto, Ontario M3C 2H2

Distributed by
North 49 Books
35 Prince Andrew Place
Toronto, Ontario
M3C 2H2
(416) 449-4000

National Library of Canada Canadian Cataloguing in Publication Data

Brown Ron, 1945-
    Castles & kings: Ontario mansions & the people who lived in them

Includes index.
ISBN 1-896757-16-2

1. Mansions — Ontario — History. 2. Historic buildings — Ontario.
3. Architecture, Domestic — Ontario — History. 4. Rich people — Ontario —
Biography. I. Title

FC 3061.B75 2001   971.3   C2001-930675-X
F1057.B775 2001

2001 02 03 04 10 9 8 7 6 5 4 3 2 1

Printed in Canada

Table of Contents

Castles &
KINGS

102/02/06

Great explorers love Polar Bear Press

DISAPPEARING ONTARIO
by Ron Brown
Images from our vanishing countryside

GHOST RAILWAYS OF ONTARIO VOL. I & II
by Ron Brown
Explore Ontario's forgotten train stations, roundhouses and railroads

GHOST TOWNS OF ONTARIO: A field guide VOL. I & II
by Ron Brown
Ghost towns to explore, how they came to be and where to find them

HAUNTED ONTARIO
by Terry Boyle
Ghostly inns, hotels and other eerie places you can visit

HIDDEN ONTARIO
by Terry Boyle
Secrets of the past

ONTARIO ALBUM
Images of the past from the private files of Terry Boyle & Ron Brown

ONTARIO MEMORIES
by Terry Boyle
Uncover the fascinating past of 73 communities we call home

ONTARIO'S VANISHED VILLAGES
by Ron Brown
Discover whistlestops, old mills, lost hamlets, relics and ruins of Ontario

TORONTO'S LOST VILLAGES
by Ron Brown
Discover a Toronto you never knew

Introduction

Most dictionaries define "castle" as a "stronghold", or "fortified mansion." The name comes from the Latin, "castrum" which means a fortified military camp surrounded by a stockade and ditch. While Ontario's many fascinating castles never played this military role, they do represent the evolution of the castle from fort to grand home.

During Europe's Middle Ages, local power rested with lords or princes, most of whom had their own collection of knights to go to war for them. To protect themselves, these warlords battened themselves down in well fortified structures. The largest of these could be small towns unto themselves, self-sustaining, with huts for the serfs and churches in which to praise God. Typically, these castles consisted of curtained walls, supplemented by crenellated battlements, with frequent arrow slits in them, in other words, the castles which we see pictured in the European travel guides.

But with the arrival of the industrial age, and national armies, the castle's military role became redundant. Owners of older castles converted them to residences, while the newly wealthy landowners built copies. Even the world's most recognizable castle, King Ludwig's Neuchwanstein Castle, the inspiration for Disney's "Sleeping Beauty" castle, was a relatively recent phenomenon. Built in 1869-86, it even contained a hot water system, warm air heating, and automatic flush toilets.

The era of the true castle had thus ended before Europeans even penetrated Ontario's forests.

Ontario's early frontier was hardly the place for castles. Homes were hastily erected, the first being little more than log shelters. Even the more elaborate dwellings were simple designs.

However, as industry expanded, and a wealthy class began to take shape, so too did Ontario's castles. Many were built to resemble the castles of Europe, usually by owners who were either homesick, or who were trying to place their imprint upon the landscape. Others, while less castle-like in appearance, were nevertheless the grand homes of a community's most influential citizens — its founders or its main industrialists. These people were a community's "king", and their grand home the "castle". Finally, there were those more modest dwellings which earned their "castle" title at the hands of derisive neighbours bent on mocking the perceived status of the castle owners.

While the earliest building in Ontario to be called a "castle" was Castle Frank, the country estate of Governor and Mrs John Graves Simcoe, completed in 1796, the first to truly resemble a castle was the London District court house built in 1827.

Then, as the railways brought more industrial growth to Ontario's cities, grand homes like Parkwood, Willistead, Rodman Hall, and Castle Kilbride began to appear. The most widely recognized castle of this era, however, is the famous Casa Loma, built by Sir Henry Pellatt to resemble the Bavarian castles of King Ludwig.

Aside from the few heavily promoted tourist castles, like Casa Loma and Dundurn Castle, Ontario's castle heritage remains little known. Yet it was the castle builders who not only placed their own personal imprint upon the early landscape of the province, but, through their industrial or simply their whimsical initiatives, helped shape the heritage of the Ontario which we know today.

While a few of the castles in this volume are public or quasi-public buildings, most remain private homes. In the case of the latter, effort has been made to ensure that these buildings can be appreciated from public vantage points, such as roads or sidewalks. The privacy of these homeowners should be respected.

As with the fairy tale castles of Bavaria, or the rugged ruins of windswept Scotland, Ontario's castles are a vital and visual reminder of Ontario's architectural and historical evolution, and one that few have considered. By documenting more than 50 such structures, this book hopes to fill that void. ✧

Ron Brown, *Toronto, Ontario*

SUNDERLAND VILLA, *Acton*

Acton, Ontario has become a popular destination for shoppers throughout the Greater Toronto Area, and even for visitors from outside the region. It is not however because of Acton's most castle-like home, Sunderland Villa, but rather for one of North America's largest leather goods stores, the Olde Hide House.

Yet the two are historically intertwined.

In 1845 William H. Storey arrived in Canada as a child. The youth apprenticed himself in the saddle business before moving to Acton in 1856 to enter into a saddle making venture with J.F. Taylor.

Sunderland Villa, now a funeral home, dominates the historic main street of Acton

William H. Storey

It wasn't long before he struck off on his own and opened a glove factory, the Canada Glove Works, expanding it into one of the largest in North America.

The town had already established itself as a leading tannery centre. In 1844 the Beardmore Company opened a tannery, and in 1899 added a massive warehouse for their hides by the Grand Trunk Railway station. The warehouse became widely known as the "hide house."

In 1879 Storey built a large Itanianate style house on the main street and named it Sunderland Villa. His glove works stood a couple of blocks to the north, while a carriage house was just behind.

Storey, like many prominent entrepreneurs, entered politics and served variously as village reeve and as county warden. When he died in 1898, more than 1,000 mourners attended his funeral. The glove works continued to operate until 1954 when the business was dissolved and the building demolished.

William H. Storey establishes Acton's glove factory

The villa served as a veterans' hostel after the first world war, and then briefly as a hotel. But by the time the Depression settled in, Sunderland Villa stood vacant. However, it didn't remain that way for long. In 1937 Victor Rumley bought the mansion and opened a funeral home, a function which it retains to this day. It stands at the corner of John and Mill Streets at the periphery of the downtown core, a district which still boasts many early commercial buildings. The coach house is now a private residence.

Meanwhile, back at the tracks, the trains no longer stop, the sidings to the warehouse have been lifted, and the station moved down the road to the Halton Electric Railway Museum outside Rockwood. The old hide house has now become the Olde Hide House, a leather goods outlet that is one of the largest in North America. Opposite the Olde Hide House, a bookstore and tea room have opened making Acton a popular local tourist destination. ❖

CASTLE KILBRIDE, *Baden*

The first thing you see as you approach the historic village of Baden in western Ontario is the trio of soaring sand hills known as the Baden Hills, a legacy of the last ice age. The next thing is the high belvedere of the massive Italiante mansion known as the Castle Kilbride.

The hills must have impressed James Livingston, who, in 1854, with his brother, John, had migrated from East Kilbride Scotland. Penniless after his migration, Livingston went to work on a local farm and then in the Perrine flax mills, one of which was located in the German speaking village of Baden.

With his newly gained experience, James, along with his brother, opened a flax mill of their own, and chose the little mill village of Wellesley. But the railways passed Wellesley by in favour of Baden, and the Livingstons moved their operation to railside.

Their real period of prosperity began with the American civil war. During that devastating conflict the supply of American cotton vanished, and the demand for linen boomed. The Livingstons opened mills in several other western Ontario towns, but always kept their headquarters in Baden. Wisely, they also operated their own farms, and therefore guaranteed not only the supply of flaxseed, but its price as well.

Not only was flax useful in the textile industry, but also in the area of construction as linseed oil was a basic requirement of paint.

Baden soon became a booming industrial town, centred on the Livingston mills, which were later known as the Dominion Linseed Oil Company.

With business thriving and his empire booming, Livingston bought a parcel of land close to his mills, and in 1876 began to plan for the construction of a building which would be the grandest in the county.

With his towering Castle Kilbride, James Livingston was the "king" of Baden

James Livingston founded Baden's leading industry

Designed by Waterloo architect David Gingerich, the house, known as Castle Kilbride, measured 44 by 42 feet, and contained a living area of 10,000 square feet. Constructed of local yellow brick, the castle featured elaborately decorated windows in iron and tin, and was topped off with an Italianate belvedere. Nearby was one of the castle's many curiosities, a yellow brick 4-seater privy.

Local newspapers enthused over not just what it had on the outside, but on the inside as well. For it would later contain features most homes of that time would never know - hot and cold water in all the bathrooms, and steam heating and gas features.

But Castle Kilbride was admired most for its artwork. And it is everywhere. Ceiling murals and medallions depict portraits, landscapes and classical images. Even the stovepipe cover has a colour portrait. The same artist, named either Scharstein or Schasstein, (his signature is not completely legible) appears to have been responsible for most of the images. In the library elaborate murals depict "War and Peace" and "Gods in Action". In the dome on the second floor the artist has depicted gods and goddesses representing the four elements of earth, wind, fire and pestilence.

But the most beguiling of all is the remarkable "trompe l'oeil" or "optical illusion" style of painting. With painted shadows which make them appear three-dimensional, these images appear as tassels draped around the ceiling of the library, and as a "statue" of a Greek goddess in the hallway. At first glance, the effect is quite convincing.

Shortly after its construction, a neighbor wired the home for the new fangled electricity. That neighbour was a man named Adam Beck, the individual most responsible for the massive hydro-electric developments at Niagara Falls.

It's a good thing that Livingston planned such a large residence, for he and his wife, Louise, went on to have a dozen children, a number of whom sadly died at an early age.

In addition to his business, Livingston became involved in politics serving as reeve, provincial MLA, and federal MP for the area. He also contributed to the local band, the library, and donated a Presbyterian church to the community.

The detailing on the woodwork on Castle Kilbride

Although Livingston's flax mills were hugely successful, his venture into car making was considerably less so, having produced a grand total of six. Louise passed away in 1904, while James succeeded her by another 16 years. The castle passed on to his son J.P and then to J.P's daughter and her husband, Laura and Harris Veitch.

After the castle had been in the family for 110 years, the Veitch's finally sold the building and the grounds to a developer and put its remarkable contents, including one of North America's finest antique toy collections, up for auction. Following the sale, local agitation to save the aging structure began to grow. Finally, in 1993 the Township of Wilmot took a huge gamble and bought the castle.

A master plan was prepared, a committee struck, and funds raised. In just nine months the Friends of the Castle had raised more than half a million dollars. Much of this came from a celebrity auction which included donations from Wayne Gretzky, David Letterman, Jay Leno, and Jean Chretien. A letter from the late Pierre Trudeau declining to donate a signed copy of his book, Memoirs, sold for $250.

The restoration included a large new addition to house the local municipal offices, new entrance, gift shop and washrooms. A large parking lot now occupies the rear portion of the property, although the front gardens are preserved. Much of the furniture, sold at auction, was recovered, as was a portion of the toy collection.

If you tour the castle you will first view a video describing the story of the Livingstons and their amazing home. You will then be lead by a tour guide through the building, one such guide occasionally performed chores for J.P. Livingston as a youth. The first element you will notice are the paintings in the main hallway, the carved dowel post depicting a lion's head, and the bronze electric light fixture high on the wall. It is here you will find the most impressive of the trompe l'oeil paintings, which are the main reason for the building's designation as a national historic site.

Just off the hallway is the smoking room with one of four white marble fireplaces purchased by Livingston from a palace in Venice. On the opposite side of the hallway, the dining room features a delicate spool work trellis over the doorway.

But it is the library which most captivates the visitor. Here you will find the most murals, trompe l'oeil tassels, and real plaster moldings. The library suite was bought from the Krug furniture factory by J.P.

in the twenties. On the ceiling is a four-shade jewelled chandelier, or "gasolier" as it was originally illuminated by gas.

The upstairs hallway is highlighted by another gasolier and an elaborately painted dome. After touring the upstairs bedrooms, one of which has been converted to a display area for the local legion, you can climb more stairs to the roomy belvedere itself, where the view encompasses the village and the lands once owned by Livingston.

Baden is located just off Highway 8 about 15 km west of Kitchener. Many of the village buildings which Livingston knew well, including the general store, hotel, and the church which Livingston gave the town, still stand. The flax mill, too, still stands, now much enlarged and put to new uses. ❖

LOUNT'S CASTLE, *Barrie*

Although attractively situated on a hillside overlooking Kempenfeldt Bay, Barrie is not a community you would visit for its built heritage. Sadly, little of it is left, most of its key historic buildings having fallen to the wrecker's ball – the ornate old city hall, the historic post office, the old railway station – none survive.

Barrie began as a military outpost, the terminus for a military portage from Toronto to the naval base at Penetanguishene. The first townsite, Tollendal, was laid out on the south shore of Kempenfeldt Bay, and the end of Yonge St. Directly opposite, on the north shore of Kempenfeldt Bay, another townsite, Kempenfeldt, marked the start of the Penetang Road.

Now apartments, Barrie's Lount's Castle still dominates its hilltop location

Development at the head of the bay, where Barrie stands today, began with the arrival of the railways in the early 1850s. Railway service began with the arrival of the Northern Railway to the settlement of Allandale on the south side of the bay where yards and a large divisional railway station with a restaurant were established. Soon the line was extended along the north shore where an attractive brick station was added across from the post office. Thanks to the railway, Barrie boomed.

Unfortunately, with the building of Highway 400, and the proliferation of urban sprawl, progress was not kind to Barrie's heritage. The most attractive buildings in town were removed to make way for slabs of concrete or glass, or for parking lots.

Nevertheless, much of the town's upscale residential district was spared such insensitive renewal and has managed to retain a number of its more prestigious homes. Grand homes like Glen Ormond, Woodlawn and Maple Hill, the latter described by Heritage Barrie as the "finest house in Barrie", all sit on a wooded bluff overlooking the bay and the lower part of the town.

But the only "castle" among them is Lount's Castle. It sits atop a prominent hill originally some distance from the centre of town and connected by a lane to the winding Sunnidale Road. Built in 1878 by William Lount, the three-storey house was designed by architect George Brown and features a steep mansard roof, and a tower with a similar mansard roof and tiles of slate. Most of the upper windows are arched. The second floor consisted largely of a ballroom, a standard feature of most 19th century "castles."

While William Lount was a noted local politician, serving as a judge and an M.P., it was his uncle Samuel who has earned the more prominent name in history books. For it was he, along with Peter Matthews who were the only two members of William MacKenzie's 1837 rebellion to be hanged for their participation.

While the interior has been converted into apartments, the exterior is little changed. The land around it, however, would shock its

original owner, having been turned entirely into a sprawling residential subdivision.

It is located at 26 Valley Drive and can be easily viewed from the road.

Despite the Barrie city council's shabby record in helping to save its historic buildings, it does have some accomplishments of which it can boast. It has successfully opened up its extensive waterfront almost entirely to the public, and has converted one of the railway's divisional buildings into a tourist information office. Meanwhile, a local TV station has committed to saving the nearby wooden Allandale railway station. ❖

ROCKSIDE CASTLE, *Belfountain*

Just as it does today, the Niagara Escarpment in the 19th century attracted the wealthy. Here they built their grand country estates to enjoy the clear air of the higher elevation, and the views from those more lofty heights.

Among those mansions and castles are the Hermitage of Ancaster, the Decew House of St Catharines, the Corran of Wiarton, Osler Castle of Collingwood, and near Belfountain, one of the Escarpment's most charming towns, James McLaren's Rockside Castle.

Before its devastating fire, Rockside looked every bit the Scottish castle

James McLaren arrived from Callander, Scotland, in 1860 and headed immediately for the hills of Caledon. Here, on a lofty promontory overlooking the Credit River, he built a true Scottish style castle, a replica of a castle in Perthshire.

Massive blocks of limestone were carved from the cliff face of the Escarpment in the Forks of the Credit gorge where several quarry operations took place through the last half of the 19th century. One by one the massive blocks were hauled by groaning wagons to be winched into place. When the castle was finished the tower rose more than 50 feet into the air. Here, McLaren would climb the circular staircase to the top from where he could see ships sailing on Lake Ontario, and the mist from Niagara Falls far on the opposite shore.

The front portion of the massive place had a rounded west wall and an arched entrance to the front door. Inside, the living room and dining room each measured 20 feet square. All in all there were 18 rooms, some with ceilings 16 feet high. Planks and beams of oak and maple were hoisted into place, while the front door alone was made with three inch oak. The property was over 300 acres in area, and included formal gardens and pasture.

Often times bearded men, clad in their rough farm clothes, would trudge up to the attic on the third floor where they held clandestine meetings. This group, known as the Grangers, eventually gained respectability and evolved into the Co-op movement which so benefits the farming community even today.

Despite the unacceptability of this organization at the time, McLaren held several reputable positions in the community. For forty years he served as post master as well as township councillor and county warden.

In 1937 the McLaren family sold the castle to a lumber company which used it as a bunkhouse, and then abandoned the property. It later resumed its role as a private residence until its one hundredth birthday. In 1964 fire raced through the stone castle destroying its contents and turning it into a blackened shell.

While there was no hope the castle could be restored to its original appearance, a new house was built around it, incorporating what remained of the walls and tower. Today, the Grange Road suggests the historic name of McLaren's secret club. It leads east from Mississauga Road to the bluff where the castle once sat, and where the new building is visible at a distance from Creditview Road.

LANGDON HALL, *Blair*

Tucked into the valley of the Grand River, like an oasis amid the sprawl of the industrial cities of Kitchener and Cambridge, lies the historic hamlet of Blair. Signs at its outskirts proclaim it Ontario's oldest inland European settlement. The pride of Blair's citizens in the community's heritage has helped to preserve its many historic structures.

One such building is the luxurious Langdon Hall.

It was here, on a high hill overlooking the wide Grand River that, in 1903, Eugene Langdon Wilks built a sprawling summer home. As his grandmother had been the daughter of New York's founder, John Jacob Astor, Wilks was comfortable with such grandeur.

Eugene Langdon Wilks' summer home more closely resembles a southern plantation

Usually the Wilks family moved between their U.S. homes and residences in Europe. But Eugene's father, Matthew Wilks, had seen in a New York paper an ad for a property on the Grand River near Galt Ontario, and decided to buy it. The property was named Cruikston Park and on it Wilks built a massive gothic mansion.

After spending some time in western Canada raising cattle, Wilks' son, Eugene Langdon Wilks, returned to the family mansion and purchased 29 acres of his father's 1000 acre estate, to which he added another 75 acres from an adjacent property. He then hired prominent architect Edward Lee Young to design his new home.

Much of the inspiration for the design came from the summer home of his uncle Walter Langdon at Hyde Park on the Hudson River in New York. (That property was later sold to a family known as the Vanderbilts and is now a U.S. national historic site.)

After Young had completed his plans, Toronto contractor Eden Smith was hired to complete construction of the estate. He altered the exterior material from wood to brick, a fortuitous alteration that has probably meant the preservation of the building.

The house he built might well be mistaken for a southern plantation home. Its two storey portico is perched on four white pillars and is set at the end of an enormous lawn, bordered by a curving driveway, an image straight out of Gone With the Wind.

While one will not see the grand staircase of the southern mansion, that was done away with by Smith, the grand hallway does possess a galleried opening to the second floor. To the right of the hallway was the ladies waiting room, while to the left was the dining room, with its high beamed ceiling.

At the rear was Wilks' billiard room, and next to that his gun room, for his passion was hunting. The second floor was made up of bedrooms and servants' quarters. The master bedroom covered the entire rear portion of the floor which contained no fewer than seven bathrooms. Meanwhile, the third floor remained unused. Incredibly, this 32-room, 25,000 square foot palace was never anything more than just a summer playground for the family. It was not even insulated and had no furnace. It did, however, boast 16 fireplaces.

After Wilks' first wife, Pauline, died in 1914 of cancer, he married Marguerite Briquet, his wife's nurse. After Wilks himself died in France in 1934, Marguerite and their children moved to Langdon Hall. Marguerite died thirty years later in 1961 and bequeathed Langdon Hall to her daughter Catherine and son-in-law Garth Thomson. Eventually they sold the property in 1982. Plans for a retirement home and housing development never materialized and in 1987, William Bennett and Mary Beaton bought the estate and created the Country House Hotel with spa and golf course, a use which it retains today.

The heritage of this handsome hotel is well complemented by that of the community in which it rests.

As early as 1800 Mennonites fleeing American persecution in Pennsylvania moved into the area. First known as Shingle Bridge after the covered bridge over the Grand, the little mill town was renamed Blair in 1858 to honour Adam Johnson Ferguson-Blair, a district judge. Now more than 200 years old, many have called the village a "time capsule." In many ways it is.

Here you can visit Lamb's Inn, which dates from 1837, Bechtel's 1854 sawmill, and an unusual sheave mill, a structure used to recapture the water power of a river and direct it back to the mill through which the river has already passed. The oldest buildings in the community are the Bechtel tannery built in 1825, and Jacob Bechtel's farmstead dating back to 1817.

YATES CASTLE, *Brantford*

While most castles look out over a lake or a river, or the town over which its builder ruled as "king", Henry Yates' castle in Brantford looks out over railway tracks.

Here, sitting at the back of an extensive lawn, on a rise of land, this Elizabethan brick mansion is in just the right place. Henry Yates was a railway promoter at a time when Brantford was lobbying hard to get itself on the railways' main lines.

When the plans for the Great Western and Grand Trunk railways bypassed the canal town, the merchants and industrialists went out

Yates' towered brick castle occupies an unlikely location across from Brantford's busy railway yards

and got their own line. Known as the Buffalo Brantford and Goderich Railway, it was opened with great fanfare in 1854. Its link to the Great Western Railway was at Paris, a short distance west. And one of the founders of the Great Western Railway was Henry Yates. He was also chief engineer for the Grand Trunk, the great Western's main rival until their merger in 1882. He co-owned the Lubric Oil Works, and served as town councillor from 1859-62.

In 1864, Yates bought up the Merrigold Villa and used the property to build an Elizabethan style grand home from which he could survey his railway kingdom. Here, on the north side of the yards, he hired John Turner to build the grand home which he would call Wynarden.

Being one of Brantford's grandest homes in its day, locals quickly nicknamed it Yates' Castle.

Yates love for his native England showed up in his castle, both outside and in. Built of red brick and stone, with yellow brick high-lights, it is a compilation of towers and gables, and looks every bit the castle. A five-storey tower, with gothic dormers piercing its roof, rises above the north, or back side of the house, while a second tower, on the west side, contains a bell which visitors were required to ring. Decorative wrought iron railings lined both the towers and the peak of the roof. An intricately decorated porch wrapped around the second storey. (Because the building was built into a hillside, the main floor became the second storey at the home's southerly expo-sure.) A high stone wall formerly surrounded its terraced gardens while a tunnel linked the home to the servants' quarters and to a pri-vate school. The latter structures still stand and are connected to the main house by a brick wall with a large wooden gate. The gate, school house and main house encase a small courtyard at the rear of the house. The gardens, modelled on Elizabethan English gardens, contained a fountain and four greenhouses.

The chimney is a joined seven-sided chimney with beading and hood moulds.

Inside the house, Yates' visitors found a ventilation system, dumb waiters, and bathrooms with hot and cold water. Yates added ornate carvings and designs throughout. The ground level of the house had billiard and drawing rooms, while the second floor contained the Yates' master bedroom, living room and den. All rooms contained elaborate fireplaces. The exterior stonework was carved into crests and emblems, while above the entrance he added the inscription "HEY 1864", referring to the date of construction and he and his wife Emily's initials.

Yates' Castle could also boast water closets and bathrooms with hot and cold running water, a rare luxury in 19th century Ontario. The stained glass windows contained hide-away shutters, the ceilings were carved in wood panels, and niches built into the walls to showcase Yates' sculptures, bells and speaking trumpets.

Yates' wealth allowed his family to winter in Atlantic City and summer at Point aux Barques. Following the elder Yates' death in 1894, the castle was taken over by his son Herbert who died in 1918. His family remained there until 1923 after which the grand old building sat empty for nearly a decade. Then, in 1932 it was converted into apartments. Sadly, the renovation resulted in many alterations such as the removal of the grand central staircase, the verandah, all the fireplaces and the ceiling mouldings.

Despite these losses, in 1989 Brantford's City council designated the castle as a heritage property under the Ontario Heritage Act.

Still, Brantford's record on heritage preservation is mixed at best. While it has designated a number of historic homes, it has also allowed the loss of its magnificent city hall. The court house, also designed by Turner, still stands as do two wonderful railway stations, that of the Toronto Hamilton and Buffalo Railway, a handsome brick and stone building, and that erected by the Grand Trunk Railway, with its rounded waiting room and tall tower. Constructed after the Grand Trunk finally rerouted its main line into Brantford, this building still serves passengers travelling on VIA Rail.

Facing this station from the opposite side of the yards is Yates' Castle. Although it has lost many of its features, its grandeur remains intact. ❖

THE WHITE HOUSE, *Brighton*

Long a landmark for Highway 2 motorists, the White House crowns a rise of land a short distance west of the town of Brighton. It was designed and built by a lawyer named John Eyre who arrived in Brighton in 1853. He also served briefly as a local member of parliament, and founded the Union Agricultural Joint Stock Company.

In 1880 he built the White House. It boasted a number of innovations unknown in existing homes, among them a full basement, and an indoor privy with running water. The three- storey building was constructed with triple brick.

Brighton's White House has been many things, including a restaurant and hotel. Today it is once again a private home

Unhappily, Eyre did not long reside there, for he died just 9 years later. It remained in trust until 1896 when it was bought by a local grocer named Samuel Nesbitt. In 1894 Nesbitt entered the canning business, an industry then taking hold in the Quinte area. But he went further than most such operators, establishing a laboratory for improving both the quality of the fruit and the canning process itself.

As his wealth increased so did his changes to the White House. In the 1920s he stuccoed the exterior and added the mansion's most distinguishing feature, its five storey tower. In 1938, after Nesbitt died, it was purchased by Irene Dickson and became known as Rene's White House Hotel. Among its guests were William Lyon McKenzie King, and Mr. and Mrs. Walt Disney.

When Highway 401 opened to bypass Brighton, the hotel closed and the White House became a restaurant. But that operation too has ceased and the White House has reverted to being a private residence. The only evidence of its former commercial role is the paved parking lot.

A short distance north of downtown Brighton stands the Proctor House. Although it lacks castle-like features, it has been restored and now serves as a museum. It was built around 1864 by John E. Proctor, then Brighton's leading industrialist. But one of the town's most noteworthy structures is neither grand nor a home. Rather, it is the historic 1857 Grand Trunk Railway station, converted through the labour of primarily one man, Ralph Bangay, and a handful of dedicated volunteers into a railway museum named Memory Junction.

BRUCEFIELD CASTLE

Brucefield is a small village nestled neatly in the rolling green farm-lands of southwestern Ontario. It is an area of traditional brick homes, country stores and solid barns. But it is the castle north of the village which turns the most heads.

Nobody seems to know exactly who built the structure, only that

Little is known about the builders of this country castle other than that they designed it after Friarton Brae Castle in Scotland

a grave on the grounds bears the date 1843. Its builders designed it after Friarton Brae castle in Scotland. And those same parties clearly knew about the bitterly cold winters which Ontario can wreak upon unwary new settlers, for the walls were constructed with no fewer than three layers of brick. Ground floor ceilings are twelve feet high, yet, of the fourteen rooms only two contain fireplaces. Two more fireplaces warm the upstairs.

The yellow brick building stands three stories high. Decorative woodworking highlights the end gables as well as that above the main balcony. A four-storey tower is topped by fanciful brickwork, carved wooden cornices and a rare pyramid roof. Servants' quarters, formerly located at the rear, burned a number of years ago.

Recorded ownership dates only from 1867 when the castle was bought by the Davidson family. The house stood vacant for more than 20 years, subject to wind, weather and the usual vandals. Finally it was rescued from decay by Earl and Jane Bensette and restored as a private home. While neither the house nor the grounds are open to the public, the castle can be easily seen from Highway 4, two kms north of Brucefield. ✥

MCCOOK'S CASTLE OR STRATHMORE,
The last of Cobourg's American Castles

In 1865 the American Civil War was over, and industrialists there could once more turn their attention to exploiting Canada's resources. The charter of the Cobourg and Peterborough Railway particularly attracted their interest. While its crossing of Rice Lake had to be abandoned due to yearly ice damage, a steamer link to the iron mines at Marmora, near the east end of the lake, made the line once more viable. It especially interested two Pittsburgh iron men, George Shoenberger and his son-in-law William Chambliss.

Once the railway began shipping iron ore to Pittsburgh via Cobourg and Rochester, the Americans began to take an interest in the town itself. To these wealthy iron magnates the clear air and long sandy beaches of this lakeside town were a welcome respite

Strathmore, once known as McCook's Castle, is one of the few surviving grand homes dating from Cobourg's days as a wealthy American resort

from the stifling and polluted air of a Pittsburgh summer, and from the war-ravaged landscape which many sought to flee. Rebel and Yankee alike put aside their weapons and turned Cobourg into a "Newport North."

The Arlington Hotel opened in 1874 launching the beginning of Cobourg's American colony. Then in the 1890s the Americans began to buy up local properties and were soon building mansions and castles unlike anything the community had ever seen. Most stretched along King St well to the east of the core of the town.

Two exceptions were Penryn Park which H.H. King had bought in Port Hope, and the Ulysses S Grant home which still stands, now Villa St Joseph, at the end of Tremaine St in west end Cobourg.

Back on King St East, the Ladds of Texas owned the sprawling Heathcote, the Albertinis bought the Interlaken next door, while the Sartoris moved into the Hill. Chambliss himself built an American-gothic mansion which he called Hadfield Hurst. For a time it served as a girls' school and is now an apartment on Green St.

One wealthy owner, a Colonel Cornell, incorporated private theatres into both his Cobourg summer home and his permanent estate in Buffalo. Other estates were known as Hadfield Hall, Cottesmore Hall, Dungannon Farm, and the most castle-like of them all, Bagnalli Hall. With its castellated towers the latter stood on King St opposite the site occupied today by East Collegiate.

One of the largest was known as Strathmore. It had been built as a summer home by a local judge named George Clark who would later become the solicitor general for the CPR. A two-storied pillared portico was added in the 1880s by an owner named McCook who gave the building its nickname, McCook's Castle. In 1906 American industrialist Charles Donnelly, one of the colony, bought Strathmore as a summer home and began to enlarge it, adding wings to each end.

The heady days of the colony lasted until the 1920s, with masquerade parties, horse shows and theatre being the most popular activities.

Then, in the 1920s, the Arlington, which had been the focus of the colony, closed. Throughout the 30s and 40s, many of the Americans passed away or moved out. The last major gathering was a wedding in 1938. Then, over a period of 20 years, the mighty mansions were demolished, and their contents auctioned.

One of the few to survive. the orgy of destruction was Strathmore. When it went up for sale in 1947 it was saved from demolition by the Ontario government who converted it into a training school for girls. Today it is the Brookside Youth Facility, a privately run correctional facility.

It stands well back from Highway 2 on the east end of the town, shaded by the tall trees of its spacious grounds. Nearby are two of the other ghosts of the long-gone colony. Opposite Strathmore and a short distance west is William Abbott's Sidbrook, a massive Beaux Arts mansion, now a private hospital. Further east stands Midhurst, formerly owned by Pittsburg steel baron, George Howe. A more conservative Italianate style of house, it remains in private ownership. One of the most beautiful of the colony's castles goes by the name of Ravensworth. Built by General Charles Lane Fitzhugh in 1897, it stands, still privately owned, on wonderfully landscaped grounds overlooking the lake. These, however, are the few survivors of this long gone era.

Like Port Hope, Cobourg has retained a wealth of historic buildings: the domed Victoria Hall which dominates the main street, Victoria College, one of Ontario's first universities, and the refurbished, and still-functioning, former Grand Trunk railway station. ❖

OSLER CASTLE, *Gibraltar*

The haunting remains of Osler's Castle are the ultimate castle ruin in Ontario. Located high on the Niagara Escarpment's soaring cuestas, these stone walls tell of a family beset by hardship and tragedy.

It didn't begin that way. Britton Bath ("BB") Osler was born in 1839, one of six children of Featherstone Lake Osler, a travelling preacher whose territory encompassed the 2,000 square miles south of Georgian Bay in the Collingwood area.

In 1857 the Osler family moved from their home base in Thornhill to Dundas. BB's youth was spent more in playing cricket and escorting the young ladies of Dundas than it was in advancing his education. His early jobs involved the drudgery of bookkeeping, although he long had a love for legal discussions. Finally he undertook a crash course in law and obtained his LL.B. at the University of Toronto in 1862.

In addition to his law practice, Osler served as local councillor and was involved in promoting the Hamilton and Dundas Street Railway.

Britton Bath Osler lived in the castle which stood here which he dubbed Kionontio, for a mere seven years before his untimely death in 1901

His early claim to fame was being named one of the four crown prosecutors assigned to prosecute Louis Riel at the now famous treason trial in Regina. He was also the lead prosecutor in one of Canada's most notorious early murder trials. When the body of an Englishman named Fred Benwell showed up in the Blenheim Swamp, Osler ruthlessly tracked down the killers. He proved that one Reginald Birchall and his wife had been luring young Englishmen to Ontario to invest in a non-existent horse farm, and then murdering them.

Following the Birchall case, Osler gained a wide reputation as a successful prosecutor in several other murder cases.

Sadly his family life was less satisfying. His wife Caroline suffered from chronic arthritis, and found the very act of moving about to be painful. Hoping that the clearer air of the land where his father had once preached would aid his wife's health, he purchased over 300 acres on the Niagara Escarpment overlooking Georgian Bay. In 1893 he began the construction of a massive summer mansion which his wife named Kionontio, Petun for "top of the hill."

Much of Osler Castle has been salvaged for its large boulders

To construct the walls, massive field stones were hauled in from the area. The "castle," as the locals called it, soon consisted of 15 rooms, topped off with turreted chimneys. Guests entered through a large stone archway and covered verandah. The rooms boasted furnishings of bird's eye maple, oak and mahogany. Most of the castle's furnishings were imported from England, and were hauled by straining teams up the steep crude road which led to the cuesta.

Water was pumped from below and fed by gravity through the house. Heat was provided from a gasoline-powered generator, as well as from elaborately designed fireplaces. The wine cellar was connected to the upper floors by a dumb waiter.

He surrounded the house with terraced lawns and rose beds where an iron gate contained the name "Kionontio."

In 1894 he was ready to unveil the castle to his many influential friends. To impress them, he hired a Grand Trunk parlour car to carry them to the fine brick railway station in Collingwood where he met them with a coach pulled by six black horses.

But the castle's location did little for the ill-fated Caroline and she died the following year.

Osler remarried in 1897 and he and new wife vacationed frequently at the castle. However, just four years later, BB Osler himself was dead. He was just 61. While the property was rented out to local farmers, the castle and its furnishings sat unattended. Eventually thieves and vandals plundered the once magnificent building, reducing it to a few stone walls.

Such is the sight which greets the hiker today. Forests have blocked the view which Osler enjoyed, while weeds and shrubs have made their way up through the floors and windows. The site lies about a kilometer west of the Bruce Trail north of Simcoe County Road 19. ❖

MACDERMOTT'S CASTLE, *Goderich*

It is fitting that the lakeside town of Goderich, touted as Ontario's prettiest place, should possess a castle that towers high above a lakeside cliff.

A first glimpse around the town's core is perplexing. It has no main "street". Rather, Goderich's downtown is eight-sided, enclosing the court house square. In fact, the entire town is laid out in accordance with an urban plan which is more than 2,000 years old. Based on a design by a Roman town planner named Marcus Vetruvius, Goderich's main roads radiate out in eight different directions through a grid network of streets. The plan, it is claimed, was

Started by Irish immigrant Henry MacDermott, his castle remained unfinished until Jessie Cameron, widow of the Hon. Malcolm Cameron, moved in

tried in only one other location in North America, Washington, DC. While the latter was ruined by an unsympathetic overlay of other streets, that in Goderich remains true to the Roman design. Some argue that the radiating pattern is at odds with a lakeside location, and was in fact originally intended for the town of Guelph.

Unlike many other towns of similar size, Goderich has been spared unsightly suburban sprawl and has retained a high proportion of its historic buildings. These include the town hall which was built in 1890 as a customs house, a stone livery stable which dates from the 1840s, the Bedford Hotel, built in 1896, and a pair of handsome brick railway stations, one built by the CPR with its "witch's hat" roof above the waiting room, and the other, erected by the Grand Trunk and still in use, with two turrets.

The building which attracts the most tourists, however, is the ancient jail. This 8-sided stone structure, along with the governor's house, dates from the 1830s, and is one of Ontario's oldest surviving jails.

And then there's MacDermott's castle. It is located on a high bluff overlooking the busy harbour area. While little seems to be known of the man, Henry MacDermott arrived from County Antrim in northern Ireland and bought the property from William Seymour, a major land holder in the Canada Company. It was this company that had undertaken the settlement of much of the Huron County area of Ontario.

Here, overlooking the harbour, which in the pre-rail era was the community's link to the outside, he began to build his castle. It is said that he modelled the mansion after one such structure in his home county. But the building was to remain unfinished. After completing two floors and part of the tower, he ran into money problems.

In 1889, he died from a fall, and his family moved out. The building sat empty for 14 years until 1903 when Jessie Cameron, widow of the Honourable Malcolm Cameron, bought the castle and finished the construction. It was while the Camerons lived there that it achieved its regal grandeur, and a new name, The Maples.

Mrs Cameron finished the tower with intricate parapets and a small balcony. Inside, the walls and floors were finished in pine. Foundation walls two feet thick were needed to absorb the shock of the blasting from salt mines a short distance away. Cameron also replaced MacDermott's gothic doors with a porte-cochere over the driveway.

In the main foyer she placed a statue of the Venus de Milo. From the drawing room, French windows overlooked the gardens which were high above the lake and the river. On the third floor a games room contained a large billiard table. When Mrs Cameron reached her 70's she installed a water-powered elevator in the tower to connect the three floors.

This gothic building once inspired a murder mystery novel, The Twenty-First Burr, written by Victor Lauriston in 1922.

For the next thirty years the castle changed owners a number of times until, in the 1940s, it was altered. Apartments were added, the porte-cochere replaced, and a number of rooms remodelled.

Today, the castle remains privately owned, but is easily viewed from St George's Crescent which, like the castle, overlooks the harbour and the lake. The stunning sunsets from the little park located here allow visitors to see for themselves why MacDermott chose the site for his castle. ❖

HAMILTON, *the city of castles*

When Allan Napier McNab arrived at the head of Lake Ontario in 1831 to build his Dundurn Castle, it was Dundas, not a muddy little village named Hamilton to which he was attracted. Dundas, after all, marked the head of navigation and the beginning of the once strategic military road to London. It contained the fine homes of anyone who counted in these early years, while Hamilton could claim little more than 100 dwellings and a half dozen taverns.

But the arrival of the Great Western Railway in 1853 changed all that. For the rail link bypassed Dundas and connected Hamilton with New York state to the east and Michigan to the west. In the 1870s and 80s more railways arrived, and the Welland Canal was enlarged to accommodate larger vessels.

The proximity of limestone to both water and rail links turned Hamilton into Canada's leading steel town. And with industry came wealthy industrialists, and their castles.

In fact, one of Canada's most highly regarded works on the nation's architecture, This Ancestral Roof, has designated Hamilton as having Canada West's greatest percentage of castles, noting that this city had seven before Toronto could even claim its first.

AMISFIELD CASTLE, *Hamilton's shame*

For all that Hamilton has accomplished in the field of heritage preservation (a mixed record at best, some might argue), Amisfield represents all that should not happen.

Amisfield was built in 1857 in an area that was then well to the south of the growing city. Here, on a 10-acre parcel and surrounded by a stone fence, stood this large Gothic mansion. Designed by architect F.J.Rastuck, it was to have been called Abbotsford after Sir Walter Scott's home on the River Tweed in Scotland.

Once one of Hamilton's grandest homes, Amisfield was ruined through unsympathetic redevelopment both inside and out

Although it lacked the crenelated towers that mark most of Hamilton's castles, its gothic gables and massive size earned it the name, "The Castle."

Following the Second World War it was divided into apartments. But it was during the 1970s that catastrophe struck. For some unfathomable reason, city council permitted the entire front of the handsome home to be utterly obliterated by a string of stores of indifferent and inconsequential design. Today, while the structure still stands, it is totally hidden from view. The paint is peeling and the grounds are unkempt. Only the rear portion of the castle can be seen from the apartment parking lot.

In contrast to the many glorious castles to which Hamilton can lay claim, and justly boast of, Amisfield will stand as the city's disgrace. ✧

The façade of Amisfield is obliterated by commercial development

CASTLE DOANE

This more modest "castle" really belongs with the story of Dundurn Castle. The original building was erected by Sir Alan McNab, creator of Dundurn. It was here at the eastern edge of his estate that he built a small brick home and covered it with stucco. It was to have been, some have theorized, a retreat for his wife should he die first.

It did not gain its castle-like appearance, however, until seventy years later when it was purchased by Robert Anderson who doubled the size and added the castellated tower. Later the house was divided

This more modest castle was built by Sir Alan McNab as part of his Dundurn Castle estate

into a duplex. In 1974, Andy Tasse bought one half of the castle, a portion which had been empty for a number of years. He subsequently purchased the other half and applied for a heritage designation.

With the heritage funding he improved the castle and installed two apartments in addition to his own quarters. The castle stands on a small lot at the north end of Lock St. An historical plaque beside the road recounts the significance of this small but historic castle.

HAMILTON'S DUNDURN CASTLE

The second most famous of Ontario's castles, Dundurn Castle, guards a bluff overlooking Hamilton Harbour.

In 1812 the American troops had crossed the Niagara River and were threatening to advance upon the west end of Lake Ontario. To prepare for a possible attack, the British troops built earthworks on a high bluff overlooking the end of Hamilton harbour, property owned by Colonel Richard Beasley.

In 1832 the site was sold to one Allan Napier McNab, a hero during the war of 1812. He soon began work on a new and grander home on the scenic bluff. He hired architect R.C Wetherell to design a mansion modelled after the family castle in Perthshire Scotland. Three years later, at a cost of $175,000, the 72-room castle was complete.

It was equipped with what were then the most modern conveniences,

Completed in 1835, Dundurn is Ontario's oldest surviving castle

including gas lights, running water, and a "dumb waiter" connecting the kitchen, which was in the basement, with the butler's pantry.

McNab's positions and connections ensured his wealth. He rose from being a Queen's Council in 1837 to president of the Great Western Railway in 1845, before it had laid even an inch of track, and then became the leader of the federal Tories. But that did not prevent him from sinking into debt and after his death in 1862, the mansion had to be sold to pay off his creditors.

For nine years it served as an Institute for the Deaf and Dumb. Then it was sold to private interests and remained there until 1899 when the citizens of Hamilton voted overwhelmingly by referendum to buy the aging castle.

A year later it was opened as a museum using furniture and display items donated by citizens from all across Ontario. A half century would pass before major renovations were undertaken in the 1950s. Then in 1967, to celebrate Canada's Centennial year, a major undertaking restored the castle to as much of its McNab-era appearance as was possible to determine.

A sound and light show was installed and a fine restaurant opened. Visits ballooned from 25,000 a year to more than 1,000 a day.

Further renovations took place during the 1990s with funding from the City and from the Ontario government's Jobs Ontario program, since discontinued by the government of Premier Mike Harris.

Now visitors can enter the drawing room and dining room areas, visit the library and smoking room before ascending the black walnut staircase to see the bedrooms, the school room where the McNab's two children were taught by tutors, the nursery and Lady McNab's boudoir. The basement housed not only the kitchen and laundry, but an ice room cooled by ice cut from the bay, and a brewery.

The castle has also become a popular location for film companies, including Disney which filmed a TV movie, The Liberators, there.

Hamilton is considered to be a city of castles, and Dundurn is the grandest of them all. ❖

"HUMANITY'S" CASTLE, *Ballinahinch*

Like its neighbour Rock Castle, Ballinahinch predates the arrival of the railways. But the steel rails were not far off in the future, and in 1850 Hamilton was enjoying a boom period. The design was originally prepared by architect William Thomas for dry goods merchant Aeneas Sage Kennedy whose Scottish heritage was reflected in the Scottish castle.

Here, where James Street ended at the foot of Hamilton Mountain, Thomas' four-storey battlemented tower loomed high above the quiet woodlands while floral carvings and gothic mouldings adorned

This grand home was named by the controversial Edward Martin after the Irish castle of his grandfather "Humanity" Martin.

A group of convalescing patients pose for the camera in front of Ballinahinch

the Tudor entranceway and windows.

In 1870 Kennedy sold his castle to Edward Martin. An aspiring lawyer, Martin was appointed Queens' Council when only 21. Along with his brother Richard he formed the law firm of Martin and Martin, one of the City's most successful practices. It was he who placed the family coat of arms above the entrance and renamed the castle "Ballinahinch" after that of his grandfather, "Humanity" Martin, in Connemara Ireland.

Martin went on to become president of the Hamilton Law Association, and served as vice president of the Hamilton Street Railway Company. In 1884 he became the founding director of the Equal Rights Association. This controversial group was formed to fight what was called the Jesuit Estates Act, legislation passed by the Quebec legislative assembly to provide a monetary settlement for lands held by the Jesuit Order in Canada. Calling it a "papist" intrusion into Canada's affairs, Ontario's Orange Order and the ERA opposed the settlement, and pushed the House of Commons to disallow the provincial act. The effort was not successful and served only to intensify the strain on French-English relations in the country.

Following Martin's death in 1904, Ballinahinch remained in the family for only another dozen years before being bought by William J. Southam, publisher of the Hamilton Spectator. From 1925 to 1940 it was the home of yet another Hamilton iron man, Frank McCune, superintendent of the Steel Company of Canada.

In the 1940s it suffered a fate common to many of Ontario's grand homes, it was divided into apartments. Today it has been further renovated and the apartments have become condominiums.

The coach house, which burned to the ground around the turn of the century, was reconstructed in the early 1980s, using contemporary photographs, and now stands at the corner of Aberdeen and James, although it is separately owned.

Like Rock Castle, Ballinahinch has been designated an historic property and displays a commemorative plaque on its gate. ✥

RAVENSCLIFFE

The finest homes in Hamilton line the stately Aberdeen Ave between Queen St and James. Most were built in the late 19ᵗʰ century by industrialists and real estate entrepreneurs. Here, at what was then the southern limit of the city, well away from the railway lines and the wharf-side factories, southern plantation columns mingle with Scottish turrets and French chateauesque roof lines. Side streets lead south from Aberdeen and slope up the foothill of Hamilton Mountain where the most fortunate could enjoy a view over their bourgeoning city.

But of this stately lot, the finest remains, arguably, the castle known as Ravenscliffe.

Ravenscliffe served briefly as the residence of Ontario's Lieutenant Governor, Sir John Morrison Gibson

Originally, this looming manor, with its soaring castellated tower, was the sole occupant of a 9 acre property owned by a Col. McGivern. Here it sat grandly at the end of a long wooded lane. In 1881 it was sold to John Proctor, one of Hamilton's leading iron men. The next owner, another iron man, named W.D. Copp, found himself in some financial distress and the house passed to the Empire Mutual Life Assurance Company which promptly subdivided the northerly half of the property.

But Ravenscliffe's most note-worthy occupant came shortly after.

John Morrison Gibson, later Sir John, was a prominent Hamilton real estate operator. Much of his time, however, was spent promoting and developing Hamilton's electrical railways, known locally as the Cataract. He succeeded in helping to establish no fewer than four lines, the most of any city in Canada. He was known, too, for passing legislation to prevent cruelty to children, an initiative which led to the creation of Ontario's Children's Aid Societies, as well as the Sick Children's Hospital in Toronto. For a time he served as president of the Canadian Red Cross. In 1908 he was appointed Lieutenant Governor of Ontario, a post which he held until 1914, with Ravenscliffe his official residence.

He died in 1929 at the age of 87.

Little has changed on the dead end street. Handsome homes still line the avenue, and Ravenscliffe still commands the approach to it. ◈

ROCK CASTLE

Like Dundurn Castle, Rock Castle predated the coming of the trains. But only by a couple of years. And like Dundurn, and Hamilton's other castles, Rock Castle occupied a prominent height of land. Here, two miles south of the harbour, where the land begins to slope upward to become Hamilton Mountain, many of the city's newly wealthy families built their estates.

Although details are unknown, the building was likely built by one Alexander Carpenter, owner of a large Hamilton foundry. While it lacked the castellated towers of most of Hamilton's other castles, Rock Castle quickly earned its name. The 30-room mansion was originally built on one-and-a-half acres of land, three stories high on the bay

Built by Alexander Carpenter, this 30-room mansion is distinguished by its two-storey outhouse

Rock Castle's main door faces no main street

side, and two on the mountain side. Oddly, although roads pass on both sides, the main door faces neither. Rather, it faces west, set in a bay with a pointed arch window tucked into the gable above it.

The doors and windows are gothic in shape while the interior boasted rooms with 12 foot ceilings and seven fireplaces. However, the oddest feature of this stone palace was its two-storey outhouse. Situated on the eastern end of the building, the separate facility is linked on its upper level by a bridge which led from Carpenter's private quarters. It is said that this allowed him to keep watch over his foundry at all times.

At the time the castle was built, Hamilton's urban fringe was still a good distance away. But with the railways, Hamilton grew southward, and soon engulfed the castle. Carpenter died in 1871, and his daughter, Margaret, inherited the old castle. Today, it is said, the place is haunted by both father and daughter.

In 1970 the inevitable proposal came to demolish the building and replace it with an apartment high rise. However, a movement started by a local student to save the building grew into a groundswell of public support and forced the City into taking over the property in exchange for more liberal zoning on other land which the developer owned.

Today Rock Castle has continued to defy development pressure and still stands, used now as apartments with many original interior features happily intact. Interior doors and stairs retain much of their original detailing, including cut crystal doorknobs. Oak floors still have their inlaid mahogany, while some of the apartment units retain original built-in bookcases. On the main floor, ornate cornices, ceiling medallions and Italian marble fireplaces still figure prominently. Sadly, the grounds are showing signs of poor maintenance. The castle can be viewed from both Arkledun Ave, which climbs the mountain to the south, and from St Joseph Dr on the north. The two-storey privy, by the way, is now used for storage. ✦

TUCKETT'S TOWERS,
the castle that tobacco built

In 1860 George E Tuckett arrived in Hamilton to make smokers out of its residents. From his tobacco factory on Queen Street North he produced the popular Marguerite cigar and the Buckingham cigarette. His son George T continued the business and in 1895 built the castle he called the Towers. It was located at King and Queen Sts, just a short distance from the factory.

The three-storey mansion features a turret and four-storey battlemented tower. He modeled the iron fence after that which surrounds Buckingham Palace in London, a nod to the name of his cigarette. A rather unusual feature inside the mansion were six pedals under the table in the dining room, each of which could be operated by one of his six children to summon a servant from the dining room. One of those children perhaps operated the pedal a bit too often and, according to contemporary newspaper accounts, earned the nickname "Fatty."

In 1920 the Towers was bought by an organization which few have heard of, the Ancient and Accepted Scottish Rite, an offshoot of the Masons and headquartered in Hamilton since 1860. In 1923 the Rite added a vast cathedral to the mansion. With its 560 seats and backdrops which include a desert, a woodland and a Greek temple, the cathedral continues to host various secret ceremonies held by costumed members.

As for Tuckett Tobacco, the firm was taken over by Imperial Tobacco which moved the operation to Guelph in the 1930s.

The Towers still contains the original woodwork of birch cherry and bird's eye maple, as well as the Tuckett's oak dining room table.

Now a Scottish Rite cathedral, this castle-like mansion was built by tobacco magnate, George E. Tuckett

MCQUAT'S LOG CASTLE, *Ignace*

It might just be Ontario's strangest castle. Not only was this lost and lonely palace built entirely of logs, but it was reputedly the work of just one man, with no help from either other men or machine.

McQuat arrived in northwestern Ontario in 1887 hoping to carve out a life as a farmer on Ontario's frontier fringe. But the life of a pioneer farmer did not agree with him and McQuat caught the gold rush fever, then raging in the area. Unfortunately, the gold remained elusive and McQuat returned with little to show for his prospecting.

Discouraged, he made his way to the shores of White Otter Lake, midway between the railway towns of Ignace and Atikokan, and there decided to remain. He went to work cutting logs from the pine forests, and slowly winched them into position.

Ontario's most unusual castle, McQuat's Castle was built by just one man

Soon the strange looking castle began to take shape. When it was finished it boasted a two storey main living area, a two storey wing, and a tower that was four stories high. And all constructed of logs. The only problem with this amazing dwelling was that it stood on Crown Land. McQuat was a squatter and was never successful in obtaining a deed to the land where he had built his castle.

McQuat was not a loner, however, and made frequent trips by canoe into Ignace. Nevertheless, he remained many miles from his nearest neighbour, a situation which led to his death. For it was in 1918 that he became entangled in his fishing nets and drowned. He was only meters away from his castle.

The building has remained empty since that day. When Ontario's Ministry of Natural Resources decided to tear down the old log castle, local heritage enthusiasts rallied against the attempt and have since that time managed to stabilize it.

McQuat's castle remains a remote destination, accessible only by canoe or by float plane. The Friends of White Otter, however, are happy to provide information on directions, and on the history of the log castle on White Otter Lake. ❖

RUTHVEN, A ghost town castle, *Indiana*

David Thompson, MP

Little can be more evocative than an abandoned mansion over-looking a silent ghost town. That is the image which the grey looming Ruthven conveyed from its cliff top perch at the ghost town of Indiana.

The early years of the 19th century were Canada's canal era. Canals such as the Erie had brought prosperity to western New York state, and the craze spread to its northern neighbour. While canals such as the Rideau were built for military purposes, others, like the Trent, the Welland and the Grand, were constructed to speed the flow of lumber, minerals and farm products.

Following the completion of the first Welland Canal in 1825, William Hamilton Merritt turned his attention to the Grand River. Settlers had moved up the banks of this wide river as early as 1806, but lacked any easy way to move their goods in or out. Stages took days, even weeks, when they could get through the bogs which passed for roads.

By the 1830s, a canal with six locks connected Brantford with Port Maitland on Lake Erie. David Thomson had been a contractor on the Welland Canal, and in 1845 moved to the bustling lock station village of Indiana on the west bank of the Grand River. Here he built a grist mill, distillery, lumber mill, and general store.

Near the village he built his dream home, a soaring Greek Revival mansion with three floors and 36 rooms. It stood close to the 80-foot cliff which formed the east bank of the river and offered him a view of the scows and schooners which glided upon the waters below him. To the north the village was laid out on a network of streets, a community which over 300 residents called home.

While his 900-acre estate was largely an operating farm, Thomson added tennis courts, gardens and riding stables. A road led north through stone gates, past the cemetery of the village and into the heart of Indiana. The Thomson's private cemetery would be located near the south end of the property.

For years Ruthven, historic home of the Thompson family, was a ghost castle in a ghost town

Inside, the twin drawing rooms each boasted fireplaces of black marble, while between them an oval staircase led upwards three stories to a roof top skylight.

Thomson served, among other offices, as first member of parliament for the County of Haldimand, and the house remained in the family until the 1980s. In its later years, it was used only occasionally and fell into a state of decay, a ghostly relic to match the ghost town beside it.

The gates at Ruthven

With the building of the Buffalo Brantford and Goderich Railway in 1875, the canal fell into disuse and was abandoned altogether in the 1890s. While other canals flourished or held their own, Indiana fell into ruin. Its population plunged from 300 to less than 25. All buildings save two disappeared.

Then, in 1994, the Ruthven mansion was declared a national historic site and renovations slowly began. Today those renovations continue. The building is open to tours at selected times during the summer, and hosts teas and other special events. It remains a work in progress.

Beside it in the ghost town, a new tea room has opened in one of Indiana's remaining structures. After touring the building you can stroll the grounds, visit the Thomson cemetery at the south end of the property, or try to find the heavily overgrown Indiana cemetery at the north. A trail leads through the Carolinian forest on the grounds, and down to the site of the mills and the lock station.

Despite the restoration, the area still seems full of ghosts. ❖

HORACEVILLE, *Kanata*

While this grand stone mansion may lack the towers and turrets of a traditional castle, it had what no other such building in Ontario could claim, its own village. Like England's medieval castles, the manor built by Hamnett Kirkes Pinhey supported a small community on its grounds.

Hamnet Kirkes Pinhey was a wealthy London importer and ship insurance broker who migrated to Canada's then wilderness in 1827. Here, several miles upstream from a crude little lumber town named Bytown he was granted a generous estate of a thousand acres fronting onto the Ottawa River. This largesse was likely a reward for his dangerous deeds running French blockades during the Napoleonic wars.

Ontario's only castle to have its own town, Pinhey's Castle enjoys a grand view over the Ottawa River.

Here, on his new land, he created his own little fiefdom. Following an established practice in England, he named the settlement Horaceville, after his eldest son.

The original house was a typical wilderness log home, and was finished in 1822. Pinhey kept enlarging the dwelling until 1849 when the final stones were hauled into place and Horaceville was complete. By then it consisted of a long two storey stone mansion which looked grandly out over the Ottawa River.

One of the first features Pinhey arranged for was a large ballroom which occupied the entire ground floor of the building's first phase. From the ballroom a false doorway flanked by two Regency windows faced the river. From the main entrance a large hallway led to the second floor staircase, while to the left of the door were the library and drawing room and to the right a large parlour.

The second floor consisted of several bedrooms and an upper privy which Pinhey nicknamed his "sanctum sanctorum".

The community which developed around the mansion included a grist mill, sawmills and the beautiful stone St Mary's Church. The site was also said to have contained a "fort." However, since there were no hostilities, others have concluded that the"fort" may have been nothing more than a root cellar decorated with a few cannons which were souvenirs from Pinhey's military days.

The farm was managed by Horace Pinhey, who married Kate Greene in the church which his father had built. While Horace lived in the older part of the house, his father and sister occupied the newer portion. Following his father's death in 1857, and his sister's relocation to Ottawa, Horace took over the entire estate.

The property remained in the Pinhey family until 1971 when the last member, Ruth Pinhey, passed away, and Horaceville was sold to the Township of March (now the City of Kanata).

Beginning in 1996, the City and the Pinhey Point Foundation commissioned restoration architect Julian Smith to undertake a combination modernization-preservation project. While ensuring that the house can accommodate a range of modern activities, as much of its original appearance as possible was retained or restored. The unusual inside shutters on the windows were restored, and the later ceilings removed to reveal hand-hewn beams. Today the house hosts art displays and community events.

While the mills and the original log house have gone, the church still stands, although it now rests on property which is separately owned, and is not part of Horaceville's public grounds.

The "sanctum sanctorum" has long given way to the requirements of more modern plumbing.

The Horaceville church stands on private property

LADY EATON'S COUNTRY CASTLE, *King*

Ontario's Oak Ridge Moraine is a legacy of the last ice age. As the great glacier began to retreat 20,000 years ago, meltwater poured a gaping crack in the ice sheet, carrying with it sand, gravel and huge chunks of ice. When the ice finally receded, it had left behind a long rugged ridge of hills, swamps and little lakes which formed when the ice chunks that were lodged in the sand finally melted. These ponds are known as kettle lakes.

It therefore comes as a surprise to many Ontarians that the Moraine

Now part of Seneca College, Eaton Hall was once the summer home of Lady Flora McCrea Eaton, widow of Sir John Craig Eaton

is in fact a land of lakes. One of those lakes was named Jonda, or Little Lake. It attracted the attention of Sir Henry Pellatt, builder of Ontario's most famous castle, Casa Loma, who in turn convinced his friend Jack (John Craig) Eaton of department store fame to buy the property which surrounded it. In 1920 on the west side of Dufferin St., in the Township of King, Eaton bought the 700-acre farm and remodeled the modest farm house. Here he held steeple chases, and hosted meetings of the Toronto and North York hunt clubs.

Soon the existing house proved too small for his ever-expanding gatherings, and Sir John commissioned a new home, one that would resemble a French chateau. Seventy-two rooms, it boasts a huge stone fireplace, library, towers, turrets, and a large formal garden, complete with fountain, overlooking the little lake.

Sir John would never see the structure for he died in 1922, fully 16 years before Eaton Hall would be complete.

During the war Eaton's widow, Lady Flora McCrae Eaton, allowed the building to be used as a military hospital, funding many of the supplies and salaries herself. After the war she moved back and continued to use it until her own death in 1970, aged 91.

In 1971 Seneca College bought the property, and converted the

Lady Eaton preparing to ride

hall into an administrative centre. In 1977 the hall was renovated to become a Management Development Centre, providing residential management training for business groups. Then, in 1994, it was altered once again, this time to offer meals and accommodation to the public. But it still plays an educational role as the serving staff are usually students training for careers in the hospitality industry.

While the interior is no more a public facility than is a restaurant, the grounds invite strollers, hikers and cross country skiers. A wide lawn leads gently from the garden down to the lake shore, where a gazebo still stands. Across the lake are the more modern buildings which house the classrooms and the offices of the college itself. The lane to the Eaton Hall parking lot winds through a forest of maple and pine, giving the estate a northern ambience although it remains only a 45-minute drive from the site of John Craig Eaton's former store in downtown Toronto, a location now occupied by the Eaton Centre.

From Lady Eaton's castle, drive a short distance south on Dufferin St to see the delightful stone St Andrews church in Eversley. Built by pioneer settlers in 1848, using stones from their farm fields, it was saved from demolition with the help of Lady Eaton.

While in the area, visit the grounds of the Marie Lake Augustinian Seminary on Keele St., the next road west. Marie Lake is another of the Moraine's kettle lakes and was the site of Sir Henry Pellatt's summer home. Lady Eaton's influence is felt here, too, as the organ in the main building was donated by her. ❖

KINGSTON'S CASTLES
McINTOSH'S CASTLE

Located at the strategic junction of the Rideau Canal and the St Lawrence River, Kingston has more history per square meter than any other city in Ontario. And it has, with some exceptions, preserved it well. Indeed, the city has designated more than 350 buildings as heritage structures.

But then Kingston was significantly more important than most other places anyway. Under the French rule, the site had been selected for a fort and trading post. Following the war of 1812, the British realized that the St Lawrence River, along which most military and economic supplies floated, was too exposed to possible attack from the

Although small, McIntosh's Castle is a replica of a Scottish castle

American forces on the south shore, and commissioned the building of the Rideau Canal. When the canal was opened in 1832, Kingston became a key military and administrative centre. It was the district capital, and briefly served as the capital of the Province of Canada.

As such it attracted the aristocracy of the day, who built their magnificent homes along the bucolic shores of Lake Ontario, well away from the swampy mouth of Cataraqui Creek through which the canal made its way. Grand places such as Summerhill, Leaside and Rockwood all looked from their extensive treed estates over the shimmering waters of the lake.

Many are deserving of the title "castle" but it was a smaller dwelling, located well back from the lake, which is actually called a castle.

It was all because a Scottish immigrant named Donald McIntosh, recently arrived from Glasgow, promised his family one. In 1849 he hired architect John Power to design a castle not near the lake but closer to the commercial centre of the town. Although modest in size when compared to the grand homes by the lake, this stone house features three wings, all centred about a castellated central tower. This distinctive home looks every bit the castle.

Unfortunately, McIntosh wouldn't enjoy it for long. A shipper and ship owner he enjoyed his good years while Kingston remained a key port. However, the shallow nature of the harbour prevented the port's expansion. Then when the Grand Trunk Railway opened its line three kilometers inland from the water, the competition proved too much for most of the lake shippers and McIntosh had to sell the unfinished castle.

McIntosh's Castle has a location as fortunate as its appearance. On the front side it overlooks City Park, close to the classical former County building, and facing the Queens University. To the east lies the City's historic residential district, with a mix of houses large and small, but all wonderfully preserved. A few blocks distant stand the historic stores of Kingston's commercial core, centred around the European style market square. ❖

SIR JOHN A's TEACADDY CASTLE

When a struggling young lawyer named John A. McDonald nicknamed his rented home the "Teacaddy Castle," he may have had his tongue planted firmly in his cheek.

There is no doubt that it was and still is one of Kingston's grandest homes. It was built in 1839 by a Kingston merchant named Charles Hales in a style then in vogue with certain architects, the Italianate or Tuscan Villa style. In a time when most of Kingston's other grand mansions were either Georgian or Gothic, this unusual style decidedly stood out.

The identity of the architect is uncertain, although one source ascribes the design to George Brown, architect of Kingston's magnificent domed city hall.

Known as "Bellevue", it was located along the shore of Lake Ontario, west of the city. Here the landed gentry were building their country homes and giving them names like Summerhill, Edgehill, Rockwood and Alwington. From the rise of

More commonly known as Bellevue, this Italianate villa was named the "Teacaddy Castle" by John A. MacDonald before he became Canada's first prime minister

land the homes enjoyed the view of the lake, while the invigorating breezes wafted in, a refreshing change from the dust and smell of the city itself.

It was largely for this reason that John A. McDonald moved his family here in 1848. Since the birth of their son, John Jr., his wife Isabella had been ill to the point of being an invalid. Their first home on Brock St did not help, being exposed to the noise, dust and odour of a nearby tavern. The move to the lakeside location seemed to help. As Isabella's health gradually improved, John could tend to his growing law practice, and to his duties as the area's member of parliament.

Sadly, just one month after they moved in, their young son died. The cause was never publicly disclosed. Just a year later, with debts mounting, John dissolved his law partnership and moved out of Bellevue.

The next year, another son, Hugh John, was born, and McDonald moved his family into a stone house on Johnson St. In 1854 McDonald became Attorney General and moved once more, this time to Toronto where Isabella died three years later.

By the time John A. McDonald became Canada's first prime minster in 1867, the Teacaddy Castle was being occupied by the first of a number of private owners. Finally, in 1964 the federal government bought the building and restored it to the period of Sir John A's residency.

Many changes had taken place in the meantime. Electricity and plumbing had been installed, and a number of the original fireplaces removed, while some doorways and cellar accesses had been covered over. Because the original plans have not survived, restoration proved a challenge. Nonetheless, when the doors opened to the public, Bellevue, complete with costumed interpreters, was a step back to the time of its most illustrious tenant.

From the entrance hall visitors could move directly into either the drawing room, dining room or back parlour which led to the gardens. The room known as Isabella's room was originally a morning room. But the young woman's ailments required that she have a main floor chambers.

The second floor consisted of the nursery, guest bedroom, servants' quarters, and, overlooking the grounds and the lake, the master bedroom with its separate dressing room. Unfortunately, little in the way of the McDonalds' actual furniture could be located. Only the cradle in the nursery is believed to have belonged to the family.

The grounds, much reduced due to Kingston's urban growth, have been replanted using gardening layouts and techniques common in McDonald's era.

Kingston has managed to retain many of its early grand homes. While Alwington was destroyed by fire, Rockwood, Summerhill, and Edgehill still stand, as does the home the McDonalds occupied on Johnson St. Most prominent among them is Sir John A's Teacaddy Castle.

Sir John A. McDonald

The main downside to Kingston's townscape is the unfortunate wall of ordinary looking hotels, approved over the last decade, that lines the waterfront, blocking the view of the water from most parts of downtown. The dreadful urban sprawl which has consumed upper Princess St and which now surrounds this historic town is better left unmentioned. ❖

SUMMERHILL

Perhaps the sprawling home known as Summerhill is more deserving of the title "castle" than does the unfortunate McIntosh. For not only does it sit grandly atop a rise of land, surrounded by shady trees, but it was considered to be Canada's grandest home in its day.

In 1836 George Okill Stuart, archdeacon of Kingston, had come into an inheritance of a large farm located on the lake immediately west of the city. By selling off lots from the farm, including a 25 acre chunk for 4,000 pounds, he was able to build the grandest home in the city.

The main features include two quarter-circle porticos and a wide bay which contains the drawing room below and the main bedroom

Known as Stuart's Folly, Summerhill was one of the grandest of Kingston's lakeshore homes

The imposing front staircase of Summerhill

above. From the two-storey central section a pair of large colonnaded wings were built, to which second stories were later added.

But in a story which seems typical of many of Ontario's castle builders, George Okill Stuart would not long occupy Summerhill. Soon after moving in, Stuart's wife found the building too damp, thanks to an underground stream which ran beneath it. As a result, in 1843, they moved back into their smaller home closer to the centre of town. While Kingston enjoyed its two-year reign as the provincial capital, Summerhill was used as government offices. Too pricey to rent out, the home then stood empty for a number of years, derisively nicknamed "Stuart's folly."

In 1853 the place was rented to Queen's University, and for five years contained most of the university's facilities, including student accommodation. Finally, in 1867, it became the official, and drier, residence of the principal and vice chancellor, a role it retains to this day. As part of the university campus, the grounds are open to the public.

The building stands on the southeast side of the campus, close to the City Park beside which McIntosh's castle stands. Its once commanding view of the lake, however, is now blocked by the buildings of Kingston General Hospital. ✧

BARRA CASTLE, *Kitchener*

Her name was Molly Marquette, and she wanted a castle.

Mrs Marquette, whose maiden name was Barra, had lived in a Russian castle in old Moscow for most of her childhood years. By 1930 however, she had married and moved to Kitchener Ontario. While here, she became expert in designing and remodeling houses. While she patiently worked on smaller homes, her wish for a castle never subsided.

Finally, her opportunity arrived. In 1930 she acquired a small house belonging to a family known as Mackay. It stood on Queen St, very close to the two historic Schneider houses. And she began to remodel it into the dream castle she had always wanted.

The south side of the building most resembled the castle she remembered in Russia. Here were the Roman-like towers and turrets. More were built on the north side of the structure as well. Although Mrs Marquette had only one leg, her determination was so great that a rumour circulated

Named for a Russian castle in old Moscow, Barra Castle was built by a one-legged woman named Molly Marquette

that she had started to build the foundation of the new section herself.

The building was never intended as a single residence, however. Rather, it was constructed as an apartment building. And she called it Barra Castle. Newspaper headlines of the day trumpeted the accomplishment as the "City's First and Only Castle Constructed By Woman Architect."

Molly had one son, Harold. A self- taught engineer, Harold had an unusual hobby, building airplanes, not model ones, but full-sized air-craft, which, it was alleged, he constructed in the basement of Barra Castle. None of the planes were ever known to have actually flown. Molly also had five daughters. They did not build airplanes.

Among the castle's more prestigious visitors were Sir Wilfrid Laurier and William Lyon MacKenzie King.

The building itself is three stories high and three bays wide. The northern entrance, which faces Queen St., boasts a pointed arched doorway with raised mouldings. Above the door, a raised plaque contains the name of the castle, along with two coats of arms. The steps leading to it include lion's head carvings and Corinthian order capitals.

The building is noted most famously for its castle-like turrets and crenellated roofline. The building encases a courtyard where a rock garden once was laid out. A walkway leads through a gothic archway to what was once a sunken garden.

The southern entrance is a large wooden door with a pinwheel design and archvolt moldings, and sidelights with diamond-shaped pains of glass. Thick walls and high ceilings continue the castle-like aspect into the building itself.

Owners over the years have included Kitchener mayor Dr Stanley Leavine, and lawyer Ken Devlin. In 1988 the building, then badly deteriorated, was purchased by Morris Borenstein and Harry Dennis with the intention of restoring its former luster.

Molly Marquette's Barra Castle stands on Queen St South, a short distance from Kitchener's famous Schneider House museum. ✧

THE CASTLE OF LONDON

It can't get more British than this. High on a bluff overlooking a river called the Thames, in a city named London, soar the towers of one of Ontario's most castle-like buildings. Although it was modeled after a noteworthy castle in Ireland, London's Middlesex County court house was never a residential building.

Ontario's first governor, John Graves Simcoe, had at first preferred the Thames-side town for the colony's new capital. But he settled instead on York, on Lake Ontario, in 1793. London would later become the new district capital, however, but it had to wait another 30 plus years.

Finally in 1826, settlement of the London District began. As its capital, London needed a court house, and one of those selected to

Never a dwelling, London's castle was built as a court house

Colonizer Thomas Talbot wanted the court house to be built to resemble his family's Malahide Castle in Ireland

sit on the commission to design it was an Irishman named Thomas Talbot. After his arrival in Upper Canada, Talbot quickly ingratiated himself with the authorities and was granted the right to attract settlers to a vast area of land stretching inland from the shore of Lake Erie.

Working from a log cabin, which he called Malahide Castle, after his ancestral castle in Ireland, he granted lands to settlers in 29 townships. He was as strict as he was eccentric. For those of whom he approved, he insisted that the requirement to clear land and build a cabin were met. For those of whom he did not approve, there would be no land at all.

Frustrated in his inability to build a replica of his beloved castle on his own property, he urged the commission to design the London court house after Castle Malahide - the real one.

And indeed, the resemblance is stunningly close. Built between 1829 and 1831, the court house measured 100 feet by 50 feet, and soared 50 feet into the air. On each of the four corners were octagonal towers, each crowned with the crenellated battlements typical of the European castle, and identical to those of Castle Malahide. Three tall pointed windows looked out from the city side of the court house, while an embayment looked out over the river. In design the castle was more house than court.

Inside, though, it was all court, with offices and cells on the ground floor, judges' chambers and court rooms on the second, and more cells on the third floor.

Major changes were made in 1877, and again in 1911, but the overall castle like appearance has been maintained.

In 1880 the court house witnessed one of Canada's most famous and controversial trials. In February of that year a mob of vigilantes strode out into the night to carry out a murderous scheme, the massacre of a Lucan area family called the Donnelly's. Reviled by most of the area's Irish settlers, the family had been accused of fires and assaults and even murders over their thirty years of living on the chilly Roman Line outside of Lucan, a rough frontier town north west of London.

On that fateful night, the vigilantes burst into the Donnelly cabin, murdering four family members, then later killed a fifth in his home a short distance away. The only witness to the executions was a 15-year-old boy who had hidden under the bed. When the vigilantes were arrested and brought to trial in the London court house, the eyes of the world were upon them. The court rooms were packed with reporters, and crowds milled around the streets outside. At the first trial, the judge had left it up to the jury as to whether the word of a boy so young could be trusted. The result was a hung jury. However, at the second trial, the judge simply told the jury not to believe the boy. Acquittal was inevitable.

Sadly, in recent years, most of London's historical downtown buildings have been bulldozed away by profit hungry developers and short-sighted municipal councils. But, despite the mayhem around it, the castle by the river still occupies its prominent perch, and remains one of Ontario's most convincing castles. ❖

KNARSBORO HALL, *Markdale*

Markdale, Ontario, is one of those places that remains little known outside its region. A quiet town, Markdale began life as a stopping place for stagecoaches carrying travelers on their way up the Sydenham Road, a settlement road that led from Toronto to Owen Sound. When the Toronto Grey and Bruce Railway came through in 1884, Markdale boomed with more businesses and residences. One of those arrivals was Dr. Thomas Simpson Sproule.

In 1880 he built what was described as a "castle-like" home, reflective of his Scottish roots, on a rise of land a short distance east

Now a funeral home, Knarsboro Hall is Markdale's grandest building

of the Sydenham Road. It was distinguished by its pillars, arched doorways and woodwork with elaborate carvings.

Italianate in style, it was designed with a tall tower and mansard roof. Guests would be ushered into a large reception area. From this vestibule the visitors could enter rooms on either side, each of which contained marble fireplaces. From the reception area a grand curving stairway lead to upper levels. The building featured French dormers with Venetian gothic windows, many of which contained stained glass. Outside, the grounds were extensively landscaped.

During his residency, Sproule served in the Senate of Canada, an office he held until his death. His wife remained in Knarsboro Hall until 1921. Then through the 1930s and 40s the grand old house served variously as apartments and a hospital until 1946 when the Canadian legion bought the house.

In 1966 it was bought by Donald May who converted it back into a residence as well as a funeral home, and restored it to reflect its early grandeur. Other than the fact that some of the grounds were converted to enlarge the parking lot, the building retains its lustre and its role as the castle of the community.

The rattle of the stagecoaches has long been replaced with the steady flow of automobiles and trucks, as the old Sydenham Road is now Highway 10. In more recent years the tracks of the railway have been lifted, needlessly some have argued. Many of Markdale's businesses have been changed to serve this new breed of travellers.

GOODERHAM CASTLE, *Meadowvale*

In 1975 the historic mill village of Meadowvale became the first community in Ontario to become designated as a heritage district in its entirety. One the key reasons is the pillared Gooderham mansion.

The Credit River tumbles from the heights of the Niagara Escarpment to flow swiftly to Lake Ontario. The Credit watershed was purchased from the Mississauga Indians in 1820 and soon after, settlers, led by Squire John Beatty, began to make their way

With its handsome pillars, the Gooderham house is a perfect fit in this historic village

upstream. The size and swiftness of the river attracted mill operators to its banks where many mill villages grew.

Meadowvale was one such village. Its first sawmills were built in the 1830s and the first gristmill in 1844. By the 1850s Meadowvale had grown to include a pair of hotels, a church, a school and at least two general stores. By then Francis Silverthorne was running the grist mill. When he was ruined financially by the Crimean War, the mill was taken over by the Toronto-based firm of Gooderham and Worts.

Soon after Charles "Holly" Gooderham, then only 18, was sent to take over the operation of the grist mill. Here, in 1870, he and his wife Eliza built a large brick mansion on a height of land east of the village, a pillared southern style home that dwarfed the simple workers' houses which lined Meadowvale's narrow lanes.

Meanwhile the mill toiled on 24 hours a day producing flour, with the leftover mash being made into alcohol. Gooderham, however, did not remain long, and by 1880 had moved away. Finally, the mill closed in 1950 and was demolished four years later.

The mansion then became a summer resort known as Rose Villa, after which it served variously as a politician's home, a seminary and an apartment. After a period of disuse, it has now become a school and the grounds have been landscaped.

The GTA's urban sprawl has finally caught up with Meadowvale and now totally surrounds the historic village. Fortunately, under the heritage designation, all buildings must retain their historic appearance. A new Derry Road bypass carries most traffic around the village, sparing the tree lined streets the gridlock that plagues most of the GTA. Like an oasis, Meadowvale's old homes, stores and hotels retain their 19th century mill town flavour. And overseeing it all is the restored Gooderham castle. ❖

EKFRID CASTLE, *Melbourne*

West of London the farm lands stretch flat and occasionally treeless to a distant horizon. The soils are deep and fertile, the summers hot and sultry. It is an area often described as Ontario's "deep south." It therefore seems an unlikely place to boast a "castle."

Yet that is exactly how area residents label a massive brick house that dominates the landscape in an area north of the hamlet of Ekfrid.

When Francis Elliot arrived from Ireland in 1820, the land looked far different. Dense forests towered high above the crude muddy trails that passed for roads. The main thoroughfare through the region was known as the Longwoods Road and had led prospective settlers into the lush lands which lined the Thames River.

Because travel was so difficult, little self-sustaining communities sprang up at frequent intervals along the forest path. One went by

Twelve thousand bricks were used to construct this country castle

the name of Mayfair Settlement and consisted of a church, sawmill, post office, blacksmith, hotel and a number of small cabins.

Anxious to provide his wife with a comfortable home in these difficult environs, Francis' son, George, built for her a massive brick home. The building cost George the sum of $7,000, a substantial amount in the 1880s, and in 1891 the family moved in.

This three-storey structure defies an apt architectural category, displaying a bit of nearly every style popular in the late 1880s. While a curved tower-like extension dominates the south section of the house, a soaring wooden dormer rises above the centre section. A wooden porch, surrounded by intricate fretwork, rises to enfold a second floor balcony. An estimated 12,000 bricks were used, while slate was placed on the roof.

Surrounded by the simpler homes of local farmers, the house soon gained its nickname, "Ekfrid Castle".

No fewer than forty-four windows allow light to pour into the 20-plus rooms. Many of the windows were constructed with interior shutters. Marble fireplaces warmed many of the rooms, while an intricately designed stairway, made of Italian cherry wood, leads to the upper floors. The attic was large enough for the children to ride their bikes and to bowl in a bowling alley.

Soon after it was built George died and the family sold the property to Christopher McCallum, freshly returned to Ontario from a failed bid to homestead on the prairies.

For a number of years following the second world war, the house sat empty and deteriorating. Finally a family moved in from Sudbury and, rather than demolish the landmark, they decided to restore it to much of its original glory.

Most of Mayfair Settlement has vanished from the landscape, and newer homes now line the Longwoods Road. But up until now nothing can compare to the Ekfrid Castle.

The building is visible on the north side of County Road 2, Longwoods Road, about 5 km west of the village of Melbourne. ❖

OAK HALL, *Niagara Falls*

What with Clifton Hill, the casino, and, of course, the Falls, it's easy to overlook Niagara Falls' castle, Oak Hall. Even though it sits high atop a 100-foot limestone cliff overlooking the thundering cataract.

And even though it was built by one of Canada's richest and most mysterious mining magnates, Sir Harry Oakes.

The site was first given out as a land grant in 1798 to United Empire Loyalist James Skinner. In 1816 the next owner, Colonel Thomas Clark, built a new house and named it Clark Hill. He died in 1837 and in 1850 a descendant, Thomas Clark Street, rebuilt the crumbling house.

Sir Harry Oakes had one of the best views of Niagara Falls from his grand castle-like home

The property passed through numerous owners before Ontario's wealthiest miner, Harry Oakes, bought it in 1924. He then hired the architectural firm of Findlay and Fowles, designers of the Table Rock House, to build for him a 37-room Tudor castle. But Oakes himself lived there for only six years, 1928-1934, before taxes drove him out of Canada.

The *porte-cochere* of Harry Oakes Niagara Falls Castle

A New Englander by birth, Harry Oakes had lasted only two years in medical school in Syracuse before heading out to search for gold. His prospecting took him to the Klondike, where, like so many others, he discovered that all the gold had been claimed. He met with no more success in Australia, New Zealand and the stifling heat of Death Valley, California. He then set his sights on northern Ontario, and soon found himself in the mining boom town of Swastika.

Here, 36 years old and nearly broke, he met up with the four Tough brothers and staked a claim near the shores of Kirkland Lake. But it was the rocks beneath the lake that held the mother lode, and Oakes staked them by himself. Within two years the shares in Harry Oakes' Lakeshore Mine went from 35 cents to $70. By age 47, Oakes was a multi-millionaire. He then built his chateau nearby before moving to Niagara Falls.

But Oakes soon became discouraged with life in Canada. First he

A number of the rooms in Oak Hall are open
to the public

was denied a promised seat in the Senate. Then the overwhelming taxes of $3 million a year sent him in search of another country to call home. With its climate and tax-free status, Nassau in the Bahamas was too good to resist and he moved there with his wife and young daughter Nancy. Here his headstrong 17-year-old daughter fell in love with and married a dashing Frenchman named Alfred de Marigny.

After donating 50,000 pounds to the St George's hospital in London, Oakes was knighted. But he would not long enjoy either his status or his wealth for in 1943 his bludgeoned body was found partially burned. His son-in-law was charged with murder, but later acquitted. No other suspects were ever found.

That year Lady Eunice Oakes donated the Niagara Falls house to the government of Canada for use as an RCAF convalescent hospital. In 1959 it was purchased by the Niagara Parks Commission who furnished the main floor in 1964 and, who, two years later, added a golf course to the extensive grounds.

In 1982 the Commission moved their offices into the house, restoring the great hall, dining room and living room to their original condition. Here are located 12 historic dining room chairs used at a luncheon for Edward Prince of Wales in 1919, as well as 51 paintings, several by W.H. Bartlett. These rooms are open to the public between 8:45 - 4:00 Monday to Friday. The remainder of the building contains the commission offices and is not available to the general public.

Oak Hall looks very much the castle. Surrounding the stone portico which covers the curving driveway, are several delightful flower beds. At the back of the building, with its patio and massive wooden doors, the view of the Falls has now been obscured by trees.

KING'S CASTLE, *Oakville*

In an era when most homes in Ontario, even those considered grand, were simple in design, the castle built by William McKenzie King was decidedly adventurous.

Before 1827 Oakville Ontario was little more than a forested cove, sheltering passing canoes and schooners. In that year, Colonel William Chisholm arrived from Nova Scotia and took up a tract of land nearly a thousand acres in area. Here he engaged his assistant Merrick Thomas to lay out a townsite. Chisholm, meanwhile, built several boats and developed the harbour at Oakville.

When William Chisholm died in 1842, his affairs were passed on

With its steeply-pitched gables, King's Castle is decidedly out of place surrounded by a modern housing subdivision

to his son, Robert, who as the head of the extended family, looked out after his many siblings and cousins. One of the many calls for help came from his eccentric cousin William McKenzie King.

King, who had spent a number of years wandering in search of gold and embarking upon unusual adventures such as whaling, returned to Oakville in 1858 and bought a parcel of land from cousin Robert. Here he built his strange looking house which he originally named "Solitude." Because of King's local prominence, and the grandeur of the house, locals took to calling it "King's Castle."

Anticipating the gothic craze which would later sweep the homes of the rich and famous, King built a four-storey home with dormers that had such a steep pitch they alone extended a storey and a half. Located on an early Indian trail, the castle sat adjacent to an even earlier tavern and horse changing station.

To most of Oakville's residents, King remained eccentric. Although it was widely rumoured that he built his castle to attract rich young women, he ended up betrothed instead to a simple housekeeper. He was no more successful at editing the local newspaper than he was at prospecting or whaling, giving up after a short effort. When he inherited a hotel from his aunt, he lost it, too, through gambling. He then proceeded to upset local Royalists by opposing the expenses of celebrating Queen Victoria's birthday.

King didn't stay long in his castle, being forced to sell it in 1859. In 1879 an ailing King died, with "no credit, no money and no hope" according to an acquaintance. The building changed hands several times and by 1902 was advertised as having both indoor plumbing and forced air heating.

A fire in 1960 destroyed the old tavern next door, and a kitchen addition was built in its place. In 1973 the castle was restored to much of its original grandeur and designated as a heritage building under Ontario's then new Heritage Act, the first residence in Ontario to receive such a designation.

The designation has helped save many of the building's features.

Five original fireplaces remain, although the marble mantlepiece from the living room is no longer in place. The parlour and dining room are separated by an elaborate arch with ribbed wood trim and a wooden keystone. A long hall down one side of the house leads from the main entrance to a broad staircase with walnut balusters. Although these and many other original features remain in place, the verandah and solarium have both gone.

Over the decades, development has eaten away at the grounds which surrounded the home. Also still standing are two other Chisholm homes, that of George Chisholm, brother to Robert, and that of family patriarch Robert. The latter, known as Erchless, is preserved beside the customs house which also opened by Chisholm. ✥

SKIBEREEN CASTLE, *Odessa*

Located in the historic mill town of Odessa in eastern Ontario, John Booth's Skibereen Castle is the least likely looking of Ontario's forgotten castles.

But, as with many others, it was the home of one of the community's kings of local industry.

Joshua Booth was the first of the family to arrive in eastern Ontario, a United Empire Loyalist refugee from the American Revolution. He entered the milling business by building the first grist mill in the Millhaven area. Booth then acquired land and a grist mill on the Kingston stage road at Mill Creek. The grist mill passed on to Joshua's son Benjamin, and in turn to his sons, Philip and John.

It was not particularly grand, but it was the home of Odessa's leading industrialists

The main street of Odessa as it appeared at the height of Booth's empire

The brothers added woolen and planing mills, which gave birth to a bustling community named Odessa. They also operated barley mills and a cloth factory.

John Booth built his large home in a part of the community known as the "Irish section," populated by immigrant labourers who had worked on macadamizing the Kingston Road. The two-storey house was built of stone walls eighteen inches thick and boasted pine floors and carved baseboards.

Because it was the grandest home in this modest neighbourhood, his Irish neighbours nicknamed the house the "Skibereen Castle," after a market town in County Cork.

In addition to the "castle" Odessa contains a number of buildings which reflect its long history. Two early stone buildings date from the 1840s, the Timmerman store, and what is now the Royal Bank building. Meanwhile, on the banks of the creek, the woolen mill still stands. ❖

CASTLE LESLIE, ORANGEVILLE

By today's standards, and indeed even by those of the late 19th century, Castle Leslie is but a humble abode. But when it was built, it was among the grandest homes in the town.

The town is Orangeville. Named after its founder, Orange Lawrence, Orangeville began as a small mill town on the banks of Mill Creek, a tributary to the Credit River. It was during this early phase of Orangeville's history that an Irish immigrant named Guy Leslie arrived and took up farming in nearby Garafraxa Township. After being appointed county court clerk in 1857, he moved into Orangeville and bought one of Orange Lawrence's town lots.

Although more Georgian than baronial, Castle Leslie was one of Orangeville's grandest early homes

Two years later he moved into his new grand Georgian style home. This was not the era of Ontario's castle building, and Castle Leslie bore none of the towers and turrets that the gothic castles would sport a few decades later. Although massive, it was a typical Regency Villa square plan. Two stories high, it boasted a wide porch supported by four wooden columns. Its double brick construction afforded a level of insulation and comfort that most of Orangeville's simple frame cabins lacked. Inside the large open vestibule a grand staircase led to the several bedrooms upstairs.

This was still the stagecoach era in Orangeville. The grand homes that the town boasts today would have to wait for the arrival of Orangeville's two railway lines. By the standards of the day, Leslie's fine home was one of the two or three grandest in town. So ostentatious was it by comparison that the other villagers took to calling it Leslie's Castle.

It is a name that remains to this day, even though the large brick mansions that accompanied the railway era, and today's monster homes, render it modest by comparison.

The railways came, first the Credit Valley Railway in 1874, and the Toronto Grey and Bruce a decade later. Eventually the Canadian Pacific Railway acquired both lines, and rationalized them by removing redundant portions of each. The Credit Valley station was removed in the early years, while the second of two TGB stations has been moved close to the main street (Broadway) to become a popular restaurant.

Orangeville has managed to retain a respectable number of its early structures, including the town hall and market place, built in 1873, and Greystones restaurant, a wonderful stone hotel that served as a stagecoach stop as early as 1852.

Leslie later moved to a house on York St in Orangeville. His two sons went on to co-invent the revolutionary rotary snowplough used by the railways to clear the massive snowdrifts that frequently bury tracks in this snow belt area.

Later the castle was divided into apartments, and much of the original interior was lost. But a lingering look at the exterior will reveal just how lovely this home was in a time when most dwellings were simple and small. Indeed it was a castle in its day.

THE COLONEL'S CASTLE,
Parkwood in Oshawa

Aman's castle may be distinguished not by its towers or turrets, but by the role of its owner in the community. And nobody had a greater role in the development of the City of Oshawa than did Robert Samuel McLaughlin.

By 1869 the family was already heavily into the carriage making business, an enterprise started by Sam's father in Enniskillen Ontario. In 1892 the 21-year-old Sam became a partner in his father's operation, which had by then relocated to the nearby town of Oshawa.

Canada's first car-maker, Col. Sam McLaughlin built a sprawling mansion north of Oshawa. The rooms and gardens are now open to the public

Col. Sam McLaughlin in front of his castle

While Oshawa had boomed with the arrival of the railway, another transportation revolution was about to burst onto the scene, and that was the pending popularity of the horse-less carriage. Sensing the trend, McLaughlin, in 1908, started the McLaughlin Motor Car Company, while his father continued in the carriage business. By 1918 competition from American auto manu-facturers like Buick and Chevrolet had become too intense, and McLaughlin sold his company to General Motors.

Sam added the rank of "colonel" to his name when he was appointed an honorary colonel in the local Ontario regiment. He would, many years later, also become a Companion of the Order of Canada.

All this time Sam and his wife, Pauline, were looking for a place for themselves and their five daughters to live. Their first home had

Pillars mark the former main entrance

burned in 1910, and although they rebuilt it, they began looking for something grander. They found the location in a 14-acre amusement park known as Prospect Park, located north of what was then the limits of the city of Oshawa.

To build their new home, they hired the architectural firm of Darling and Pearson, known for having designed the magnificent North Toronto railway station for the CPR. By 1917 the mansion was finished and at $100,000 was considered to be Canada's most expensive home. They called their castle Parkwood.

Guests entered through four two-storey pillars and into a foyer from which a modest curving staircase led to the second floor. Here they may have found daughter Eileen playing on a pipe organ whose pipes were secreted in the hallway walls. A $10,000 Steinway player piano was the centrepiece for the drawing room with decoration handpainted in Hamburg, Germany.

In the dining room a mahogany table was set under a remarkable chandelier of Bohemian glass. On the wall portraits of three of the family's five daughters still hang. The dining room led into a bright and airy breakfast room. Here the McLaughlins would be served on one of seven sets of dishes, one for each day of the week.

The sunroom, added later, overlooks the extensive lawns and gardens which stretch away on the south side. Overhead, the ceiling was painted with a mural called Gods of the Wine Festival. In this room guests would often be entertained by a live orchestra.

The McLaughlins were a very active family, for located north of the main entrance were nothing less than an indoor swimming pool, squash court and bowling alley.

Although the mansion contained 25 bedrooms, the five daughters shared three. Two other bedrooms were set aside as "bachelor apartments" for whenever the daughters' suitors would be invited to stay over. Later in life Sam and his wife Adelaide would inhabit separate apartments. The shower in Sam's contained seven heads.

All in all Parkwood contained 55 rooms and had 11 fireplaces.

But it wasn't just the indoor luxuries for which the McLaughlin

Many public holidays and other events were celebrated at Parkwood

mansion was famous. It was the gardens. Here the designers and landscape architects created a series of garden landscapes, including a magnificent formal garden with fountain and tea house, a sunken garden, a terrace and an intricate Italian garden. The gardens are still maintained and most of the flowers for them continue to be grown in the on- site greenhouses.

After Adelaide died in 1958, aged 85, the Colonel lived on at Parkwood until, in 1972 he too died, aged 101.

He bequeathed the estate to the Oshawa General Hospital which set up the Parkwood Foundation and opened the site to the public. Here you can freely stroll the grounds and enjoy the magnificent gardens. Guided tours of the house itself are available for a small paid admission.

Today Oshawa has sprawled northward and surrounded the grounds. Nevertheless, the spaciousness and the beauty of those grounds and the magnificence of the Colonel's castle remain intact. ◈

KING CAPRON'S CASTLE, *Paris*

The founder of Paris, Ontario, Hiram "King" Capron, would not likely recognize his castle today.

Capron moved to Upper Canada from the United States in 1822 to make his fortune. Here, along with two other enterprising young settlers, Joseph Van Norman, and George Tillson, Capron chose a cove on Lake Erie where the three began Ontario's first iron ore furnace. Technology of the day dictated that bog ore was fired to make iron implements such as ploughs and kettles. A village called

Started by Hiram "King" Capron, Penmarvian remained modest in size until finished by industrialist John Penman

The beautiful tower on Penmarvian

Normandale developed up around the furnace and grew to a population of 400. When the furnace shut down a few years later, the village became a ghost town.

But Hiram Capron had always had his mind set on an area known as the forks of the Grand. Here, where Smith's Creek flowed into the Grand River, Capron bought a large parcel of land and laid out a townsite. Because of the extensive gypsum beds in the area, a product used in the making of plaster of Paris, Capron named the townsite Paris.

Capron made his fortune grinding the gypsum, and earned his prestige by assisting in the establishment of churches and a library.

By 1850 Capron was worth nearly a quarter of a million dollars and he decided to build a grand new home overlooking the river. He had well earned his nickname "king" Capron, and the king was about to build his castle.

Known as Riverview Hall, it was a five-bay stone house with pillastered cornices, a grand home, but a far cry from the building which it later became. Sadly, his wife Mary died shortly thereafter, while the king lived on until 1872. In 1887 a local industrialist named John Penman bought Riverview Hall and began to add an extensive array of towers, turrets, and arches, until it resembled a castle. He renamed it Penmarvian.

Today Penmarvian has become a retirement home, and has retained all of its grandeur. While Capron's carriage house still stands (larger than most houses in Paris) little can be seen of the original Riverview Hall which King Capron knew. The grounds are still extensive and well treed, however, new growth now obscures the view of the river. It stands on Grand River St North.

Capron's first house still stands as well, a modest dwelling at 8 Homestead Rd.

Paris is blessed with several unusual houses. Asa Wolverton's southern plantation style manor stands on Grand River Street South. Like Capron, Wolverton was an American-born industrialist. Yet another American, Norman Hamilton, built the house known as Hamilton Place, a Greek Revival style house, built entirely of cobblestones. This unique construction technique was introduced to Paris by still another American, Live Boughton, and consisted of laying identically sized cobblestones in mortar in the manner of bricks. Paris has about a dozen buildings constructed in this manner. A downtown store contains a plaque to commemorate the world's first long distance phone call placed by Alexander Graham Bell from his original home downstream in Brantford. ❖

CASTLE VILLENEUVE, *Picton*

The ground in Picton shuddered, and windows rattled as a deafening explosion filled the air. By the time the dust had cleared, a shocked community looked at the charred ruins of what had been one of its oddest houses, the whimsical Castle Villeneuve.

Picton is one of those places that, in proportion to its size, boasts an inordinate number of grand homes. While it was never an industrial town, as was Hamilton, it did attract those who made their money in shipping. One of the earliest harbours on Lake Ontario, Picton was funneling settlers into Prince Edward County

This eclectic but grand home was functioning as a restaurant when it was destroyed by fire

as early as 1783. It was known as Hallowell's Bridge until 1837 when it changed its name to Picton.

One of the port's early arrivals was a young lawyer named Phillip Low. He quickly established his notoriety when, just three years after he arrived, he led a battalion of loyal troops against William Lyon McKenzie in the battle of Montgomery's Tavern during the 1837 rebellion. By 1855 he had founded and was president of the Grand Trunk Telegraph company. Thanks to the building of the Grand Trunk Railway, and its need for telegraph communication, Low's company expanded to operate 65 telegraph offices between Montreal and Buffalo.

In 1840 he purchased a simple farmhouse on a bluff overlooking the harbour. Then he began to add towers, turrets, wings and fanciful windows and doors. He named the eclectic building Castle Villeneuve, after his mother's family connection to Admiral Villeneuve who had commanded the French fleet against Admiral Nelson at the battle of Trafalgar.

Its latest incarnation was as a restaurant until a gas leak erupted into a violent explosion, destroying the legendary place.

CLARAMOUNT, *Picton*

Of all Picton's grand homes, Claramount survives as Picton's castle heir-apparent. Villeneuve's other next door neighbour, Claramount was not built until 1906. Three stories high, its six hollow wooden columns, arranged in a semi-circular pattern, reach two of those stories, and are topped with terra cotta Ionic caps. The building took full advantage of its location on a small peninsula and its view of the bay with spacious porches.

Claramont was Castle Villeneuve's neighbour

Its owner was a young lawyer named Edward Malcolm Young who named it after his wife Clara. Young died in 1936 and for twenty years Clara rented out rooms to tourists. Then in 1956 it was divided into apartment units. While it was never known as, nor much resembled, a castle, Claramount is the only survivor of the three grand homes that overlooked the bay.

Many of Picton's other grand homes line the opposite side of the harbour and are arranged along Main St and Hill St.

While Picton's main downtown street, Johnson Street, contains a number of early historic commercial structures, its heritage integrity has been compromised by incompatible fast food outlets and other modern intrusions.

RYLAND'S RICKARTON CASTLE, *Picton*

Castle Villeneuve was not Picton's only castle. In 1860 Colonel George H. Ryland bought a 100 acre parcel overlooking Picton Harbour and converted the simple house which was on it into a decidedly castle-like mansion. While it lacked the size and the eclecticism of Castle Villeneuve, its crenellated tower and ramparts made it more castle-like in its appearance. Designed after Warwick Castle in England, Ryland named it initially the Warwick House.

He added a large square three-storey tower with a crenellated parapet around the top. He then altered the roof structure of the original house to give it a crenellated roofline as well. Stone quoins set off the corners, while medieval mouldings could be found above the win-

Castle-like in appearance, Rickerton served briefly as an Anglican boarding school and later a tavern

dows. A Tudor style arch was placed over the main doorway.

While Ryland's castle was much smaller than its next door neighbour, Castle Villeneuve, it too enjoyed a fine view across the bay.

Between 1866 until 1877 it struggled as the Ontario College, a Church of England boarding school. But its isolation relative to Ontario's larger cities proved its undoing and it was sold to a local ship owner, Arthur W. Hepburn. One of his ships was named the "Rickarton" and he gave the name to the castle at this time.

The castle remained in the Hepburn family until 1944 when it was used briefly as command headquarters for the local Hastings and Prince Edward regiments. After lying vacant, Rickarton was converted to a hotel and tavern, retaining many of its interior features such as the ballroom with its molded plaster cornices and Egyptian columns.

Then in the late 80's it was left vacant once more until it was heavily damaged by vandals and demolished. ◈

PENRYN PARK, *Port Hope's Castle*

Few would argue that Port Hope contains Ontario's best preserved collection of 19ᵗʰ century stores and houses. Its location on the swift flowing Ganaraska River assured its initial prosperity as a mill town, while its small harbour gave it an all-important shipping outlet. During the early years of the 19ᵗʰ century many grand homes were built, primarily on the east side of the river. During this period the community, first known as Smiths Mills, briefly adopted the name Toronto. However, to avoid confusion with, not today's Toronto, but with Toronto Township, the name was changed to Port Hope.

Although the town of Port Hope boasts many grand homes, Penryn Park is its finest country castle

The arrival of a pair of railway lines, the Midland and the Grand Trunk, ushered Port Hope into a boom period which led to a further influx of grand homes. Many of these were placed prominently atop the lofty bluffs on the west side of town where the two railway stations were located. By the 1870s Port Hope had boomed to a population of 6,000.

And there it stayed. Cobourg, just 6 miles east, had the better port. With the shipping of iron ore from the Marmora mines, to which it was linked by the Cobourg and Marmora Railway, Cobourg became the busier of the two towns. Industries passed Port Hope by.

For lovers of heritage that was a good thing, for the buildings which would likely have been removed in the name of prosperity remained in place. They survived into an era when heritage buildings began to be seen as a valuable treasure to hold onto. As a

A small statue decorates the grounds of Penryn Park

result, Port Hope can claim Ontario's best preserved 19th century main street, and two historic residential areas, the older of the two dating to the 1830s and 40s, all of which represent 19th century landscapes that have been very little altered.

Here are some of Ontario's oldest and most magnificent homes. King St offers a street lined with some of Ontario's oldest houses, including the Bluestone and Little Bluestone which were built in 1834, St Mark's church from 1822, and the Canada House built in

1800. Meanwhile, Dorset St contains many of the mansions from the railway era, including Fairmount from 1858, the Wimborne House from 1859, and the massive pillared Hillcrest built in 1874.

But one of the most castle-like is that known as Penryn Park.

The original "Penryn" on Victoria Ave, was built in 1832 by Commander John Tucker Williams, a veteran of the 1812 war. Penryn Park was erected 27 years later by Williams' son, Colonel Arthur Williams. The younger Williams was, like his father, considered a war hero after having commanded the Midland battalion against the Metis during the Riel rebellion. At the battle of Batoch, it was he, ignoring a superior's order, who led a daring charge against the entrenched Metis. The surprise charge defeated the Metis and, according to some, turned the tide against the rebels. Within days Louis Riel had surrendered, and the rebellion was over.

But he would not long savor the honour, for he died shortly thereafter of pneumonia.

Penryn Park was even grander than the older Penryn building. It is considered a "gothic" style of house, with a steeply pitched roof and gables, pointed arches, and a large tower on the driveway side. A wide verandah which extends the length of the house looks south over a series of ridges to the waters of Lake Ontario in the distance.

In 1894 the house was sold to one Henry King of Pittsburgh, who, like many others from Pittsburgh had taken up summer residence in the Cobourg and Port Hope area.

A small but curious little house sits behind the larger home. This was added in 1894 by King who used it as a billiard parlour. With its high peaked roof it complements Williams' castle. Penryn Park has served as a restaurant, and has been part of the Port Hope golf course for 50 years. ❖

THE BIGELOW HOUSE, *Port Perry's Castle*

Port Perry is one of Ontario's forgotten treasures. A quiet village, it lies on the shore of Lake Scugog, the most southerly of the Kawartha Lakes. In the days before rail, steamers sailed the little lake, connecting Port Perry with other wharf side villages such as Caesarea and the now vanished Port Hoover. Many steamed up the Scugog River to dock at Lindsay.

With the arrival of the Whitby and Port Perry Railway, the little port boomed. Because it now had an iron link to the outside, industrialists began to move in. One of those daring individuals was Joseph Bigelow.

Built by Port Perry's leading industrialist, the Bigelow house dominates this historic town from its hilltop location

When sketched for the county atlas in the 1880s, the Bigelow house enjoyed rural surroundings

He had originally moved to Lindsay with his family where his father entered the milling business. In 1851 Joseph and his brother Joel moved to Port Perry to open a general store. When Joel moved to Chicago to start up a real estate business, Joseph took over a planing mill and began making barrel staves.

His next business venture was to build one of the premier commercial blocks on the main street, a handsome structure known as the Royal Arcade. By the 1870s he had become the most influential businessman in the village and decided to erect a home to match his status.

Every king needs his castle, and Bigelow's was to be a massive Italianate mansion on the highest point of land. He hired Oshawa architect H. R. Barber to design his dream home. When finished it was regarded as perhaps the finest example of such a house in southern Ontario.

From the main entrance-way, doors led to the dining room, parlour and Bigelow's own office, while a grand staircase led to the bedrooms and servants' quarters upstairs. The central tower soars four stories above the wrap-around porch. But unlike many contemporary homes, this one lacked fireplaces. Bigelow's wife, Elizabeth, objected that they were too dirty.

The house today remains little altered, and still occupies its large lot at the corner of McDonald and Cochrane Streets.

Much of Port Perry's main street remains as Bigelow might remember it. Most of the 19th century commercial buildings survive. The Royal Arcade burned in the disastrous fire which devastated the downtown in 1883, but was rebuilt in even grander style than before. In more recent times, unsightly overhead wires have been removed, and period streetlights added. Most of the stores now sport signs typical of the period as well. So authentically does Port Perry's main street harken back to its early years, that it has become a popular location for movies and television commercials. At the foot of the main street, the site of the railway station and yards is now occupied by an attractive lakeside park, while the station itself was moved across the street to become a flower shop.

Port Perry is one of the most appealing lakeside getaways in the Greater Toronto Area, a hidden treasure, where the "castle" Bigelow is still the king of the hill. ❖

CROSBY HALL, *Richmond Hill*

Historically, Richmond Hill has little to offer. Once a busy farm town, centred around its mill, Richmond Hill has been overwhelmed by Toronto's urban sprawl, and looks it. Mall after mall has popped up along Yonge St, Richmond Hill's main artery. Endless fields of houses spread seemingly to the horizon, while the historic downtown core has been compromised by uninteresting new businesses. All of which

One of the few remaining historic buildings in this rapidly changing Toronto suburb, Crosby Hall was built by Parker Crosby in 1863

makes the presence of an historic house like Crosby Hall that much more significant.

By comparison to Ontario's other "castles" Crosby Hall is modest in scale. The Hall dates from 1863 when it was built by one Parker Crosby and was, in its day, considered the "most palatial" place around.

The lot upon which it sits was originally owned by a refugee French Royalist named Chevalier Augustus Bointin. In an attempt to escape the atrocities of the French Revolution, count Joseph de Puisaye led a group of French aristocrats to settle on 5,000 acres along Yonge St north of the fledgling hamlet of Richmond Hill. He named the settlement Windham, after the British Secretary of War, William Windham, who had helped the migration. But the harshness of the winters and the toil needed to open new land were too much, and, when the monarchy was restored, most of the royalist refugees returned to France. A plaque on Yonge St north of Elgin Mills Road commemorates this ill-fated colony. The last evidence of the colony, a wonderful French chateau, the home of Henri St George, a son of one of the original royalists, stood on the shores of Bond Lake, but it too has gone.

Crosby hailed from Cumberland England, and designed the hall after a manor house there. Two gabled wings flank a recessed entrance to give the place a U shaped appearance. With its elegant octagonal cupola and 12 rooms it looked grandly over a lot of some 30 acres in area. As the local newspaper noted, Crosby Hall featured a "neat cupola, and indispensable verandah." It contained 12 rooms, a kitchen, a wash house and woodshed.

While Crosby could not be considered the "king" of Richmond Hill, he was one of its leading merchants. After arriving in Canada in 1844, he moved to Richmond Hill in 1861 where he opened what was called the "fireproof" store. It replaced his original dry goods store which had been destroyed by fire.

When Parker's son, Isaac, took over his father's business, he renovated Crosby Hall, adding a porch and replacing the original clapboard with brick.

After serving as a private residence until 1920, Crosby Hall was purchased by the Bedford Park Floral Company, one of Richmond Hill's many floral businesses, to house company managers. The Hall has now lost its porch, while the acreage which once surrounded it has been totally urbanized.

In 1978 it became Richmond Hill's first heritage structure to be designated under Ontario's Heritage Act.

RODMAN HALL, *St Catharines*

The elegant Rodman Hall is one of Ontario's oldest surviving "castles." More English manor than traditional castle, this hillside mansion was constructed in 1853. The building was significant as much for who built it as for how it looked.

The hall was constructed by Thomas Rodman Merritt, son of one of Ontario's most famous canal builders, William Hamilton Merritt. The elder Merritt was responsible for the construction of the early Welland canals, and the now vanished Grand River Canal.

The younger Merritt inherited his father's business sense, evolving from general store keeper to operator at a flour mill and owner of a

More English manor than Scottish castle, Rodman Hall was built by Thomas Rodman Merritt, son of William Hamilton Merritt, promoter of the Welland Canal

Thomas Rodman Merritt

fleet of ships. By 1853 the 29-year-old Merritt had accumulated enough wealth to launch the construction of a massive Jacobean manor on a bluff overlooking Twelve Mile Creek.

The floors contain inlaid patterned hardwood, the ceilings are ornamented with elaborate plaster carvings and mouldings, while the fireplaces were made of Italian marble.

Merritt planted his extensive grounds in a variety of ornamental trees and shrubs, an atmosphere it retains to this day. The meandering walkways are lined with pine, maple, willow and black walnut trees. The grounds, which once extended south to the railway, east to his father's canal, north on St Paul Cres, and west to Pelham Rd, are now a fraction of their original size.

With his wife Mary Benson, Thomas Rodman Merritt lived there most of his married life, and in 1903 they celebrated their 50th anniversary at Rodman Hall.

The Hall remained in the Merritt family until 1959 when it was sold to the city as an art gallery. Since the acquisition the building was restored, a new addition added, and the grounds cultivated after having lain overgrown for many years.

In 1974 the National Museums of Canada declared the landmark a National Exhibition Centre. Displays have included works by local regional and national artists including both historical and contemporary art. Its permanent collection now numbers more than 800 works, including paintings, sculptures, prints and drawings, most of them Canadian.

As you enter through the main door, you will see a stained glass partition with the Merritt coat of arms between the foyer and the main hall. The art rental and exhibition spaces were formerly a pair of drawing rooms with French crystal chandeliers. What was once the oak panelled dining room is now a gift shop.

One of the most striking features as you enter the main part of the building is the massive stain glass window at the top of the wide staircase. The rooms on the second level consisted of a billiard room, morning room and several bedrooms.

According to their pamphlet, the Rodman Hall Arts Centre also offers "lectures, artists' visits, concerts, films, children's theatre, and art instruction for all ages."

Rodman Hall is located on Bellevue Ave near the intersection of Ontario and St Paul Sts. in St Catharines. ❖

THE CASTLE IN THE BUSH, *St Mary's*

Built by the founder of the beautiful stone town of St Marys, the Castle in the Bush earned its name, not from its architecture, but rather from its having been the grandest home of its day.

In 1841 George Tracy arrived in the forests of Blanshard·Township in western Ontario where he purchased 400 acres on the Thames River. In 1850, with the arrival of the Grand Trunk Railway still a half dozen years away, Tracy divided his farm into town lots. But until the railway arrived in 1857, sales were slow. Nevertheless, he made enough profit to start construction on his castle.

He hired New York architect Robert Barbour who used smooth faced limestone as a building material, and designed a two storey home with double gables on either side of a two storey recessed verandah. Although not a large building, it did sit grandly on its hill-top location amid the uncleared forests. Locals quickly nicknamed it the "Castle in the Bush."

In 1858 Tracy moved to Wisconsin, selling his home to a newly-arrived millowner named Daniel McDougall who named the estate Cloudesdel Hall. The next owners, the John Weir family, gave it yet another name, calling it Cadzow Park after the estate of the Duke of Hamilton in Scotland. Weir earned his wealth from Ontario's booming flax industry. He was to be the castle's last private owner, for in 1925 the estate was bought by the local Rotary Club and turned over to the town.

For the next half century the town used the castle to house town employees until, in 1978, it became the town museum. For the 20 years previous the local Women's Institute had used a few of the rooms to display artifacts. Today, however, the house has been fully restored and is a fully operating museum.

While the "Castle" in the Bush may not resemble such, St Marys does claim another building which is decidedly more castle-like. In 1879 with the town booming from the arrival of the railway, work began on the Oddfellows Temple and Opera House. Built at a cost of $22,000, this Scottish Baronial castle rose sixty feet in the air. Battlements stretched along the entire roofline which was punctuated by a middle gable, and small turrets at each end. Six tall arched windows lined the second floor, while eight smaller windows were placed along the third.

The gable contained the vaulted chamber used by the Oddfellows for their secret rites and ceremonies. While the theatre occupied the second floor, the ground floor was leased out to commercial businesses. During the twentieth century, the wonderful building was used for industrial purposes including harness making and then, incredibly, as a flour mill, a function which it served until 1973, after which it stood vacant. Now designated as a heritage structure, the Opera House houses apartments.

St Marys clearly rates as one of Ontario's prettiest towns. Remarkable stone structures are everywhere, from the town hall, to the stone arch bridge and the St Mary's Junction railway station. Built in 1857, this ancient depot is the only one of the Grand Trunk's original stone stations in Ontario to have remained unaltered.

VALLEY HALLA VILLA,
Scarborough's Castle On The Rouge

It is North America's largest urban park, a forested oasis surrounded by tedious urban sprawl, and it has its own castle. The Rouge River is one of the Toronto area's most historic rivers. The site of an ancient Seneca village, the Rouge stretches from a marsh on Lake Ontario to the sandy hills of the Oak Ridge Moraine.

With the arrival of European settlers, the Rouge became home to mills, shipbuilding and a phoney oil boom. There was even a short-lived proposal to turn it into a canal. These however have all vanished and today the Rouge, with its hillsides covered in pine and hardwood forests, attracts hikers, naturalists, photographers and even mountain bikers.

With its castle-like stone tower, Valley Halla Villa was built by one of Canada's first health food promoters, Robert Jackson, maker of Roman Meal bread

It was here in 1936 that a millionaire named Robert Jackson decided, at the age of 70 to build his dream palace, a castle which he would call Valley Halla Villa.

Jackson was the inventor of the wildly popular Roman Meal bread, a health product which earned him riches when so many others were suffering the hardships of depression-era Canada. After having survived a near fatal brush with arthritis, Dr Jackson, a medical doctor, was one of the first to get into the health food business. Following the first world war he began lecturing to promote exercise, a diet of fruit and above all, his special bread known as Roman Meal bread. He pointed to his own appearance as an example of how this program would keep its users looking young. (It was discovered following his death in 1941 that he had been falsifying his age and that this self-proclaimed "82-year-old" was in fact a mere 76.)

In 1935, nearing the age of 70, Jackson hired architect C. Wellington Smith to design a castle on the forested valley wall of the Rouge River. Here Smith created a 20-room gothic structure with a stone tower as an entrance. Following a fire which gutted the castle while it was still under construction, Valley Halla Villa was finished in 1936. William Beesley, a carver whose work can also be seen at Toronto's old City Hall and in the Queens Park legislative building, put his talents to work carving elaborate works on the oak and walnut paneling which lined the rooms.

The building, with its turreted main entrance, is constructed of stucco over cement, with field stones used for the chimneys and trim. A long winding driveway leads from a set of gates atop the crest of the valley wall down the slope to the carriageway which overlooks the valley. The turret which marks the main entrance lies on the opposite side of the building.

The most remarkable feature of the interior is the two storey 15-foot high ballroom. A massive stone fireplace, with the provincial coat of arms carved above it, dominates one end, while at the other end a balcony offers space for a small chamber orchestra to entertain

Valley Halla's gate shows signs of wear

guests. A sunroom at the east end of the ballroom overlooks the valley as well.

A wide stairway with brass railings leads from the main hallway to the bedrooms of the second floor. One end of the hallway leads to a dining room with room enough for 30 guests (although it is not known if it was ever used for entertaining). Fruit and Roman Meal bread would no doubt have been on the menu. After dinner, guests could enjoy a large solarium which led off the room. In it Jackson raised orchids for his pleasure. Another doorway leads from the hall into a study which contains another stone fireplace.

But the outside is as stunning as the inside. A formal garden flanked by a pair of octagonal towers stretches to the north, while the pathway to the main tower contains stone pillars topped with wrought iron lamps and crosses a man-made stream which leads between small ponds.

Jackson did not enjoy his 20-room mansion for long for he died a few years after its completion. After passing through a variety of private hands, and after having been proposed as an official residence for the then chairman of Metro Toronto, Paul Godfrey, the castle was taken over by the Metro Zoo. It lies on the east side Morningside Ave opposite the zoo itself, and is not open to the public, although it can be seen at a distance from the Rouge River Provincial Park.

Carefully preserved and used on occasion for film shoots, the Metro formerly used it to house zoo officials. ◈

COTTONWOOD,
The Mystery Mansion of Selkirk

Much mystery surrounds the Cottonwood Mansion. Here, on the flat Haldimand Clay Plain that stretches inland from the shores of Lake Erie, a grand 17-room Italianate mansion looms above the wide open farm fields.

When it was built, and how it earned its evocative name remain a mystery, as does exactly how its owner acquired the money to build it.

William Holmes Jr. arrived in the area from his native Brockville in 1832, and two years later married Mary Hoover, daughter of a local land owner. Soon afterward, they vanished from the records

It is a mystery how this Italianate mansion, which dominates the flat farmlands around it, got its name

and nothing more was heard of the couple for another ten years. Then, just as suddenly, they reappeared, with money enough to establish themselves as land speculators and money lenders.

In 1865 Holmes decided to build, on land inherited by his wife, a home unlike anything the local farmers had ever seen. Rising above their fields was a two-storey brick mansion, measuring 6,000 square feet and topped by an elegant belvedere. The bricks were variegated clay mixed with yellow beach sand from the nearby lake.

Following the death of his wife in 1869, Holmes married a much younger Cynthia Anderson who gave birth to a daughter Lillian, and it was she, not Cynthia who, upon Holmes' death in 1892, inherited Cottonwood Mansion. Lillian sold the estate in 1911. Until 1988 it stood frequently neglected and was stripped of many of its original fixtures.

In that year, Larry Hamilton, a descendant of the original landowner Jakob Huber, bought the crumbling castle and pledged to restore its early lustre. He created the non-profit Cottonwood Mansion Preservation Foundation, while the local community raised a remarkable quarter of a million dollars to begin the restoration work.

Even more remarkable was the discovery of one Helen Smiley, Lillian's daughter, living in Oregon. Her knowledge proved instrumental in guiding the restoration of the mansion, as did her possessions, which were donated by her family following her death.

Today, much of the mansion is as William and Cynthia Holmes would remember it. In the entranceway, a doorbell, complete with porcelain knob, is still operated by the original wire installed in 1875. Thanks to early photos, the detailing on the woodwork has been exactly replicated.

Off the hallway is the parlour, now known as a music room, containing one of the two fireplaces incorporated into the mansion (most of the heating was by wood burning stoves). The drapes in this room are original, and were among the items provided by the family of Helen Smiley. The dining room, which contains the other fireplace, is now named to honour Florence Neff Young, who donated to the restoration project a 12-piece china and silver setting, and half the residue of her own estate, a sum which amounted to over $100,000.

Other items in the dining room were acquired either at auction or are on loan.

A second parlour, known as the southeast parlour, was apparently used originally as a smoking room, and then as an apartment for an aging William and Cynthia.

Fifty-seven stairs then lead to the second floor and the belvedere. Four bedrooms and a grand ballroom dominate the second floor while on the third floor, a foyer lies at the base of the final steps into the belvedere.

From that level, the view extends north, west and south to the lake. Oddly, there were no windows overlooking the farm fields to the east.

Cottonwood today hosts meetings, family receptions, and weddings, and also serves as a repository for donated archival material and genealogical information on area families. While much generosity has helped restore the building to its current condition, funding remains an ongoing problem, particularly in light of government cutbacks, and donations are encouraged.

Cottonwood lies on Regional Road 53, about 4 km south of Highway 3. Hoover Point on Lake Erie, named for the anglicized Jacob Hoover, is about another 5 km south. ❖

RICHARDS' STONE CASTLE, *Snow Road*

The forgotten hills of northern Frontenac, formerly a county, contain some of Ontario's most scenic landscapes. Rolling meadows, ringed with forest show off the simple but well-kept cabins of the early settlers. Well off the beaten path, the area contains no high-speed highways, no malls, no fast food outlets. Rather it is a land of general stores, small churches, and a lively community spirit.

The river that runs through it was a major reason that anybody came here at all. The Mississippi River, a much smaller version of its Yankee namesake, was a main highway for loggers. Most of the tim-

This impressive stone home stood out in an area long dominated by the simpler log and frame homes of the area's pioneer descendants

ber was heading downstream to the large mills at Almonte and Carleton Place. But a number of smaller sawmills were built along its banks as well.

To encourage settlers to clear the land and help provide much needed labour for the lumber camps, roads were surveyed into the hills. Because of the obstacles of rivers and ridges, few of these early routes were straight.

In 1860 the first road surveyor through the area was John Snow, and the road was named after him. At the point where the Snow Road crossed the Mississippi River, Peter McLaren opened up a lumber depot which became known as McLaren's Depot. Here a handful of homes clustered around the store and lumber camp.

In 1883 the Kingston and Pembroke Railway was built as far as the river where the village of Mississippi Station developed as a temporary terminus. Shortly after, the river was bridged and another station was placed on the north side of the river. Named Snow Road Station, it became the site of yet another village.

Most of the area's early homes were built of logs or planks. While many homes in Perth, then a two day's stage ride away, were built of the ample limestone deposits which hovered near the surface, it was unusual to find such a house in the hills near Snow Road, particularly one that resembled a castle.

Most of the land along the north shore of the river was owned by a local lumber baron, Robert Geddes. It was to this area that William Richards moved from North Adams Massachusetts in 1883, once the railway facilitated travel into the area.

Here he built a three-storey mansion using stone quarried from just across the river. The grand home was offset with a stone tower on the road side giving a it decidedly castle-like appearance and making it the grandest home in the area. Richards' castle took two years to complete and was ready for its "king" by 1889. Inside, a curving staircase led from the spacious foyer to the upper floors.

While the house still stands grandly beside Snow Road, a short

distance east of Highway 508, the area is no longer the tranquil wilderness it was when Richards arrived. Today, vacationers travel in from Kingston and Ottawa to the summer cottages on the river or the shores of Dalhousie and Millar Lakes. Each summer a rollicking music festival takes place in the delightfully named hamlet of Ompah (pronounced Um-pa), and is promoted as the "Ompah Stomp."

Still, the area is, by comparison, a tranquil escape from the sprawl and gridlock of urban Ontario.

THE DEACON'S CASTLE,
Bell Rock, *Sudbury*

Perhaps it was the gritty pragmatism which typified Ontario's north-land that discouraged the castle builders. With the exceptions of the McQuat Castle near Ignace and Harry Oakes' mansion in Kirkland Lake, northern Ontario has few grand homes which fall into the castle category. While the Ermatinger House in Sault Ste Marie, and the Mather-Wells house in Keewatin are large and lovely homes, they would not be out of place in most of Ontario's well-to-do neighbourhoods.

Sudbury's Bell Rock house, however, is just a bit grander than most.

In 1908 a rising young lumber executive named William J Bell, then general manager of the Spanish River Lumber Company, selected a rocky outcrop overlooking Sudbury's Ramsey Lake for his grand new home. Up to that time, the crest had been the site of the odd looking "Deacon's Castle", a hand-hewn "fort" built by a local hermit who, many assumed, had been in the armed services at some point.

On his 155 acres, Bell built a coach house, an out house for storage and laundry, and the lovely large stone mansion. While the main house was constructed of coursed cut stone, the others were assembled with mainly rubble stone. The hill was at first a sad looking barren outcrop of rock, but under the guidance of landscape architect, John James, it was soon alive with lawns and gardens.

The house itself was three floors, with office, living room and kitchen on the main floor. The dining room with its stained glass windows presented a wide view through a bay window. Most of the main floor rooms were lined with rich wood paneling. Four bedrooms and a bathroom were located on the second while the third was used mainly for storage. Most of the rooms sported oriental carpets, and many were heated by large fireplaces.

Staff at the house included a chauffeur/gardener, a receptionist/house-keeper, a laundress/ charwoman, and in later years, a nurse. Several animals were kept on the property including horses, cattle and chickens. In 1911 Bell brought in Sudbury's first car, although there were few places to drive to at the time.

Bell, meanwhile, continued his rise in the lumber industry, becoming president of the Spanish River Lumber Company in 1926, a position he held until 1932 when he sold the company.

William and his wife Katharine were both philanthropists. Katharine worked with local churches, bringing in the first Victorian Order of Nurses, and organizing the Sudbury Horticultural Society. William in 1926 donated most of his property to be used as lakeside recreational grounds.

William Bell died in 1945 at the age of 87. Katharine survived him by nine years, dying at 90 in 1954.

Even after death, the Bells continued to give. Their will bequeathed $125,000 to the Salvation Army, while the house and grounds were given to Memorial Hospital. Unfortunately, as the house lay vacant, it was gutted by fire. Eventually, in 1966 it was purchased by the Chamber of Commerce and transferred to Laurentian University which operates it today as a museum and art centre.

CASTLEFIELD, *Toronto*

In the late 1820s Yonge St was still a rough dirt trail, often a quag-mire in the spring and during wet weather. While York remained a muddy hamlet down on the bay, many of the newly arrived upper classes were purchasing lots along the road for their country estates. It was on a then remote section of Yonge St between the hamlets of Eglington (spelt with two "g"s then) and the mill town of York Mills that a young English lawyer named James Hervey Price bought his 200 acre estate lot.

James Hervey Price began the castle building craze in Toronto with his Castlefield built in the 1820s

At the end of a long treed avenue he built a castle- like mansion which he named Castlefield. Indeed the grand home did resemble a small castle. The main portion stood two stories and was topped with four crenellated turrets. The two wings were a storey-and-a-half each. Beneath the towers a massive door led into a cavernous foyer lined with black walnut woodwork.

The city clerk, Price worked closely with the man who would be the city's first mayor, William Lyon Mackenzie. Although Price did not fully support Mackenzie's rebellion in 1837, he did allow the rebel leader to hold his meetings in Castlefield. While on the run from the government forces, Mackenzie hid briefly in Price's castle before escaping to the United States. For having harboured the rebel chief Price spent 13 days in jail.

In 1841 Franklin Jackes bought Castlefield from Price. It was Jackes' son William who sold the estate to developers in 1885. The castle itself stood for another thirty-three years before being demolished.

With the coming of streetcars development intensified, and the hamlet of Eglington disappeared as well beneath a wave of stores. Only the old general store survives from Castlefield's rural days. Now a wine store, it stands on the east side of Yonge St near the corner of Roselawn. And of the old castle itself, the only evidence that it ever stood here rests in the name of the streets, Castle Knock and Castlewood, while Castlefield Ave traces the old lane which led to the castle. ✧

CASTLE FRANK, *Toronto*

Being Canada's largest city, Toronto can claim the largest number of monied individuals, a characteristic that was not the case two centuries ago. At a time when Montreal and Halifax were sizeable cities, "York" was a collection of a few dozen houses on a grid of muddy streets. By the 1820s it could offer a few grand homes, such as the Berkeley House, designed after an English manor, and the Campbell House, a brick Georgian mansion. While the Berkeley House ended it days ingloriously as a warehouse, the Campbell House was relocated and survives to this day.

Lady Elizabeth Simcoe

In the midst of it all, there was "Castle Frank".

To say that Elizabeth Simcoe, wife of Upper Canada's first lieutenant governor, John Graves Simcoe, was displeased with her husband's new posting, would be to understate her feelings. By 1793 Simcoe had been forced to alter his proposed location for Upper Canada's new capital from London on the distant Thames, to the more convenient harbour at the mouth of the Don River.

Being from Yorkshire, Simcoe named the site York. His affinity for his native country led also to several other Yorkshire place names appearing in the vicinity, such as Scarborough, Whitby and Pickering.

But the familiarity of the names didn't help Mrs. Simcoe. The area around the harbour was damp, and the air was filled with clouds of mosquitoes, both of which filled their canvas tent, their sole abode. She and the governor lost little time in searching for airier grounds upon which to build a grand home fit for the head of the colony, and more suitable for entertaining.

At first they leaned toward the heights of Scarborough, but the distance from the new townsite was too great. They then turned their attention to a series of sugar loaf hills along the river which Simcoe had named the Don (again after his home area).

There, late in 1793 in the name of their two-year-old son Francis, they bought 200 acres. High on the west bank of the river where they decided to build their country retreat, a home which they would call Castle Frank. Construction proceeded through 1794 although the

The second Castle Frank, now largely forgotten, was decidedly more castle-like in style and was built by Sir Edward Kemp around 1900

Simcoes were too busy to visit the site. The threat of war and the death of their daughter Sophia had kept them in Newark (Niagara-on-the-lake) for much of that year.

During 1795 Lady Simcoe travelled frequently to the high bluff, occasionally taking tea with a new neighbour, George Playter, who had built a cottage to the north of the castle. Travel was either by boat up the Don, or by horse along a trail which followed roughly today's Parliament and Winchester Sts, and through an open pine forest.

Although they chose to name it Castle Frank, the appearance was anything but castle-like. Rather, it was designed on the plan of a Greek temple. Measuring 50 by 35 feet, the large log structure boasted porticos on each end, supported by sturdy pine logs 16 feet high. Four windows along each side contained 16 panes of glass each. A large chimney stood in the centre of the unfinished interior. The log building was covered with clapboard siding, while heavy shutters protected the windows. Being built into a hillside, the basement contained windows which looked out over the gully. Mrs Simcoe used this lower level for sleeping when the temperature was too hot in the main room.

Because the castle lacked interior rooms, whenever the Simcoes stayed there they needed to erect canvas sheets for privacy. But even there they could not escape the torment of the mosquitoes. "On the second day after some heavy thunder showers, the mosquitoes were more troublesome then ever," Mrs. Simcoe lamented in her diary. "It is scarcely possible to write or use my hands, which are occupied in killing them or driving them away." Even here she was forced to retreat to the protection of her mosquito net.

It was a torment they didn't long have to endure. By July of 1796, Mrs Simcoe and her ailing husband were on their way back to England. She bade a final farewell to the "dear place" as she later called it, and "cried all day." John Graves Simcoe died ten years later, while the son after whom he and his wife had named the castle, was later killed in the battle of Badajoz. He was only 21.

Peter Russell, Simcoe's successor, used the castle for social events. After that the castle stood empty and rotting, attracting little interest even from marauding Yankees in 1813 who were looking for the governor's "castle." A crumbling log house was not quite what they had in mind. Finally, in 1829, a party of careless fishermen burned the shell to ground.

But that was not the end of "Castle Frank". Sometime around the turn of the century Sir Edward Kemp, a wealthy manufacturer, built a new "Castle Frank." The two-storey 24-room brick mansion stood a short distance north of the original structure. Although Sir Edward died in 1929 the second castle stayed on until it was demolished in 1962 to make way for a new high school. The name of the school? "Castle Frank" (now Rosedale Heights Secondary School). The name lives on because of the subway station which serves the area. ❖

TORONTO'S OTHER CASTLE, *Graydon Hall*

Second in size only to Casa Loma, Graydon Hall is Toronto's forgotten castle. While it resembles more a grand manor than a castle, its location on a rise of land overlooking the broad valley of the Don River gives it a decided dominance.

Like Toronto's other castle, it was a latecomer, being finished in 1936, more than two decades after Casa Loma.

The era which followed the first world war was one when Toronto's wealthy were beginning to build their grand country estates north of the city's expanding fringes. The height of land along the slopes of the Don Valley, wooded and rolling, had particular appeal.

Graydon Hall was one of a number of grand homes built by Toronto's upper crust in the rolling farmlands by the Don River north of the city

Bayview Ave attracted most of these estate builders. A direct route along an early farm road into the city, it skirted the west wall of the valley, offering pleasant views and forested hills. Among Bayview's grand homes were Sunnydale Farms built by Joseph Kilgour, president of Canada Paper Company. Millionaire mining promoter David Dunlap added the Donalda Farms in 1914, while Sir Clifford Sifton, one-time Interior Minister in the government of Sir Wilfred Laurier, built a lofty red brick estate in 1923 at the corner of Lawrence Ave. and what is the current route of Bayview Ave. Glendon Hall, home of E.R. Wood, founder of Canada's largest bond dealer, Dominion Securities, came the following year and is today part of the campus of York University. In 1931 J.S. McLean, head of Canada Packers, moved into an estate called Bayview, a mansion which is now part of Sunnybrook Hospital complex.

Other places like Donningvale, Penryn and Windfields soon followed. But the grandest of them all was Graydon Hall.

It took its name from its proximity to the site of the Gray mills, one of the many vanished mills of the Don River. The estate of Henry Rupert Bain, not a name preserved in legend, however, he was an astute broker and financier. When he was just 25 years old, he set up his own brokerage house. During the great depression he moved from financing municipal bonds to going for the gold, financing, among other projects, the profitable Pickle Crow gold mine.

With those proceeds he bought a 100-acre farm on the east side of the valley and built the largest home the Toronto area had seen since Sir Henry Pallett went broke with his ill-fated Casa Loma. The 29-room fieldstone house cost him $250,000, a small sum today, but an enormous amount during the depression.

The house boasted 14 bedrooms, limestone trim and a 10-car garage, this in a time when few roads were even paved. From his stone terrace, Bain could look out over his formal gardens and golf course, while the wide valley of the Don spread out below him. His four gardens focused on a fountain. These included a west exit gar-

The entrance to Graydon Hall

den with its tree-lined view of the large lawn, and a rose garden as well as a secluded water garden with natural stone edging. The landscaping was done by the prestigious firm of Dunnington, Grubb and Stensonn.

On the opposite side of the house was the main entrance where a balcony was built on top of the port-cochere. The main hall was lit by a large window and the date 1936 was etched into stone above the doors. Walnut paneling, hand painted wallpaper, antique rugs and ornate moldings graced the interior. Among the visitors to Bain's house were Vivian Leigh, Katherine Hepburn, Mary Pickford, and Michael Redgrave.

Bain's marital situation took a strange twist when, in 1951, shortly after his friend Reginald Watkins married Bain's ex-wife, Bain in turn married the former Mrs Watkins.

In 1950 Bain sold off a portion of the estate property to E.P Taylor, and a year later sold Graydon Hall itself to Nelson M. Davis, head of a transportation empire which took in more than 50 companies.

Two years later Bain died while vacationing in Mexico. He was only 54. His estate by then had soared in value to nearly one and a quarter million dollars which the courts decided would go to his first wife.

By the 1960s, Toronto urban fringe was at Graydon Hall's doorstep. Don Mills had been laid as a leading edge planned suburb, while the 401, opened only a few years prior, was already crawling at 15 miles an hour. In 1964 most of the grounds were sold to developers. Today, backsplits and apartments have closed in on the once magnificent estate. The only evidence of the former spaciousness which characterized Bain's castle is a small park on the west side of the hall.

If views from the terrace have been blocked, so have most views of the building. A fence and unsympathetic parking lot obliterate the view from Graydon Hall Drive, while shrubbery hinders the view from the park.

For a number of years, much of the building stood empty, overgrown and vandalized. Now however, after careful restoration both outside and in, much of it for the Junior League of Toronto's Designer Showcase event in 2000, Graydon Hall has regained its glory and now includes a fine dining restaurant with catering and conference facilities.

HOLLAND HOUSE, *Toronto*

Throughout the closing years of the 18th century, castle-houses were the rage among the English landed gentry. It was a period of gothic revival, as the architects would call it, and copy castles were a common manifestation of that trend. As witnessed in Price's Castlefield, it soon spread to the new estates sprouting up around York.

John Henry Boulton was one who traced his ancestry to the landed gentry of England, and wanted a home to reflect his lineage. He and his brother, D'Arcy, builder of the still-surviving Grange, were sons of D'Arcy Boulton Sr, who had served as both attorney general and solicitor general for the new colony. While Junior preferred the

On a site now occupied by the Royal Bank Plaza, Holland House was another of Toronto's early copy-castles

leisured life of a gentleman farmer, J.H. followed in his father's footsteps, becoming solicitor general as well.

At this time, anything west of Jarvis St, the heart of the new town, was considered countryside. And it was on a site near what is today Wellington and Bay Sts, that Boulton built his country castle. Although he named it after a 17th century family mansion near London, he modeled it after either Belvoir Castle, designed in 1801 for the Duke of Rutland, or after Luscombe Castle in Devonshire, a building designed by architect John Nash. In any event, Boulton's affinity for the British aristocracy was undeniable, and it showed in Holland House.

When the house was first built, it bore more of a resemblance to his brother's Grange. But within a year he had hired a recently-arrived English architect named John Howard to convert it to a castle. He named it Holland House after his birthplace, Holland House in London, which his father had rented from Lord Holland.

And Holland House looked every bit the castle. Although it was made of brick, Boulton had it covered with stucco which was in turn etched to resemble stone, again to make it more castle-like. Even the chimneys were constructed to resemble castle turrets. Its appearance was not lost on York's other inhabitants who nicknamed it simply "The Castle."

Comparisons with Castlefield are tempting. Both had the same overall massing, with a three storey entranceway flanked by a pair of lower wings. But while Castlefield was crowned by four turrets, Holland House featured instead a large circular tower where three arches led to the main entrance. Some contemporaries compared it to the redesigned Windsor Castle in England.

Originally it fronted onto Front St, then the shore of Lake Ontario, and provided a view over Toronto harbour. A carriage way wound its way to the entrance.

But Boulton was a political gadfly, and within two years of moving in, he was sent packing for comments unflattering to the government of the day. He re-emerged as Chief Justice of Newfoundland, but did-n't last long there either, losing that position in 1838, and he returned to his Toronto castle. He remained there until he died in 1870.

During that time, he witnessed changes to the surrounding landscape that he never had thought possible. Toronto quickly expanded west, engulfing his one-time country estate with stores and hotels. Below Front St the lake was filled in and railway tracks and stations soon obliterated his view of the lake.

Following Boulton's death, Holland House was occupied briefly by Alexander Manning, president of the Toronto Malting and Brewing Company. It was also used by the Ontario Reform Association and was once proposed as Ontario's Government House. But from 1890 until 1904 the place sat largely vacant.

Then, in that year, Toronto's most devastating fire destroyed most the buildings in the Bay and Front St areas. Holland House miraculously survived. However, the flurry of rebuilding which followed took Holland House with it, and it was replaced primarily with warehouses. Today the site is occupied by the Royal Bank Plaza.

With Toronto's "countryside" now 50 km away, it is hard to stand at Wellington and Bay and imagine John Henry Boulton's castle in the country. ✤

NORCASTLE, *Toronto*

Ever since its development as an upscale residential enclave, Rosedale can justly claim street after street of "castles." Only one, however, actually earned the nickname of "castle." Located on what is today Glen Road, this massive brick mansion was built by a local property owner named Edgar John Jarvis, descendent of the famed Sheriff Jarvis who had conceived of the Rosedale area many years earlier. With its tall crenellated tower, he named the house "Norcastle" for its proximity to the North Iron Bridge over a local ravine.

When A.E. Gooderham bought the estate in 1905, he renamed it Deancroft, the maiden name of Gooderham's mother.

But it was Gooderham's wife, Mary Reford Gooderham, who distinguished herself as matriarch of the castle. From 1912-15 she headed the Imperial Order of the Daughters of the Empire, and made the

One of Rosedale's many grand homes, Norcastle is now gone

castle their headquarters. She later served on the Red Cross executive, the Royal Canadian Institute, and the Women's Auxiliary of the
Conservative Party of Canada. For her efforts during the war, she
received a medal from the French government, one of only four
women to be so honoured.

While a few of Rosedale's early mansions still stand, still grand,
Norcastle is not among them. It was demolished and the property
divided during the 1960's into smaller lots for the modest bungalows
which stand there today. ⟨⊹⟩

SIR HENRY'S CASTLES

No castle builder in Ontario went from riches to rags more certainly than did Henry Pellatt, the man who built Casa Loma.

When one thinks of castles in Ontario, Casa Loma is the first to come to mind. When he built it, Sir Henry Pellatt (he was knighted in 1906 for his role in developing hydro electricity in Ontario) was among the richest men in Canada. Using training gained in his father's brokerage firm, which he entered at age 17, Pellatt made a number of hugely successful investments. Recognizing the growth potential of the Canadian prairies, he invested in the Canadian Pacific Railway and the Northwest Land Company, a move which

Designed after King Ludwig's Bavarian castles, Casa Loma is Ontario's most famous castle, even though Sir Henry Pellatt never completed it

quickly earned him $4 million. He became involved in Brazilian power developments, the predecessor to today's Brascan. He was also involved in the Grand Trunk Pacific Railway, and the Kitsumkallum Timber Company of BC. In fact, his penchant for investment, some of it virtually sight unseen, earned him the nickname, "Henry the Plunger."

A world class athlete, Pellatt in 1879 won the world championship for the one mile race, including a 12-second dash over the final 100 yards, a feat unsurpassed until it was broken by an American named Jesse Owens in 1930.

In 1911 he hired Edward J. Lennox, Toronto's most respect-

ed architect, to design a castle. Not just any castle, but rather one inspired by the 19th century castles of Bavaria's King Ludwig. Over a period of three years, three hundred workers assembled a massive castle with 98 rooms, and 25 fireplaces. It was located on a 10-hectare block of land which he had purchased (in his wife's name) on Wells Hill on the Davenport Escarpment, a long ridge which offered a view of the growing city below and the lake in the distance.

Until the castle was complete, Pellatt continued to occupy his grand home at the corner of Sherbourne and Bleeker Sts, then an opulent neighbourhood which included his father's residence. This house too had reflected Pellatt's love of castles. The three storey

Pellatt returns to Casa Loma for the last time, shortly before his death

building was topped by turrets and had an overhanging balcony and a $7500 stable.

Pellatt's castle was the ultimate in opulence. The Great Hall boasted a 70-foot oak beam ceiling and a 40-foot window containing 738 panes of glass. The conservatory was crowned with a $12,000 stained glass dome backlit by 600 lights. From his study, secret passages led to both the second floor and the basement, should unwanted visitors come calling. The main floor hallway was designed to be a replica of a hallway at Windsor Castle, and was named Peacock Alley.

His bedroom measured 40' by 60' and contained a secret compartment in a pillar. The adjacent bathroom, which cost $10,000, contained six taps.

The castle also boasted 30 bathrooms (only 15 of which actually had baths). The designs included two bowling alleys, a shooting gallery, a roller skating rink, and an 18-meter swimming pool. None of these, however, was ever completed. The basement was large enough to sleep an entire regiment, and had room enough left over for a 1700 bottle wine cellar. Pellatt ensured that Casa Loma was as modern as it was possible to be at the time, with electric lighting, central vacuuming and piped ammonia to cool the wine cellar. The castle was the first residence in Toronto with an elevator.

Casa Loma's grand hallway, Peacock Alley, was built to resemble the grand halls of Windsor Castle

Although the exterior is covered with stone, the building is in fact built of steel reinforced concrete. A contemporary critic described Sir Henry's castle as being a mix of "17th century Scottish baronial and 20th Century Fox."

From the basement a 243 m tunnel led to the castle-like stables where each horse had its own name in 18 carat gold, and a carriage house where Pellatt once stored Toronto's first electric car.

Not too surprisingly, it all cost a lot more than Sir Henry had anticipated. The $250,000 which he estimated it would cost was spent on the walls alone. Add to that the $30,000 building permit. Heating bills ran $25,000 a year, the 40 servants $22,000 and then there were the taxes: $12,000 a year.

Even though the Pellatts occupied the castle for a decade, they never finished it, nor could they fully furnish it. In 1923, Pellatt's Home Bank went bankrupt, leaving him $1.7 million in debt and the Pellatts moved into a five bedroom apartment on Spadina Rd known as the Spadina Gardens. It was here, in April of 1924, that his wife,

Mary, died suddenly. Now short of money, Pellatt auctioned the contents of his beloved house on the hill, but earned only $131,000, a fraction of what he had hoped for. Pellatt then turned the property over to the City of Toronto. In 1927 Pellatt remarried, his second wife being Catherine Merritt, granddaughter of William Merritt, promoter of the Welland Canal. They moved into a home on Crescent Rd in Rosedale. She died, however, just two years later. After living out his last days in a small house in Mimico, which he shared with his chauffeur, Sir Henry died in 1939 with cash assets of only $185. At his zenith, Sir Henry Pellatt had been worth $17 million.

After the Pellatts vacated the castle, proposals for the building included a convent, a monastery, a men's club, and a home for the Dionne quintuplets. There was even a proposal to convert the castle into a luxury hotel to be called the Chateau Pellatt. Plans were submitted for 96 suites and 56 single rooms, no two of which would be alike. The shooting gallery and bowling alley would be completed, and Turkish baths and a gymnasium added. When this plan faltered, the castle operated for a season as a nightclub featuring the then famous Glen Grav's Casa Loma Orchestra. Finally, the building was acquired in 1936 by the Kiwanis as a public treasure, and has remained so ever since.

But Casa Loma wasn't Henry Pellatt's only home. He was, after all, in the land business. Weekends saw him at his 600-hectare farm located on Marie Lake, a glacial lake just south of King City. His neighbors to the east were the prestigious Eatons. Here he kept pheasants as well as elk and deer given him by King George V. He was noted for falling asleep on his horse, which managed to make its way back to the stable on its own.

One reporter described his visit to the estate in 1915: "Once through the big granite gates that guard the entrance to the farm, there is a mile and a quarter drive before the bungalow is reached, for the estate is more than two miles long. And delightful as has been the drive, a yet prettier sight awaits the journey's end... the lake itself, lying an irregular sapphire, set about the wooded hillsides and grassy slopes."

Among the guests to the estate were the Girl Guides, a group with which Lady Pellatt was actively involved. While visitors were lavishly entertained, and mingled with the resident deer, chickens, holsteins and ducks, they were not allowed to swim in the small lake for the water was used for drinking.

In 1938 the farm was sold for $95,000 to the Basilian monastic order, and today is the site of an Augustinian retreat. The gate and brick barn, the largest and most modern in the area, reflect Pellatt's passion for castle-like structures. The chicken house was almost as impressive as the barn, while the milking shed resembled a miniature castle.

He owned a pair of summer homes as well. A mini-castle stands today on the shore of Lake Couchiching at the north end of Orillia. Surrounded now by modern housing, this two-storey stone building, erected around the time of the first world war, occupies the site of Southwood, a summer home formerly occupied by Pellatt's father.

He also owned a summer home on Lake Ontario at the east end of Toronto in a neighborhood today known as the Beach. Known as Cliffside, it stood beside the summer resort of Victoria Park. It later passed into the hands of his son Reginald and stood into the 1930s until it was torn down to make way for apartments and a parking lot.

One of his wealthy neighbours was the railway builder Sir Donald Mann whose mansion, Fallingbrook, sat on a steep cliff overlooking the lake. Although it burned many years ago, the gate house still stands, a distinctive and anomalous Tudor-style house on Kingston Road a short distance east of Fallingbrook Avenue.

Victoria Park itself became the site of the Harris Filtration plant. One of the few contemporary buildings still standing is the intriguing turreted house known as the Chateau des Quatre Vents (house of the four winds), a structure which was built in 1891 and enlarged in 1919 by Emile Gagnon.

While Sir Henry died nearly penniless, his built heritage lives on. ❖

HUTCHISON HOUSE, *Whitby*

A neighbour to the Sheriff Manor was another castle-like house, known locally as simply the Hutchison House. Its resemblance to the manor is quite remarkable. It has two castle towers, is two stories in height, and boasts Italianate windows along the second floor. An embayment extends prominently into the eastern yard.

School inspector Robert Alexander Hutchison occupied the house from 1913 until his retirement in 1943. Hutchison died in 1961 at the age of 88. The building today, while still enjoying a large yard, has been converted to apartments. It stands at the corner of Byron and Colborne Streets. ❖

This grand town home was a scaled down version of the much grander Trafalgar Castle

TRAFALGAR CASTLE, *Whitby*

If it looks like a castle, sounds like a castle, and was styled after an English castle, then it must be a castle. Oddly, Trafalgar Castle, now a girls' school, remained a residence for a mere 12 years.

Nelson G Reynolds, sheriff of Ontario County, harboured a grand dream, especially for a sheriff. He would, on the eastern outskirts of the fledgling town of Whitby, built himself a castle. Here he imagined, he would entertain kings, queens and princes.

The palatial home was begun in 1859 and finished three years later. How Reynolds, on a sheriff's salary, could afford the $70,000 needed for his monumental castle, remains unanswered to this day, keeping in mind that in those days, even a solid brick home cost lit-

Although it has served most of its life as a girls' school, Trafalgar Castle was originally the home of a local sheriff named Nelson G. Reynolds

tle more than $2,000 to build.

The building was the work of renowned architect Joseph Sheard, an English wheelwright turned architect. In designing Reynold's castle, Sheard was influenced by such magnificent English structures as Hampton Court and St John's College.

For construction material, Sheard opted for buff brick, and embellished the building with battlements, buttresses and eight-sided turrets with Reynold's coat of arms placed above the main entrance. On entering, one was confronted immediately by the broad staircase, and the painted windows that lit it. In the bedrooms were mantlepieces of white marble, while those in the drawing rooms were of rosso antico.

Elaborate carvings surmounted the doors and encircled the chandeliers, statues were tucked in fanciful corner alcoves.

When it was finished, residents from miles around flocked to see what was likely the only castle they had ever seen. Most, after all, were still living in simple cabins of frame or log.

At first it seemed as if his dreams would come true. Soon after moving in, he entertained the Duke of Connaught, and the third son of Queen Victoria, Prince Arthur (after whom Port Arthur was named).

But his reverie was to be short-lived. The expense of keeping the place up soon caught up with him, and in 1874 he was forced to sell. At first it seemed as though the Ontario Agricultural College would move in, but the board of governors opted instead for a site in Guelph. Finally, in 1874, he sold the castle to the Methodist church for a girls' school, a role which it plays to this day. The price, $35,000.

Much of the original interior has been respectfully retained. The building dominates its extensive treed grounds at the corner of Gilbert and Reynolds Sts in Whitby, just a few blocks east of Brock St., the town's main thoroughfare.

After the school opened, the Methodists began a number of additions and alterations. A new wing was almost immediately added and named the Ryerson

The principal's office after the castle became a girls' school

Wing after Egerton Ryerson, founder of Ontario's public school system. In 1895 the servants' wing was demolished and replaced with Frances Hall, named after the daughter of Hart Massey, co-founder of the Massey-Harris farm implement company. A gym and pool were added in the early 1900's and a new chapel in 1956. The latest addition was the Kemcke Wing built in 1984, named after Craig Kemcke, the school's principal.

The school was officially opened by Lord Dufferin, Governor General of Canada in 1874, and has witnessed a string of dignitaries since then. Writers and artists like Lucy Maude Montgomery, Arthur Lismer and A.Y Jackson have all paid homage, as have four governors general, 10 lieutenant governors, and at least two prime ministers.

Now under the auspices of the United Church of Canada, the school functions as a private secondary school, offering courses from grade 7 to OAC.

Whitby contains a treasure trove of other historical structures including the former town hall which houses the archives, several historic main street structures, including the hotel, and the historic turreted Grand Trunk railway station, now an art gallery. ❖

SHERIFF'S MANOR, *Whitby*

Following his financial eviction from his beloved Trafalgar Castle, Reynolds didn't entirely give up on castle building. Now chastened, he moved to the west side of the main street and there, in a considerably less pretentious neighborhood, he built another similar, although considerably more modest structure. Alas, his stay here didn't last much longer than did his residency at the castle, and by 1885 this house, too, had changed hands.

The new owners were the Golds, Reverend Matthew and his wife Elizabeth. Like Reynolds, who was a sheriff, the Golds possessed wealth beyond that which their occupation would have otherwise inferred. In this case it was Elizabeth's inheritance which elevated their life style to that of castle-dwellers.

When it was discovered, however, that Elizabeth was borrowing heavily to finance her favorite charities, the Golds separated. Elizabeth died in Toronto at the age of 83, while the Rev Matthew survived to the ripe old age of 103, dying in England.

The central tower and the flat roof are distinguished by their battlements, while the interior contained a solarium. Many of the windows were of stained glass, while a secret passageway led to the garage. Otherwise, little is known of the architectural detailing, as the building has been altered and enlarged over the years.

In 1904 the castle was bought by a wealthy local industrialist named Fred Hatch who enlarged the house to eight times its size. Among the prominent visitors were auto makers such as William Buick, Charlie Chevrolet, Rufus Olds and Col Sam McLaughlin, whose carriage factory in Oshawa became the basis for the massive General Motors operations in that city.

Hatch also owned a large property at Port Whitby named Heydenshore, to which another equally noteworthy, and considerably more notorious figure was said to visit. The era was that of Prohibition, and the figure, Chicago mob boss Alphonso Capone.

Finally, in 1973, chef Peter Solyom, an immigrant from Hungary, bought the building and converted it into a restaurant, a use that continues to this day. The building is located at the corner of Bryan and Dunlop Sts. ❖

When he could no longer afford his castle, Sheriff Reynolds built a much smaller version of his original home

WILLISTEAD, *Windsor*

If a castle is the centre from which its master controls his domain, then Willistead is very much the castle even though the Tudor style woodwork and stone porticos are more typical of an English country manor. Willistead was the heart and focus of Hiram Walker's company town, Walkerville.

In 1859 Hiram Walker opened a distillery on the south shore of the Detroit River, opposite his home town of Detroit. As business expanded Walker added a railway line, and laid out an attractive company town. Soon, the Walker family decided to build a mansion that befitted both them and their town.

In 1906 Edward Walker, Hiram's son, hired Albert Kahn,

Built by Edward Walker, Hiram Walker's son, Willistead is the centrepiece of Walkerville

renowned Detroit architect, to build that home on a 16-acre property at the south end of Walkerville. Using the latest construction techniques, Kahn designed a manor that looked straight out of Shakespearian England with exterior half-timbered walls and gables. The walk-in basement contained central heating and two coal-burning furnaces, which supplied heat to hot water radiators. The entire building was wired for electricity.

As you enter the grand building, you are confronted with a massive 42-foot great hall with oak paneling. Just off the cavernous chamber, a wide stairway with carved railings leads to the second floor. The dining room is distinguished by mahogany

American distiller Hiram Walker founded Willistead, one of Canada's most beautiful company towns

wainscotting and a plaster ceiling with Tudor roses from which hangs a massive brass chandelier. On the wall a fireplace is made of Italian marble. Look carefully along the wainscotting to find the secret walk-in vault where the Walkers stored their valuables.

Beside the dining room was a French-style salon into which the women guests could retreat to enjoy the damask-covered walls and the della robbia motifs above the marble mantle, while the men shared their cigars and brandy. Another favourite with the ladies was the conservatory with its flowers and expansive view of the estate grounds.

On the north end of the manor were Walker's billiard room with carved wood paneling and a 6 x 12 foot billiard table. Mahogany doors hidden in the walls separated the billiard room from the morn-

Statuary decorates the public grounds of Willistead

ing room. The well-lit library contained more paintings than books, as Walker was an avid art collector. The oak panels and beamed ceiling gives this room the ambience of the English country manor. One prominent feature of the library is Hiram Walker's desk, ornately carved with cherubs on top and carved legs. He had reputedly purchased the massive desk at the Chicago World's fair in 1883.

The second floor contained the Walkers' bedrooms and guest suites, each with its own bath. A Baldwin Grand piano with player piano mechanism is featured in Mrs Walker's sitting room.

A number of changes have been made to the second floor, for example the guest rooms have been opened to make a large gallery, which is rented out for meetings and banquets and which frequently displays the work of local artists.

The third floor was set aside for the servants' quarters.

A website for the City of Windsor describes the home as "a modest family residence for a childless couple." With no offspring, the Edward Walkers deeded the home to the city which used it variously as a library, and a municipal office; it now functions as a conference and reception centre. The public may visit two afternoons a week, although the grounds are open as a public green space at all hours. On the grounds you may also see the former coach house, now a meeting hall, and the gate house which was originally the residence of the groundskeeper.

After visiting Willistead, stroll north along Kildare Ave to see the grand homes of the distillery's management. Closer to the plant are the columned bank, the former hotel and the red stone company office. At this point you can access the VIA Rail station, or the walkways along the Detroit River. Downtown Windsor and the Casino lie to the west of Walkerville. ❖

CASTLE CARBIDE, *Woodstock*

Located in the rolling farmlands west of Kitchener, Woodstock can be counted as one of Ontario's better preserved historic communities.

The townsite was acquired and laid out in 1832 by British Admiral Henry Vansittart as a continuation of a plan started by Governor John Graves Simcoe to create a string of military settlements through western Ontario. At this time St Paul's church was built. Woodstock's oldest building, it survives to this day.

Shortly after, in 1851, the new town hall was built. It, too, survives, now a designated historic site. Within three years, the Great

One of Woodstock's many grand homes, this mansion was built by inventor Thomas "Carbide" Willson

Western Railway had laid its line into town, later adding an attractive Italianate railway station, which also survives, and still sees passenger service. Designated under the Heritage Railway Station Protection Act, it is one of Canada's oldest continuously operating rail passenger stations.

But it is along the aptly named Vansittart Street where Woodstock boasts one of Ontario's best collections of grand historic homes. Several claim high gables and towers, but it is the house built by Thomas "Carbide" Willson in 1895 that many claim to be the most castle-like in appearance. The cost, $90,000, was the most any house had cost in Woodstock up to that time.

While the architect is not identified, the designer of one of its most distinctive features is well documented. The stained glass window, located on the large circular tower, was originally designed by the Tiffany Glass Company for Lafayette College. The window depicts Alcuin, an 8th century educator from York England, and Charlemagne, and is named "Truth, Master and Pupil." The house, with its offset tower, is described as Queen Anne Revival style, a style which became popular in the later years of the 19th century.

An inventor, Willson attained his wealth through the discovery of a way to produce calcium carbide, an element essential in the production of acetylene gas. Indeed, a secret room still containing some of his scientific equipment remained hidden until recent years. In recognition of his accomplishments, the University of Toronto awarded him its first McCharles prize in 1909.

Most of Willson's work took place in Merriton and Shawinigan Quebec, where he had established carbide works. He moved to Ottawa in 1901 and died in New York in 1915.

In 1977 the City of Woodstock designated the house as a heritage home under the Ontario Heritage Act.

Bibliography

Adamson, Anthony, and M. MacRae, *The Ancestral Roof*, Toronto 1963.

Angus, Margaret, *Bellevue House, A National Historic Park*, Ministry of Indian Affairs and Northern Development, 1969.

Angus, Margaret, *The Old Stones of Kingston*, Toronto, 1966

Architectural Conservancy of Ontario, Quinte Branch, *A Decade of Sundays, Quinte Walking Tours*, Vol 1, Belleville, 1994.

Ashenburg, Katherine, *Going to Town, Architectural Walking Tours in Southern Ontario*, McFarlane Walter and Ross, 1996.

Barrie LACAC, Heritage Barrie, *Grand Homes Tour*

Beach Gary et al, The Wilmot Heritage Book Committee, *Photographic Memories, Wilmot Township, One Hundred and Fifty Years*, English Garden Publishers, New Hamburg, 1999.

Beatty Stephanie and S. G. Hall, *Parkwood*, Boston Mills Press, 1999.

Bell Rock, Laurentian University Museum and Art Centre

Bond, Y., *The Ottawa Country*, Queens Printer, 1968

Boyle, Terry, and Peter J. Stokes, *Under This Roof*, Doubleday, 1980.

Boylen, J.C *The Story of Castle Frank*, Rous and Mann Press, Toronto, 1959

Byers, Mary, and M. McBurney, *The Governor's Road*, University of Toronto Press, 1982

Byers, Mary and M. McBurney, *Homesteads*, University of Toronto Press, 1979

Byers Mary, J. Kennedy and M. McBurney, *Rural Roots*, University of Toronto Press, 1976

Canada, Minister of Canadian Heritage, *Bellevue House, National Historic Site*

City of Brantford, *Designation Report for Wynarden (Yates' Castle)*

Cruikshank, Tom, *Port Hope, A Treasury of Early Houses*, 1987,

Cruikshank, Tom, P.J. stokes, and John de Visser, *The Settlers Dream, A Pictorial History of Older Buildings of Prince Edward County*

Dendy, William, *Lost Toronto, Images of the City's Past*, McClelland and Stewart, 1993

Denison, John, *Casa Loma and the Man Who Built It*, Erin, Boston Mills Press 1982

Duncan, George, *Early Houses of Richmond Hill and Vicinity*, Richmond Hill Historical Society, 1995.

Greenhill, Ralph, Ken MacPherson, Douglas Richardson, *Ontario Towns*, Oberon Ottawa, 1974

Haldimand LACAC, *Memories of Haldimand, When the Lakes Roared*, 1997

Hubbert, M.Y., *Split Rail Country, A History of Artemesia*, 1986,

James, Doug and the Port Hope LACAC, *Historic Port Hope, Vol 1 And 2.*

Kalman, Harold, *A History of Canadian Architecture, Vol 1*, Oxford University Press, 1994.

Koch, Henry, Various Articles, Kitchener Waterloo Record, 1985

Knowles, Paul, *Castle Kilbride, the Jewel of Wilmot Township*, Commemorative Collectibles, New Hamburg, 1994

Langdon Hall Country House Hotel, *Langdon Hall, One Hundred Years of History,*

Litvak, Marilyn M. *Edward James Lennox, Builder of Toronto*, Dundurn Press, 1995

Lundell, Liz, *The Estates of Old Toronto*, Boston Mills Press, 1997

Markdale and Flesherton, a written heritage,

Martyn, Lucy, *Toronto, 100 Years of Grandeur, the inside stories of the great houses of Topronto and the people who lived in them,*

Ontario Ministry of Tourism, *A Guide to Provincial Plaques in Ontario,*

Oreskovich C. *The King of Casa Loma*, Toronto, 1982.

Otto Steven, *Rockside Castle*, Cuesta, 1993

Port Perry, Explore Out History, Port Perry Star, 1991

Robertson, John Ross, *the Diaries of Mrs John Graves Simcoe*, Toronto, 1911

Scadding, Henry, *Toronto of Old, Collections and Recollections*, Toronto, 1873.

Scarborough Local Architectural Advisory Committee, *Home Sweet Scarborough*, 1996

Schofield, Richard, M. Schofield and K Whynot, *Scarborough Then and Now*, Scarborough Board of Education and Scarborough Historical Society, 1996

Spilsbury, John R., *Cobourg, Early Days and Modern Times*, 1981

Stacey, Alan. *History Along the Trail, Kionontio (Osler Castle)*, Bruce Trail News,

Vicary, Alison and M Clark, *Independence and Plenty, an Illustrated History of Shedden Fingal and the Surrounding Area,*

Walking Tours of Port Perry

Wilson, L.W, and L.R. Pffaf, *Early St Marys, St Marys* on the Thames Historical Society, 1981

Williams, Lorraine, Don Mills, the home of little-known stately homes, The Don, September, 1984.

Winter Brian, Historical Whitby, various articles in the Whitby Free Press.

Acknowledgments

Marilyn Armstrong Reynolds, Kingsville Gosfield Heritage Society

George Duncan, Heritage Coordinator, Town of Richmond Hill, Dept of Planning and Development

Lynne Gibbon, Orillia Public Library

Mark W. Hall, Architect, M.W. Hall Corporation, Toronto

Susan Lankheit, Orangeville LACAC

Rae McFarlane, Huron County Historical Society,

Brian Malcolm, Parkwood, Oshawa

Jean Mills, Bruce county Historical Society

Evan Morton, Curator tweed and Area Heritage Centre

Barbara Orr, Manitoulin Historical Society

Don Payne, Heritage Halton Hills

Mrs Jean Schaefer, Goderich

Richard Schofield, Scarborough LACAC

Patti Shea, Kitchener LACAC

Gordon Sweger, Grenville County Historical Society

Donna Thompson, Save Our Heritage Committee, Brighton

Lewis Zandbergen, Stirling Historical society

Brent Zatterberg, Lennox and Addington County Historical Society

City of Woodstock, LACAC.

Hamilton Public Library, Local History Files

Muskoka Lakes Museum

St Marys Museum

Websites:

www.hpl.hamilton.on.ca/collections/landmarks/dundurn.htm

www.canadiangarden.com/community/graydon_hall

www.city.windsor.on.ca/parkrec/Willistead_manor/architecture.asp

http://members.xoom.com/_XMCM/cottonwd/history.htm

www.tonw.kirklnadlake.on.ca/oakes.html

Photo Credits

All images are from the Ron Brown Image Bank, with the following exceptions:

City of Toronto Archives, 70, 141, 143, 144, 151, 158, 159

Hamilton Public Library, 44, 51

Archives of Ontario, 21, 75, 167

Public Archives of Canada, 62, 103, 169

Index

T3-BHM-336

The Spa Less Traveled

Discovering Ethnic Los Angeles, One Massage at a Time

By Gail Herndon & Brenda Goldstein

Photographs by Courtney Brillhart

Prospect Park Books

Copyright © 2011 by Gail Herndon & Brenda Goldstein

All rights reserved. No part of this book may be reproduced or transmitted in any form or by any means, electronic or mechanical, including photocopying, recording, web posting or by any information storage and retrieval system, without permission in writing from the publisher.

All information in this book was verified when the book went to press. Please forgive the authors and the publisher if the establishment you wish to patronize has changed or is no longer in existence—these things happen.

Designer & photographer: Courtney Brillhart
Editor: Colleen Dunn Bates
Assistant editor: Gina Magnuson
Assistant photo editor: Natalie Weinstein

Published by Prospect Park Media
prospectparkmedia.com

Distributed to the trade by
SCB Distributors
scbdistributors.com

Special Sales
Bulk purchase (20+ copies) of The Spa Less Traveled is available to companies, organizations, mail-order catalogs and nonprofits at special discounts, and large orders can be customized to suit individual needs. For more information, contact Prospect Park Media.

Library of Congress Control Number: 2011927388

ISBN: 978-0-9844102-7-9

First edition, first printing
Printed in China on FSC-certified, sustainably produced paper.
thespalesstraveled.com

We dedicate this book to our parents:

Christine & William Herndon
and
Bonnie & Marshall Goldstein

Who've traveled the world and birthed the spirit of adventure in us

With love,

Gail & Brenda

A portion of the royalties from the sale of *The Spa Less Traveled* will go to Oasis, a nonprofit that works to stop human trafficking. Find out more at oasisusa.org

Acknowledgements

Special thanks to our dear friends for their feedback and support: Didi, M'Liss, Debra, Desiree, Akio, Yui, Brenda, Randi, Beth, Keith, Betty, Cherylnn, Deb, Sujata, Reuben, Mary Ellen, Jack, Sandie, Maria and Lisa.

Thanks to our cultural attachés who assisted with the vocabulary words:
Su, Maria, Ginny and Akio.

Big thanks to Keith for his reviews of the men's Korean spas. Thanks also to Detective John Bonomo for his insights into regulating massage businesses.

To our creative designer, Courtney Brillhart, thank you for the energy and enthusiasm you added to this project.

To Steve, thank you for your spectacular gift with words—and your mad Google skills.

To Colleen, Shepherdess of all Good Things, thank you for taking our project and creating something even better than we could imagine.

Gail & Brenda

Table of Contents

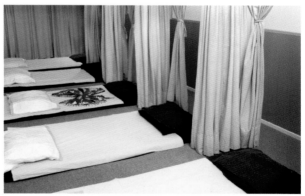

A typical Thai massage room

Introduction:
Cultural Exchange, the Spa Way

We Googled. We Yelped. And we found that most of L.A.'s authentic ethnic spas weren't getting a fair shake. That's because they're being compared to a different kind of treatment, the Swedish massage. Odds are you've had a Swedish massage; it is, after all, the most popular kind in the United States, a mild and completely relaxing treatment. But that's just one experience, and it's definitely not the way all massages were meant to be. After all, we're in Los Angeles! There's so much more to experience. Not only is the county of Los Angeles home to 9.86 million people, it boasts the largest Chinese, Thai, Korean and Japanese populations outside their home countries. So many of these immigrants brought with them meaningful customs and rituals. Just as you expect their languages and foods to be different, so should the anticipation for massage. And have we got some surprises for you!

The goal of this book is to help you understand each treatment and what's in store for you. There's nothing more enlightening than experience. Over the last several years, we've been privileged to be able to explore some of the purest ethnic enclaves in Los Angeles, rich in history and culture. And we were blown away. Visiting the places listed in this book is the only way to discover which spa treatments work for you. The more you try, the more you learn what you like… and don't. Being informed about how a certain therapy may help you can make your experience more physically and emotionally satisfying.

Be sure to read the introduction page for each massage type, as well as the glossary.

Going to L.A.'s ethnic spas will open you to new worlds. Despite soft-drink billboards and American fast-food restaurants just down the street from the majority of the spas listed, they really do offer a good look into other cultures. The people who work at the spas may have left behind a country, but they have, in large part, re-created it in their businesses. So please don't be put off by limited English and certain, shall we say, colorful habits. After all, you won't find eggs cooking or underwear drying in the sauna at Burke-Williams! (You'll have to read the book to find the place we saw that.) But your world will expand and your body will be transported.

If you picked up this book, you don't need selling on the many benefits of massage. But we do want to sell you on the rewards of exploring the diverse cultural neighborhoods Los Angeles has to offer and to expose you to their respective body treatments. Think of this as your own cultural exchange program, without the passport requirement or heinous air travel. We'll be your guides.

Escape. Explore. Enjoy!

Gail & Brenda

Chapter 1 – **The Ethnic Spa Basics**

MAKING THE MOST OF *THE SPA LESS TRAVELED*

Spa treatments are all about relaxing, and it's hard to relax until you know what to expect. So here's our short list of what's in the book and how you can make the most of it.

Glossary: A good place to start, particularly if you're not sure which treatment you'd like to try, or even what is actually involved in a specific treatment.

Spa Etiquette: Reference this section for spa pointers, advice on tipping your masseuse and the panty/no-panty debate.

Chapters: Each chapter provides an overview of a particular ethnic enclave, a brief history of the community, a description of the signature treatments and a guide to a great massage.

Keys: Icons quickly convey the information you want to know without having to read through the text. At a glance, for instance, you can see the price range, if the spa accepts credit cards, how authentic the facility is and if it's co-ed.

Authenticity: You can start your spa explorations closer to home, and then we'll help you work your way to other neighborhoods for more authentic experiences.

Vocabulary: We translate some of the most frequent words you might need to know in a spa setting. Start with "hello" or "thank you" and build up your vocabulary. You'll be pleased, and they'll be impressed.

Why We Like It: These short and sweet summaries help prioritize your destinations and respective spa treatments. We've included suggestions for nearby shops and restaurants that you might want to visit while you're in the neighborhood.

Recipes: We share a few simple recipes to help you re-create your spa experience at home.

Licensing: What you should know about training, licensing and certification.

Spa Relaken

Human Trafficking/Prostitution: This is a serious topic, and we felt it could not be glossed over. Read this section to learn what it is and what to do if you suspect human trafficking or prostitution.

Index: Stuck in traffic? Turn to our handy index of spas by neighborhood to learn where you might pull off the freeway and get a massage. The best stress relief possible!

One important note: We've done our best to bring you the most up-to-date information, verifying everything prior to printing. Please know that hours, websites, pricing and the like are subject to change by the owners and are outside our control.

Many hundreds of massage facilities blanket Los Angeles County, but if they didn't pass muster with us, we did not include them. This is not meant to be a comprehensive book—it's a curated book. If you have a favorite that didn't make the cut, e-mail us. We'd like to meet you there, and we may possibly include your spot in the next edition.

Most importantly, use this guide with a friend. You can be braver together (this is particularly helpful when the two of you do Chinese cupping), you can laugh together (a given if you both take the ice-cold plunge after the Russian platza treatment), you can feel safe when exploring together, and you have someone with whom to practice foreign words. Spa going is so much more enjoyable when shared. And that's how we wrote this book.

THE MANY BENEFITS OF MASSAGE

Even a single massage can have a measurable benefit, and if you can incorporate more of them into your life, all the better. Massage directly impacts the muscular, nervous, circulatory and immune systems. You can enjoy treatments singly or in concert with other therapies. Massage is not a

self-indulgence, but rather it should be a regular (even weekly) part of your routine of self-care, good health and wellness.

Many scientific studies have detailed the good things massage does for the body, but we'll give you just a brief list. If you're curious about something specific, look online for the most up-to-date research.

- Detoxes your body
- Reduces depression
- Alleviates mental fatigue
- Reduces heart rate and blood pressure
- Improves the body's immune response
- Lowers levels of stress hormones [which can make you gain weight]
- Increases blood circulation
- Relieves pain
- Reduces muscle fatigue
- Combats insomnia
- Relieves physical fatigue
- Improves digestion and elimination
- Relieves headaches due to eye strain and tension
- Boosts levels of endorphins and serotonin, which control pain and regulate mood

Since this is a book about our personal experiences, we can tell you what benefits we've noticed since beginning our research:

- Our circulation has improved, and as a result so has our skin tone.
- We've had no trouble sleeping. None whatsoever.
- Due to its stretching nature, Thai massage has improved the flexibility in our legs and hips.
- Being alone with our thoughts in a sauna or hot tub helps us problem-solve and recalibrate for the next day.

The bottom line is this: We've learned how to relax, which has given us more balance in our lives. Like you, we've struggled to take time for ourselves. But we've moved into a place of unabashedly enjoying our time having treatments, because they make us better equipped to handle stress and put life's problems into perspective. We invite you to join us, at the spa and on the journey toward improved health.

SPEAKING SPA: A GLOSSARY

As we've traveled L.A. (and the world) to experience various ethnic massages, we've learned that they have a lot in common. These are truly healing arts, practiced for generations as part of a larger lifestyle approach to good health.

Prenatal, lomilomi and Swedish are fully relaxing massage choices. This book, however, is primarily devoted to therapeutic massage. This type involves more specific manipulations of the body, addressing the nervous, circulatory, lymphatic and other systems. We hope reading about these types of massages makes you more comfortable and ready to try something therapeutic and/or enjoyable.

Acupressure: This traditional Chinese method of massage uses the fingers to apply pressure to specific areas of the body along meridians, or channels, to impact the body's energy. Meridian points are found all over the body, including the face, head, fingers and toes. Pressure on these meridians releases muscle tension and promotes healing by improving the flow of energy throughout the body. Specific points along the meridians are also used in acupuncture. You might also see this called shiatsu massage.

Aromatherapy: Typically an add-on to a massage, aromatherapy involves the scents of essential oils, primarily from herbs and flowers, which are both inhaled and applied to the body. Most essential oils require a "carrier oil" to allow them to be applied directly to the skin. Depending on the scent, the effect can be both physically and emotionally beneficial. Essential oils can address headaches, sore muscles and indigestion, among a host of other conditions. Peppermint, for instance, is particularly reviving for sore feet. As you gain experience with aromatherapy treatments, it will become easier to see the connection between scent and emotions. Specific scents can ease fatigue, anxiety and grief, for example. A good therapist can suggest something for your particular need.

Ayurvedic Massage: Also known as *abhyanga*, Ayurvedic massage is typically performed by one or two therapists who anoint the entire body with a warmed herbal oil, the base of which is typically sesame oil. The massage both begins and ends at the head. After the massage, some oil remains on your body and hair, which is why a warm shower is part of this service. It is part of the Indian approach to health care, which integrates massage, herbs, yoga and meditation. Ayurveda is a Sanskrit word that translates to "science of longevity." A primary tenet is that there can be no physical health without mental health, and vice versa. One of the benefits we've noticed following this massage is a deep night's sleep.

Banya: A *banya* is a Russian sauna heated by rocks that emit an intense heat. The temperature often exceeds 200°F, the upper limit for most types of saunas. The traditional banya involves a ritual. After showering, head to the banya and lie down on one of the lower benches. The higher up you move in the sauna, the more intense the heat. Lying down will allow you to stay longer and achieve more physical benefit—the idea is to stay as long as you can. It'll be easy to get a good sweat going. When you've reached your limit, rinse off in the shower, then run to the closest cold pool and jump in. The ritual involves repeating this process several times. If you're up for it, you'll find you can build up a tolerance for a longer stay in the banya, and then you'll definitely be looking forward to the cold plunge. When your body is sufficiently loosened up, typically after your third trip to the banya, a *platza* follows. (See Platza.)

In the banya at Vōda Spa; photo by Edward Duarte

Body Scrub: A.k.a. total body exfoliation. Koreans take the gold medal for perfecting this art of skin polishing. Masseuses wear mitts designed to scrub the dead skin cells from your entire (and we mean *entire*) body. This procedure is not for the shy, as you are typically one of many naked women lying on tables in fairly close proximity.

The masseuses, all donned in their working garb of black bras and matching panties, scrub, rinse and scrub again before rinsing, oiling and rinsing again, all in preparation for the big milk-bath finish (and by bath we mean they pour milk on your wet, naked body). As the tables are all lined up, there's something assembly-line about it, but there's no denying the results—softer and smoother skin, just like a baby's.

Cupping: This ancient Chinese technique involves using small cups to create suction on the body by generating a vacuum. Typically the practitioner extinguishes a match inside a glass, plastic or bamboo cup and immediately places it on your back along the meridians. This forms an air-tight seal, causing the blood to rise to the surface of the skin. The process is supposed to open the meridians and allow your internal energy to move freely throughout the body. If the cups are left alone, an even stronger suction is created, which pulls your skin into the cup. It looks like mini-cupcakes under a glass, depending on your level of back fat. Our favorite method is when they use a little oil on the back first, which allows the therapist to move the cups around, creating a pleasant suction feeling. Cupping may be used on your neck, shoulders and the backs of upper arms. After the cups are removed, you'll be left with dark red circles, like hickies on your back. The longer the cup stays in one place, the more intense the circle color. These will last a couple of weeks, which is why you might choose this therapy during the winter months. Any backless, strapless or even short-sleeve outfits may set people to talking! The treatment should not be painful, but you may feel a little discomfort as skin is pulled into each cup.

Deep Tissue: This technique involves slow-moving strokes with deep finger pressure on stiff areas, including the neck, back and shoulders. The intent is to realign the deeper layers of muscles and connective tissue, thereby releasing chronic patterns of tension and pain and, it is hoped, improving mobility and body alignment. The massage stroke may go with or across the grain of muscles and tendons. You may recognize some of the same strokes from Swedish massage, but because the pressure is deeper and concentrated, it is more intense and can sometimes be uncomfortable for short periods. If you prefer a lighter touch, this is not the massage for you. However, if you have knots or chronic muscle tension, this focused method might be very beneficial.

Hot Stone: For centuries, the Chinese, Native Americans and Hawaiians have used heated, smooth, palm-size stones during massage. Stones are most commonly placed on the forehead, stomach, chest, back and along the spine and are both left to rest and gently used during the course of the massage. Wherever they are positioned, the seeping heat relaxes the nervous system, and a subtle warmth spreads. Made of a particular kind of volcanic rock, these stones hold their heat for a long time. Oil is used to transfer the heat from the stones to the body. The warmth often brings pain relief, and you'll also benefit emotionally, because the warmth reduces mental fatigue. You may also notice an improvement in muscle function, because hot-stone treatments typically improve circulation.

Thai stretching at Lamai Thai

Indian Head Massage: This is part of a holistic Ayurvedic bodywork system from India, where the head, neck and face are massaged with the purpose of clearing blocked energy channels. The theory goes that blocked channels cause negative energy to build up, contributing to illness and pain. You may be fully clothed or asked to remove your top to allow the masseuse access to your shoulder blades, where the massage typically begins. It includes the upper back, shoulders, upper arms, neck and, finally, the head. The movements flow smoothly, and the pressure to the head is quite gentle, sweeping away stress and tension. Oil is used on your head, so plan your outing accordingly. Choose this type of massage if you have insomnia, suffer from headaches or eyestrain and/or hold tightness in your jaw, neck or shoulders. Another name for this type of massage is *champissage*.

Jim Jil Bang: These Korean family saunas typically have two distinct areas. The "wet" area is where you go first to shower, get a body scrub, soak in a tub and/or take a sauna (dry or wet). Since clothing is not allowed here (that's right, you're naked), it's for women only. Please do not bring a bathing suit—aside from not being necessary, it's not allowed. The men also have a wet zone. The other area is co-ed and is "dry," offering various saunas (clay, jade, gemstone, salt), massage chairs, a large lounging area with a heated floor and a restaurant or café; some even have WiFi. Since it's co-ed, everyone is clothed in the facility-issued T-shirt and shorts or robe.

Lomilomi: A healing art that comes from the ancient Polynesians, *lomilomi* actually means "massage" in the Hawaiian language. The therapist uses fingers, palms and elbows in long, continuous, sweeping strokes (think of the gracefulness of the hula). It can feel like ocean waves washing over you, particularly since different areas of your body may be massaged at the same time. This effect is magnified if you get a "four-hands" massage—two people massaging you is a very luxurious experience. Like the Chinese, Hawaiians consider energy flow and believe thoughts and tension can block energy in the body. Lomilomi is supposed to unblock energy flow, addressing not only physical pain but mental, emotional and spiritual issues. A blessing or prayer is commonly performed before the massage begins, with the masseuse gently placing his or her hands on your back. Or you may be asked if there is any healing you would like to receive. Nut oils, such as macadamia and coconut, may be used. If you get lomilomi while in Hawaii, you may find the methodology different on each island, as there are varying schools of thought about how the massage should be performed.

Massage Therapy: Massage practitioners use their hands (and sometimes arms, elbows and even feet) to manipulate the body's soft tissue; techniques include kneading, vibration, compression, stretching and tapping, some of which may be done while the therapist is holding or moving your body. The massage may be dry or with the aid of oils, lotions or scrubs. Massage may also be used in combination with other therapies to relieve pain, reduce stress and improve health and well-being.

Maya Abdominal Massage: This technique is done on the abdomen and pelvis to reposition internal organs and relieve tension in the diaphragm. Practitioners believe that the activities of normal daily life can cause reproductive organs to shift in the womb and obstruct the flow of blood, lymph vessels, nerve pathways and energy in the body. These blockages can inhibit the delivery of hormones, fluids and nutrients to the organs, creating constriction in the tissues and congestion in the abdomen and pelvic areas. The goal of Maya abdominal massage is to put the uterus back into place, improving both reproductive and digestive functions. This therapy is supposed to help with infertility, lessen painful periods and treat a displaced, fallen or prolapsed uterus. The therapist will have you strip

to your underwear and lie on a massage table. Your upper and lower body will be covered, but your stomach (from just under the bustline to your pubic bone) will be exposed. The therapist uses the fingertips of both hands to apply pressure vertically and diagonally, from the pelvic bone and ribs toward the belly button. It feels like your insides are being rearranged from the outside, which is interesting, to say the least. But it's much harder to wrap your head around having someone other than your gynecologist manipulate your ovaries. The massage is not painful, but you may find your stomach is a little tender afterward. Therapists are typically happy to share self-care techniques that you can do at home. A few cautions: Maya abdominal massage should not be attempted during your period, if you wear an IUD, or if you are in the first trimester of pregnancy.

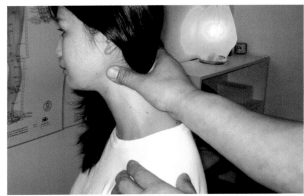

Shiatsu at Rolling Hills Shiatsu Center

Pregnancy Massage: Pregnancy massage (sometimes called prenatal) adapts to the needs of pregnant women. Support is given to the back, hips and the precious belly with a body pillow positioned between the legs. You lie on your side for this massage, and if there is a pregnancy table with a cut-out for the belly, you'll get the chance to lie on your stomach and enjoy massage on your back. Deep-tissue massage on the legs, abdominal massage and work on the feet are not a part of a pregnancy massage and should be avoided. This is meant to be a completely relaxing treatment.

Platza: This is Part Two of the Russian traditional massage performed in the banya, the super-hot dry sauna. The *platza* is a rigorous massage performed with a bouquet of oak, birch or eucalyptus leaves that have been soaked in warm water. The masseuse, who is bestowed with the title of platza master, both taps and strokes your backside as you lie face down on one of the lower levels in the sauna. The leaves release essential oils during their agitation, which are said to draw out impurities in the body. The process also improves circulation and the metabolism. This is also known as *venik* massage.

Reflexology: This treatment focuses on the reflex points of the feet and hands. Based on an ancient Chinese system, reflexology is grounded in the notion that the nerve endings in the sides and bottoms of the feet, hands and ears correspond to particular muscles and organs throughout the body. Therefore, massaging these pressure points is said to stimulate and improve circulation to the internal organs, contributing to healing. First, feet are usually soaked in a hot tea bath. The massage that follows is usually dry, with no lubricant. Tools of a reflexology masseuse are thumbs, fingers, knuckles and often a wood or plastic implement with rounded ends. This can be a very relaxing treatment, but that's not a typical first response. Don't be surprised if a spot or two on the bottom of your feet makes you jump!

Shiatsu: This Japanese massage technique applies finger pressure (*shiatsu* means "finger pressure") to specific energy (*tsubo*) points on the body. This results in improved circulation. Similar to acupressure, shiatsu concentrates on unblocking the flow of energy and restoring balance to promote self-healing. While you're in a reclining position, the masseuse applies pressure with the finger, thumb, palm, elbow or knee to specific areas of the body, following along the meridians. Shiatsu is a combination of many techniques, from rolling, brushing and patting to pressing, sweeping and vibrating, all gently stretching the body to loosen joints and muscles. The treatment brings a sense of relaxation while stimulating blood and lymphatic flow.

Stretching massage at Plai-Fah

Sports Massage: Sports massage is a type of Swedish massage designed to improve athletic performance by focusing on the muscles used in a particular athletic activity. This is accomplished by stimulating the circulation of blood and lymph fluids. Trigger-point therapy (akin to acupressure) is also often incorporated to break down knots in the muscles and increase your range of motion. It can also be beneficial after an intense athletic event and help speed recovery from athletic strain.

Swedish Massage: A more general treatment, Swedish is the most prevalent massage technique around. It involves long strokes and kneading with light-to-medium pressure.

Massage oils facilitate the extended movements, which are oh-so-soothing. Sleep is a frequent visitor to the Swedish massage bed, because this is such a completely relaxing treatment. We suspect this is why we've seen a few criticisms about other types of massage. To the Chinese, pain is good. To the Thai, stretching will find the limits to your range of motion. Both can be intense compared to Swedish. We believe that massage is a therapy, an art form, a healing ritual. It's not something you sleep through, although if you do it frequently enough, that could happen! If you are looking for a more intensive massage or harder pressure, go for a deep-tissue massage.

Thai herbal balls

Thai Massage: With roots in ancient Thai culture, this bodywork aims to unblock trapped energy and improve vitality by applying pressure along the body's energy pathways. You will typically be given fisherman pants—not just large but huge-waisted unisex pants with two ties at the back that should be wrapped around the waist and tied at the front. You may also be offered a loose top. The massage is typically performed on a mat, futon or raised bed on the floor, giving the masseuse room to move more freely around and over you. The touch is slow and rhythmic, beginning and ending at the feet. No oil is used in a traditional Thai massage, though it's used in a combination massage, typically Thai/Swedish. The masseuse generally follows the Sen (energy) lines on the body, similar to the meridians in Chinese massage, yet the Thais do not connect the Sen lines with internal organs. You'll find out just how flexible you truly are in a Thai massage—toward the end of the treatment, the masseuse will use her hands, forearms, elbows and feet to stretch you. She may try to fold you like a pretzel, using her body weight to position you into various poses. Often called Thai-yoga massage, it is akin to doing yoga without having to think about it.

Thai Herbal Ball: This herbal poultice is an add-on to a Thai massage. When first out of the steamer or microwave, it's hot! The therapist will touch your body with it only for seconds. After a minute or two, she'll use it as part of a deep rub, typically along the Sen lines on the back, neck and shoulders. After it cools a bit more, your masseuse may stroke you with it. It's a good therapy to relieve sore muscles and to stimulate circulation. We've found the deepest sleep after this has been added to an afternoon Thai massage. Richly aromatic, the ball comprises galangal (a member of the ginger family), kaffir lime and tamarind leaves, turmeric, camphor and other herbs and spices. Tiny older women once raised us off the floor, quite swiftly and effortlessly, until we were totally suspended like drapes over their feet, our bellies toward the sky. You'll have to read the Thai Massage chapter to find the place that practices the Thai herbal ball this way!

Tui Na: This ancient Chinese system is most commonly used for musculoskeletal problems. Massage is performed at your pain areas and along acupressure points, meridians and joints. *Tui* means "push" and *Na* means "grasp" in

Chinese, and both are liberally used, along with stretching, pulling, rolling, kneading, pressing, rubbing and tapping. It works by stimulating the flow of both blood and energy in the body. As there are several methods or schools of Tui Na massage, you may find no two alike. It's great for those seeking a focused therapy to treat chronic problem areas, including the lower back and shoulders. Stimulation of acupuncture points balances internal organs, so this therapy is also effective for those with digestive problems and insomnia. This therapy is often used in conjunction with other modalities, including acupuncture, cupping, compresses, the application of salves and/or the burning of an herb known as mugwort.

Walking Massage: Also known as *ashiatsu* or barefoot shiatsu, this Japanese technique is the combination of the Japanese words for foot (*ashi*) and pressure (*atsu*); you can also find walking massages in Indian, Thai, Chinese and Philippine cultures. The therapist supports her weight by holding on to bars attached to the ceiling, adjusting the amount of compression on your muscles and soft tissue through her grip. You'll find it close to magic that someone's feet actually feel like soft baby hands—the strokes are deep, long and flowing. Because of the weight, this qualifies as a deep-tissue massage, but it can initially feel like a Swedish because of the softness of the masseuse's feet. If you are muscular and have a hard time finding a masseuse who can work you deeply enough, this is a great choice.

SPA ETIQUETTE

For those who are trying these therapies for the first time, we have some guidelines to help navigate your visit.

Appointments. We definitely recommend making an appointment. While many of the spas say they take walk-ins, they often don't have enough staff on hand to accommodate unexpected arrivals. Help them schedule their workers ahead of time by calling ahead.

Payment. Although many spas say they take credit cards, they may add a service charge, so we've indicated this in the listings. Cash is always preferred—plus, it's nice to give a tip in cash, even if you're paying by credit card. Don't be surprised if places ask you to pay before you get the service. You can always reserve the tip for afterward.

Panty-No Panty. We've learned that therapists will work on you however you dress. If you want to leave your bra and underwear on during a massage, go right ahead. If you are more comfortable going commando, then by all means, go for it. Most places make a concerted effort to keep your exposed areas covered. If you feel you need more coverage, adjust the sheet or towel yourself.

Tipping. We recommend a minimum 20% tip, but if you're getting a steal of a deal, like an hour foot massage for fifteen bucks, why not tip $10? It's still a deal. Our practice has been that for any massage under $50, we tip $10. You're welcome to give more, but it's offensive to give less. If you give less, you may get some attitude and be prepared for some grumblings. We bring cash to give the tip directly to the therapist.

What to Bring/What Not to Bring. Bring an elastic, scrunchie or banana clip to hold your hair up if it's long. If you're going to a sauna or steam room, bring flip flops, as they are not always provided. But leave all jewelry at home.

Communicate. People always say to tell your therapist your preferences. But what if talking (in English) isn't an option? You can still communicate. Facial expressions, body movements and gestures can effectively convey what you want and don't want. For example, if the pressure is too hard, pull away. If you don't want one of your hands massaged? Before the massage begins, sign an "X" with one finger over the other hand. Get creative, but let your wishes be known.

Be Respectful. Turn off your cell phone when you arrive. Take the time to observe your surroundings and acclimate to the sights, sounds and smells. Even though others around you may not be following this, lower your voice when speaking. Many of the services are in communal rooms or rooms sectioned off with a sheer curtain. Everyone will be able to hear what you say.

Shower. Important to do before you leave home, but just as important to do again when in a Korean or Russian spa, and not just before a treatment. Always shower before using the saunas, steam rooms or pools.

Drink Up. It is important to drink water both before and after your massage, since toxins will be released from your body. Help them out, literally.

But Don't Eat. Your massage will be more pleasant if you don't have a full stomach, so don't eat a big meal before you go. Think about having a bite afterward, as you explore the surrounding neighborhood.

Relax. Get in the habit of arriving a little early for your massage. Use the time to get to know the layout of the facility or simply relax. This will help get you in the proper state of mind to more fully enjoy your treatment.

Listen to Your Body. Be sure to note how you feel after the massage and for the rest of your day. Becoming aware of how your body responds to a certain therapy is important, particularly if your initial response to the treatment wasn't favorable. It may become a favorite as the day progresses.

How Often to Massage. This really depends on what's going on in your life and what you can afford; keep in mind that the majority of the spas in this book are substantially less expensive than the mainstream chain luxury spas. We've found that having a massage once a week really helps manage the stress of the week. When we can't go during the week, we love our weekends out, when our exploring will include a massage, a bite to eat and a little shopping. It's probably safe to recommend that you should go more often than you go now.

Night and Day. We visited the majority of spas during the daytime, and that's how we'd suggest you start. Businesses look different at night, and a place that looks so serene during the day may be lit up like Chinese New Year at night.

PRECAUTIONS

Massage should not be pursued by anyone with the following conditions:

- A recent surgery
- An infectious skin condition
- An open wound or rash
- A recent chemotherapy or radiation session, unless permitted by your physician
- Heart disease or blood clots; check with your physician—there is a risk of blood clots being dislodged
- Pregnant women should check with their doctor first, and if given the green light should have a massage only by therapists certified in pregnancy massage

LICENSING

In California, massage parlors and self-employed massage technicians must obtain a business license, which must be current and posted on the premises. Employees do not need a business license, but they must be certified, either as a Certified Massage Therapist (CMT) or a Certified Massage Practitioner (CMP), and their certificates must also be posted. A CMT must complete at least 500 hours of formal training at an approved school, and a CMP must complete at least 250 hours.

The certifying agency is the California Massage Therapy Council (CAMTC), and it requires that massage therapists undergo background checks, fingerprinting and verification of their training. If you have any questions about a therapist, you can look them up on the CAMTC's website, camtc.org.

HUMAN TRAFFICKING/PROSTITUTION
THE WHITE ELEPHANT IN THE MIDDLE OF THE ROOM

Aren't these places simply fronts for prostitution and human trafficking? We simply cannot answer that with 100% certainty. But we can tell you that any place with a business license is regularly inspected by both city and state agencies.

All cities have their own zoning regulations and ordinances. We suspected Arcadia holds to a high standard because massage businesses are required to post a sign that says: "In cooperation with the Arcadia Police Department, our doors are to remain unlocked at all times for periodic inspection to insure our professionalism." It turns out this posting is required by code. An interesting conversation with Arcadia Detective John Bonomo led to a quick online search for the application documents for massage therapists. These documents detail which licenses workers need to have, dictate a dress code, explain requirements for record-keeping of services performed, specify hours of operation, and even stipulate the wattage of light bulbs, among other things. New business owners have to submit to a background check and be fingerprinted. Not every city, however, has such high standards.

That said, please know that the facilities listed in this book are held to the same standard as the big chains like Burke-Williams. If a business doesn't abide by its city's laws, it will be cited. If violations are not addressed, the business will be shut down. If you note anything untoward, please contact the local police department.

A GUIDE TO THE ICONS

Co-ed

Men-only

Women-only

Appointment required or suggested

Food on premises

Credit cards accepted

GUIDE TO PRICES

The following price guide is for a typical one-hour treatment, not including tip.

$ $25 or less

$$ $26-$50

$$$ $51 and up

Chapter 2 – **Thai**

YOGA IN A MASSAGE

Thai massage dates back more than 2,500 years. Like the origins of the Thai people themselves, its history is unclear. Thailand was at the crossroads of ancient migration routes, which saw many cultures passing through. Because of its proximity to China and its position on one of the main trade routes from India, Thailand has had many cultural and religious influences. Thai medicine also appears to have been impacted by both Chinese and Indian (Ayurvedic) medicine, and massage is one of the components of Thai medicine.

Traditional Thai massage combines gentle stretching movements with whole body massage. During the massage, the therapist applies pressure along energy lines (*Sen*). This activates the body's pressure points and energy lines, allowing tension to be released. The idea is that when joints are opened in this manner, the body's energy is allowed to flow freely. This flow of energy is a similar concept in China (*chi*) and India (*prana*), yet in Thai massage, the *Sen* are not connected to the internal organs.

Following the massage manipulation of major Sen lines, the therapist will move you in a series of yoga-like stretches and postures. This is why Thai massage is sometimes called "lazy yoga"—you may be stretched into forward and backward bends, spinal twists and the cobra, locust and plough positions, among others. These are used to activate and balance the energy systems of the body, similar to the intent of acupuncture and Shiatsu. The combination of energy activation and physical stretching is what makes Thai massage unique.

There's something lovely about doing yoga without having to think about it. You don't have to know the names of the poses, for starters. And unlike a yoga class, the poses are not called out. The masseuse will gently assist you into all positions, s-t-r-e-t-c-h-i-n-g you out.

Lamai Thai

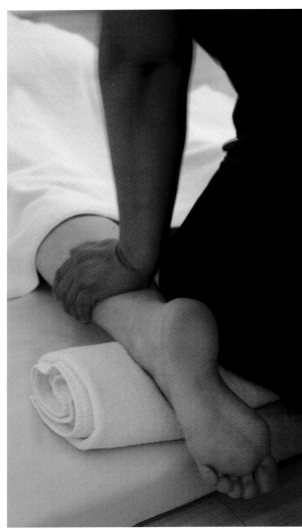

Thai massage at Pattaya Healing Massage

We've all heard that stretching is important, but do we really understand why? The amount of movement a muscle can have is determined by the difference between its length when relaxed and when fully contracted. When muscles are tensed, they become shorter, even if you're not consciously contracting them. This can happen through overuse, but more often (especially as we age), it comes from not using them enough or from emotional tension. The result is progressively more restricted movement, leading to stiffness, aches and pains—all not-so-lovely characteristics of the aging process. Okay, you had us at aging process!

Movements are often done in a gentle rocking fashion, stretching you a bit further each time—but don't worry, you won't be stretched beyond your capacity. But be prepared. If you say your thigh is tight or hurts, that doesn't mean the therapist will leave it alone. In fact, quite the opposite will occur. Since one of the goals is to improve your flexibility and range of motion, she will indeed continue to work on the area that you just said hurts! So if you really don't want a certain body part stretched, make that known up front. Hand gestures and facial expressions go a long way in conveying your message.

Traditional Thai massage always starts at the feet, works up to the head, and then ends back at the feet. If performed traditionally, it should also be dry—that is, without oil—though you may find it combined with Swedish, a relaxing, all-about-the-oil style of massage. Thai massage is best performed on a thin padded mattress on the floor or a low bed. If not performed in a closed room, a large room may be subdivided into "rooms" with drapery or sheers, affording some privacy.

You will often be provided unisex clothing—a loose shirt and huge-waisted pants, called fisherman pants. Only a few places we went to had diagrams on how to put them on correctly. What you need to know is that they tie in the front. If only pants or loose shorts are provided, that's a hint that you'll be topless, but you'll remain fully covered by a sheet or towel throughout your massage. Some smaller places do not provide clothing; we usually keep our underwear on, because Thai therapists twist you all around, and it's nice to be covered.

SIGNATURE TREATMENT: *THAI HERBAL BALL*

The herbal ball is a medicinal poultice that was first used in Thailand in the 14th century, when war-weary soldiers returned home. Today it is used to alleviate pain and inflammation by opening the pores and bringing a focused heat to the area to induce relaxation. It is especially good post-partum. The "ball" is a piece of muslin fabric filled with a variety of Thai herbs—primarily prai, lemongrass, turmeric, kaffir lime and camphor. Ask if you can take yours home after your treatment—you should be able to get another two or three uses from it. You'll just have to recruit a partner. And if you're interested in making your own, check out the recipe in our Creating a Home Spa Experience chapter.

A FEW WORDS IN THAI

ENGLISH	THAI PRONUNCIATION
Hello	sawa dee-ka
Good-bye	la-kon
Yes	chaì
No	mai chai
Thank you	khop khun kha
Pain	poo-what

Buddha shrine in Thai Town

THAI TOWN

Thai Town centers on Hollywood Boulevard between Normandie Avenue and Western Avenue in Hollywood, near Los Feliz. It's just north of the 101 Freeway and southwest of Griffith Park. The Metro Red Line at the Hollywood/Western station gets you there.

HISTORY

Thai Town got its formal designation on October 27, 1999, when the L.A. City Council named this particular half-mile stretch of Hollywood Boulevard as such. (Both Bangkok, Thailand's capital, and Los Angeles are known as the City of Angels.) As you would expect, the area is ripe with all things Thai, from home furnishings and silk clothing to restaurants and massage spas. This neighborhood is also home to many Armenians.

On the first Sunday in April, the community celebrates the Thai New Year, called Songkran. It is the largest cultural event outside Thailand. Thai families come together to participate in the Thai New Year water ceremony, when people pour water on the hands of revered elders and ask for blessings, although it can often devolve into teenage water-gun fights. You'll find traditional arts and crafts, wonderful food, distinctive clothing, martial arts exhibits and other street performances. Learn more at thainewyear.com.

It might be worth your while to time your Thai massage experience to coincide with Thai New Year, as many spas will have discounts in celebration of the holiday.

THAI MASSAGE IN THAI TOWN/ HOLLYWOOD

Chaba Thai Massage
4960-D Hollywood Blvd., Los Angeles 90027
(Corner Kenmore)
323.953.8980, chabathaitherapy.com

Hours: Daily 10 a.m.–9 p.m.

Facilities: A tiny place nestled deep in the corner of a mini-mall, this place usually leaves the front door locked, so make sure you call for an appointment. It has only three rooms, two with massage tables and one with a raised platform and a padded mat.

What to expect: Pay for the massage first. You'll be given a large T-shirt and a pair of traditional Thai shorts; change your clothes in the room and lie down on the table. They will wash your feet with a warm towel and begin the massage at your feet. The focus is your comfort and enjoyment, so feel free to let them know if something does not feel right or if you want your therapist to repeat a maneuver.

Services offered: Thai, deep-tissue and hot-stone massage, plus facials and waxing.

Parking: Two spots in the lot, some side-street parking.

Why we like it: Don't be deceived by the look of this place—if you want an authentic Thai massage by a true professional, ask for May and you'll get a treat!

Jasmin Day Spa
4718 W. Fountain Ave., Los Angeles 90029
(Corner Vermont, behind Children's Hospital)
323.663.1536, jasmindayspa.com

Hours: Daily 10 a.m.–10 p.m.

Facilities: Located upstairs, this place has six nicely decorated private rooms with massage tables and curtains as doors.

What to expect: A traditional, relaxing, yoga-like massage. The therapist used her hands, elbows, knees and feet to massage our bodies.

Services offered: Thai, Swedish and deep-tissue massage.

Parking: Lot in front.

Why we like it: This little gem offers a true traditional Thai massage. The place is clean and smells good, the rooms are neat and private, and the therapists are professional. If you live in the area, or work at one of the many hospitals nearby, stop in for a restorative treatment.

THAI

LA Face & Mind
4850 Hollywood Blvd., Los Angeles 90027
(Corner Edgemont)
323.668.1885, lafaceandmind.com

Hours: Daily 10 a.m.–9 p.m.

Facilities: Located in a mini-mall (like so many others), this Thai massage place has eight rooms, one with a massage table and the others with padded mats on raised platforms on the floor.

What to expect: Pay first, and know that there's a $3 charge if you use a credit card. They'll ask if you prefer a man or woman therapist, so let them know. Take off your shoes before you enter the massage area, and they'll ask that you turn off your cell phone. The rooms are lined down a hallway, four on each side, with walls separating the rooms and curtains serving as doors. You'll be given a pair of baggy shorts to put on, either over your underwear or not, your choice. Since you're on a mat, you can ask for a U-shape pillow to rest your head when you are face down. The therapists perform Thai massage that incorporates hot stones, which really help reduce the stress and tension in your muscles. If you're especially tense, the therapists may use Thai balm, but they always ask first before applying it.

Services offered: Thai massage.

Parking: Lot in mini-mall.

Why we like it: Our therapists and the receptionist were all very accommodating, introducing themselves, asking our names and what we needed and making sure we were comfortable and the pressure was just right. They pride themselves on practicing the art of Thai massage.

Nuch Royal Thai Spa (formerly R4U)
5300 Hollywood Blvd., Los Angeles 90027
(Corner Hobart, east of Western)
323.461.4400, nuchroyalthaispa.com

Hours: Daily 10 a.m.–10 p.m.

Facilities: The sixteen massage rooms (including some for couples) all have raised platforms, and the massage is performed on a mat.

What to expect: First you'll change into the provided halter top and shorts, and then they'll wipe your feet with a warm towel and begin the massage. No oils are used—this is really a traditional Thai massage. Let them know if you prefer a male or female therapist.

Services offered: Thai, Thai herbal ball, Swedish, deep-tissue, four-hands and pregnancy massage, plus foot reflexology, body scrub and facials.

Royal Thai Spa

Parking: Lot in front or side-street parking.

Why we like it: The new décor adds to the charm and authenticity of your experience. The place is clean, colorful and smells good. Make sure you check the website for specials.

Thai Sabai
5261 Hollywood Blvd., Los Angeles 90027
(Corner Harvard)
323.485.2800, thaisabai.com

Hours: Daily 10 a.m.–10 p.m.

Facilities: Tucked away in a Thai Town mini-mall, this was one of the first places we went for a traditional Thai massage. The surroundings are pleasant, and the eleven massage rooms, separated by thin walls that don't connect to the ceiling, all have mats, as well as hooks to hang your clothes and bags. Two separate rooms are used for acupuncture. The therapists trained in Thailand at the Wat Po College of Traditional Medicine (their certificates are on the wall in the reception area).

What to expect: Your massage will be done on the floor on a Thai massage mat. You'll be given two loose pieces of clothing: a halter-style top that leaves your back exposed, and a pair of shorts. All the moves are yoga-like stretches, and since this is a traditional massage, the therapists do not use oil. There's a service charge for credit-card payments.

Services offered: Thai, sports and pregnancy massage, foot reflexology, skin care. Gift certificates available.

Parking: Lot in front, validated valet parking on weekends.

Thai Sabai

Why we like it: It lives up to its name—*sabai* means relaxed or comfortable—which is exactly how you'll feel after a massage here. Don't forget to sign up on the website for promotional discounts.

Another location at in Westwood at 1951 Westwood Blvd., Los Angeles 90025, 310.801.3912.

Top Thai Massage
5123 Sunset Blvd., Ste. 213, Los Angeles 90027
(Sunset Center Plaza, between Normandie & Kingsley)
323.663.3439, topthaimassage.com

Hours: Daily 10 a.m.–9 p.m.

Facilities: Nestled in the upper left corner in the Sunset Center Plaza, accessible by stairs only, Top Thai has eight rooms with mats on the floor and one room with a massage table.

THAI

What to expect: A simple place that offers professional Thai massage, which is given on mats in rooms separated by white curtains. They'll provide you with a pair of boxer shorts and a loose camisole; you can keep your underwear on or take it off, your choice.

Services offered: Thai, Swedish and deep-tissue massage.

Parking: Lot in front.

Why we like it: They provide a true full-hour traditional Thai massage on a mat, so just lie back, relax and enjoy.

See also Top Thai in Studio City.

BEYOND THAI TOWN

ARCADIA

Spa Thai Essence
1010 Baldwin Ave., #201, Arcadia 91007
(Near Fairview)
626.446.8601, spa-thai-essence.com

Hours: Daily 10 a.m.–9 p.m.

Facilities: Located upstairs via stairs in the back, this is a small place with only three rooms, all with massage tables.

What to expect: You must have an appointment. When you enter the room, you'll take off your shoes and clothes and lie face-down on the table. If you get a scrub, there is a shower to rinse off, and they'll give you a towel.

Services offered: Thai and Swedish massage, herbal Thai ball, body scrubs (milk, sesame, ginger or coffee), facials and oat body mask.

Parking: Behind the building in a lot or street.

Why we like it: There's true pride of ownership here. May, the owner, greets you and makes you feel very welcome. She takes a real interest in your goals for your massage and concentrates on those areas. It's quiet and peaceful, with no talking or cell phones ringing—a real pleasure!

ARTESIA

R&R Thai Spa
18008 Pioneer Blvd., Artesia 90701
(Between Artesia & 183rd,
across from Oasis Plaza)
562.809.8772, rrthaispa.com

Hours: Daily 10 a.m.–9 p.m.

Facilities: In an unassuming building, this small place has six individual rooms and one large room that can accommodate three people. The rooms have curtains for doors; some have walls, and others are separated by curtains.

What to expect: You can wear whatever you like; we chose to strip down to our underwear. They'll keep you covered with a towel and as comfortable as possible. The massage is provided on a table, and they'll walk on you if you ask.

Services offered: Thai, Swedish, foot and facial massages.

Parking: Private lot on the side of the building.

Why we like it: Reasonable price for a good Thai massage in a clean, friendly environment.

A&K Body Care
9210 Alondra Blvd., Ste. D, Bellflower 90706
(Between Virginia & Santa Ana)
562.804.0876

Hours: Mon.–Sat. 10 a.m.–6 p.m.

Facilities: This is a place you might overlook because of its dowdiness and its location in a corner of an older little shopping center, but it's a clean, well-run facility, with certified therapists who give a good massage. It has six tables total, two in each of three rooms, which are separated by medium drapes.

What to expect: We had the combo Thai-Swedish massage, which started traditionally with us face down. Our feet welcomed the wipe-down with a hot, wet washcloth, and then the therapist made the traditional slow, steady walk up the back of our legs with her palms. A lot of time was spent on the upper back, and after the requisite kneading to work out the kinks, she added oil, reversing the order—now from the neck, shoulders and back down to the butt, legs, thighs, calves and feet. We were then wiped down with a warm washcloth, and our legs were stretched before we turned over. The massage-oil-wipe-down process was then repeated on the front side.

Services offered: Acupressure, reflexology and deep-tissue, Swedish, Thai and combo massages.

Parking: Free parking in the mini-mall.

Why we like it: Ask for Pat. She gives an amazing massage.

Joy's Massage Therapy
16100 Woodruff Ave., Bellflower 90706
(At Alondra, in the Big Saver Foods center)
562.867.7744, joysmassagetherapy.com

Hours: Wed.–Mon. 10 a.m.–9 p.m.

Facilities: This lovely place has nice bright lighting in the public areas, lockers, a steam room, showers and seven generously sized rooms, one of which is a couple's room; the rooms have actual doors, too. All masseuses are licensed and certified. A licensed aesthetician is also on staff.

What to expect: You're provided fisherman shorts but no top, and you'll slip under a thin sheet on a massage bed. It starts with a warm foot wipe-down, followed by applying pressure to points on the toes, soles and the balls of the feet. For the traditional Thai massage, no oil is used. After massaging up the calf, thigh and butt, your legs are splayed for some stretching. We had just as much stretching as massage at Joy's, and it was great! Then it's on to the back, arms, neck and some shoulder stretches before turning over. After a massage on your front side, your legs are splayed one at a time to give a good stretch into the inner thigh. At the end, you'll sit with legs crossed, and the therapist will raise you like a table top with her feet. You'll hang there for probably less than a minute, but it feels longer.

Services offered: Thai, Swedish, shiatsu, sports, deep-tissue, hot-stone, pregnancy and combo massage, as well as aromatherapy, reflexology, body scrub, steam room and facials. Gift certificates available.

Parking: Plenty in the shopping center.

THAI

Why we like it: The owner, Joy, does everything right here. We loved our services and the ambience. And that upside-down table move is like magic. Ask for Jem if you want a challenging stretching session.

BURBANK

Chaba Herbal Spa & Thai Yoga Massage
1212 N. San Fernando Blvd., Burbank 91504
(Between Bethany & Cornell)
818.557.6261; chabamassage.com

Hours: Daily 10 a.m.–10 p.m.

Facilities: A tiny oasis in a little strip mall. All six treatment rooms are private and clean.

What to expect: Pay for your service first. They offer a traditional Thai massage on a bed, and therapists use a lot of warm towels to loosen up your muscles and clean you off, if you opt for a treatment with oil.

Services offered: Thai, Thai herbal ball, Swedish and deep-tissue massage, plus body scrub and reflexology.

Parking: Lot in front.

Why we like it: Its claim is true—this places provides sincere Thai hospitality and promotes wellness in a holistic way. It also offers a 15- or 30-minute massage if you want to get quick relief. Bottom line—it's truly accommodating. Ask for Jasmine.

Gio's Thai Massage
116 S. San Fernando Blvd., Burbank 91502
(Between Olive & Angeleno)
818.612.0932, giosthaimassage.com

Hours: Daily 10 a.m.–10 pm.

Facilities: It's a little hard to find because it's inside and upstairs from Gio's Brooklyn Boxing Club, which has the same address. Stand there long enough (as we did) and the guy working at the club will lead you to the stairs to the massage area.

What to expect: Up the stairwell is a narrow hallway that doubles as the waiting and reception area. The walls are painted in deep, warm colors and Thai woodwork and rich fabrics decorate the space; they've made good use of every inch. Five rooms have massage beds. Soft music played in the background as we changed into the shorts provided

and lay face down, with rolled pillows placed strategically for our forehead and neck comfort. The massage stayed true to tradition, starting with the wipe-down of the feet. We were kept covered by a towel while we were massaged and finally stretched. Our massages ended with some back-stepping.

Services offered: Thai, Swedish, deep-tissue, combo, pregnancy and sports massage.

Parking: Free parking in back at 201 E. Angeleno Ave., and you can enter the back of the store, where signage is better. Or park on San Fernando.

Why we like it: They not only have small space heaters in the rooms but also crockpots to keep the massage lotion warm.

THAI

CANOGA PARK

L.A. Thai Massage Therapy
22211 Sherman Way, Canoga Park 91303
(Corner Farralone)
818.703.7028

Hours: Daily 10 a.m.–10 p.m.

Facilities: Stuck in the corner of a strip mall, this little place is deceptive from the front. Inside are private rooms with tables or massage mats on the floor; a large couple's room is handsomely decorated.

What to expect: This is a lovely traditional Thai massage. All the employees wear scrubs-like uniforms and wash their hands carefully before and after they give massages. Since they do not provide you with anything to change into, you get undressed and stay in your underwear if you wish. They will keep you covered with a towel.

Services offered: Thai, Swedish and deep-tissue massage.

Parking: Lot in front.

Why we like it: Professional massage in clean, private rooms on a mat or massage table, as you prefer.

The Massage Clinic
7551 Topanga Canyon Blvd., Canoga Park 91303
(Topanga Canyon & Saticoy)
818.703.1114, themassageclinics.com

Hours: Daily 10 a.m.–10 p.m.

Facilities: On the edge of a tiny mall with very limited parking, this little place has just four private rooms, each with a massage table and a door.

What to expect: You'll undress in your private room and lie face-down on the massage table under a sheet. As the therapists move from one part of your body to the next, they take care to make sure that only the section they're working on is exposed. They usually use oil, but you can request that they not. If they do use oil, they wipe it off at the end with warm, damp towels.

Services offered: Thai, four-hands and couples massage, as well as foot reflexology.

Parking: Some spaces in the mall.

Why we like it: Real private rooms with doors, and the therapists made sure they understood our needs and preferences, checking regularly about the pressure and if we were okay.

CHATSWORTH

Angel Thai Spa
21108 Devonshire St., Chatsworth 91311
(Corner Variel)
818.341.3080

Hours: Daily 10 a.m.–9:30 p.m.

Facilities: This small mini-mall place offers Thai massage on a raised bed.

What to expect: Walk into a large, open waiting room and take off your shoes. Each of the five rooms has a massage table and curtains instead of a door. They do not provide clothes, so wear what you're comfortable in, or take off what you wish. They'll provide a sheet to cover you.

Services offered: Thai, Swedish, deep-tissue and combination massages.

Parking: Lot in front.

Why we like it: Thai massage on a comfortable table in a small, quiet and private place. The therapists' certificates are posted on the wall.

Bambu Body Works
10020 Canoga Ave., Unit B, Chatsworth 91311
(Between Devonshire & Lassen)
818.339.4172

Hours: Daily 10 a.m.–9 p.m.

Facilities: Located in the auto-body area of Chatsworth, this place is a hidden treasure. From the outside it looks like every other building on the street, but once inside you feel like you're in someone's home. The attractive rooms are separated throughout the building, so there's a sense of privacy.

What to expect: A phenomenal traditional Thai massage. The therapists we've had were trained in Thailand and then certified in California, and they work in rooms that are handsomely decorated with Asian art and movie posters. Choose between a traditional mat or a massage table, then undress, lie down and get ready for an amazing massage. We were stretched, pulled and pushed in every direction, and while it was tough at first, at the end we felt great! A $2 service charge for credit-card payments.

Services offered: Thai, Swedish, deep-tissue and combination massages.

Parking: Lot behind building.

Why we like it: Hip atmosphere and amazingly talented and professional therapists—one of the best body-work massage around!

Sunlee Spa
21113 Devonshire St., Chatsworth 91311
(Corner Variel)
818.576.8900

Hours: Daily 10 a.m.–10 p.m.

Facilities: Another shabby-looking place in the corner of a mini-mall. But go inside and that impression will change. The tiny front office is nicely decorated, and the four rooms down the hall are attractive, with curtains as dividers and massage tables instead of mats on the floor.

What to expect: Best to make an appointment as this is a small place. Wear whatever you're comfortable in; they'll cover you with a sheet if you undress completely. We enjoyed a traditional Thai massage with lots of stretching and relaxing moves.

Services offered: Thai, Swedish and combination massages.

Parking: Lot in front.

Why we like it: Small, clean and comfortable, with good therapists who know their craft.

CLAREMONT

Mint Leaf Natural Products & Thai Massage
250 W. First St., Ste. 148, Claremont 91711
(Between S. College and S. Indian Hill)
909.399.0200, mintleafthai.com

Hours: Daily 10 a.m.–8 p.m.

Facilities: A beautiful little place in Old Town Claremont. Spend some time browsing the natural and homeopathic products; we picked up some mini Thai herbal balls and little herb pouches for tea footbaths.

What to expect: All massages are performed on padded floor mats, and a top and pants are provided. We opt for the traditional Thai whenever possible and have always received superb treatments.

Services offered: Thai and Swedish-Thai combo massages, with an optional Thai herbal ball add-on.

Parking: Plenty on the street in front.

Why we like it: You'll get a true Thai massage in a beautiful facility in a lovely little city. Factor in time to walk through Old Town Claremont afterward and keep your Zen on.

CULVER CITY

Five Senses Spa
4349 ½ Sepulveda Blvd., Culver City 90230
(Corner Lindblade)
310.391.9212, fivesensesspa.net

Hours: Daily 10 a.m.–9:30 p.m.

Facilities: A lovely little place where the therapists wear matching uniforms and the five rooms have massage tables. Walls and sliding doors divide the rooms.

What to expect: Pay for your service first. The rooms are attractive if a bit small. Undress to the level you wish (we usually keep our underwear on for Thai, because of the stretching) and slip under the sheet. We had the Thai herbal ball massage and loved it. A nice touch: They place a flower floating in a bowl just below the hole in the massage table. There's a shower to use before or after your massage if you like.

Services offered: Thai and deep-tissue massage, Thai herbal ball.

Parking: Lot in the back.

Why we like it: The delightful staff pays constant attention to your every need. Ask for Asia or Linda.

Swanya Thai
4324 Sepulveda Blvd., Culver City 90230
(Between Wagner & Lindblade)
310.313.1699 or 310.313.1799, swanyathaimassage.com

Hours: Daily 10 a.m.–9 p.m.

Facilities: A pretty storefront with rooms for individuals and couples.

What to expect: A traditional Thai massage in lovely surroundings. After you pay, you'll receive a big pair of Thai fisherman's pants and a top (for women). When you make your appointment, specify whether you want a room with a table or a traditional floor mattress.

Services offered: Thai and Swedish massage, Thai herbal ball, body scrub.

Parking: Street or behind the building; enter on Wagner Street.

Why we like it: Aesthetically appealing with a calm atmosphere, this is a great place for a couple's massage.

Thai Yoga Massage & Thai Teak
10720 Washington Blvd., Culver City 90230
(Near Overland)
310.559.5881; thaiyogamassageonline.com

Hours: Daily 9 a.m.–9 p.m.

Facilities: This is primarily a Thai furniture store with an area upstairs for massage. Although massage is the secondary business, they know Thai massage well. The three beautiful rooms have mattresses on the floor and are partitioned by pretty draperies. It's far enough from busy Washington Boulevard that noise is not an issue. There are three other locations in Santa Monica and Venice.

What to expect: Loose shorts are provided. The massage was great—thorough, challenging in the stretches, and ultimately relaxing. Why did we book only an hour?

Services offered: Thai, Swedish, deep-tissue and back massages.

Parking: Small lot off Washington.

Why we like it: We'd come here just for the furniture, so that makes it a two-fer. The massage is authentic and a bargain. Check out the website for great pictures, other locations and the promotional offers. At this location, ask for Ning.

Eagle Rock Thai Spa
2501 Colorado Blvd., Ste. A1, Los Angeles 90041
(Eagle Rock, corner of College View)
818.726.9989 or 323.982.1320, eaglerockthaispa.com

Hours: Daily 10 a.m.–10 p.m.

Facilities: In a little raised strip mall, this place is hard to see from the street, but worth seeking out. There are six clean, pleasant, curtained massage rooms, three with mats on the floor and three with massage tables.

What to expect: Pay first, and since they don't provide clothing, undress down to your underwear or however you're comfortable. They give you a bottle of water after your service, which is a nice touch.

Services offered: Thai, deep-tissue and Swedish massage, plus facials.

Parking: Lot in front or street parking.

Why we like it: It's a very good traditional Thai massage.

Thai Hands Emporium Salon
2750 Colorado Blvd., Ste. 3, Los Angeles 90041
(Eagle Rock, between the 2 Freeway & Eagle Rock Blvd.)
323.259.5098

Hours: Daily 10 a.m.–8 p.m.

Facilities: Right by the Westfield Mall, this is a clean, small place that offers traditional Thai massage. Three rooms have mats on a platform, and the other two rooms have massage tables. Walls separate all, with curtains for doors.

What to expect: Pay first, and know that there's a small charge if you use a credit or debit card. Wear something comfortable or strip down to your underwear and choose either a mat or table massage. They'll cover you with a towel, start at your feet and work their way up to your head, pushing, pressuring and stretching you along the way. A very relaxing massage in a quiet setting.

Services offered: Thai and deep-tissue massage.

Parking: Lot in front.

Why we like it: Refreshingly simple, clean and inexpensive. They have a sister store, Tranquility Nook, 2274 Colorado Blvd., Eagle Rock.

ENCINO

Narai Thai Spa
18063 Ventura Blvd., Encino 91316
(Between Lindley & Newcastle)
818.609.9400, naraithaispa.com

Hours: Daily 9:30 a.m.–9:30 p.m.

Facilities: Narai has a pleasant reception area and five large massage rooms with massage tables or floor mats. Towel warmers are in each room.

What to expect: A traditional massage that begins with a warm wipe-down of the feet. We were covered with a sheet, except for the area being worked on. We both had great massages and were offered a cup of hot tea afterward.

Services offered: Thai, Thai herbal ball, deep-tissue, shiatsu, Swedish, sports, combo, hot-stone and pregnancy massage, plus reflexology, skin care, facials, waxing and eyelash extensions. Gift certificates available.

Parking: Plenty in the private lot in back.

Why we like it: Ask Cindy, the owner, for the internet rate, which is typically lower than what's posted on the website, and check the site for specials and early-bird rates. Ask for Pinky if you want to try some unusual stretches for your neck, face and hips.

Vara's Thai Massage
17301 Ventura Blvd., Ste. 4, Encino 91316
(Corner Louise)
818.788.1234

Hours: Daily 10 a.m.–10 p.m.

Facilities: Vara's has seven "rooms" sectioned off with cream-colored Thai fabric. Their floors are raised, with mattresses and assorted pillows.

What to expect: Loose pants are provided. We got lovely traditional massages and thoroughly enjoyed this facility and our experience.

Services offered: Thai, Swedish, deep-tissue and combo massage.

Parking: Two-hour free parking on Louise or behind in the Coffee Bean & Tea Leaf lot.

Why we like it: It's nice and quiet. Ask for Janie, who pays extra attention to the neck and shoulders.

THAI

GLENDORA

Sukho Thai Healing Center
519 W. Baseline Rd., Glendora 91740
(Between Grand & Glendora)
626.335.4488, mysukhothaimassage.com

Hours: Daily 10 a.m.–8 p.m.

Facilities: This little place has a large, striking Buddha relief at the end of the reception room. Dark wood furniture and floor and a calming color palette create a refined atmosphere. Three of the four rooms, separated by thick drapes, have mattresses on a raised floor, and one has a massage table for those who have difficulty getting up and down. The owner, Toi, has experience accommodating people with special needs.

What to expect: We got the Thai massage with the herbal ball add-on. The herbal ball always intensifies the treatment, and we add it on whenever we find it. The massage followed protocol, and our bodies were kneaded up one side and down the other. A little crockpot kept the herbal ball warm, and the therapist used it on the upper back, shoulders and neck. Next came some standard stretches, and then we turned over and enjoyed more compression, kneading and stretching. We called it delightful.

Services offered: Thai, Swedish and combination massages, with optional Thai herbal ball add-on and facials. Gift certificates available.

Parking: Private lot on the side off Baseline.

Why we like it: What a great find! An authentic massage, easy parking and a great price. Check the website for discount coupons, and ask for Toi.

GRANADA HILLS

Silver Sand Spa & Massage
17050 Chatsworth St., #101, Granada Hills 91344
(In the 99 Cents Store center)
818.363.9580, silversandspa.com

Hours: Daily 10 a.m.–8 p.m.

Facilities: In the 99 Cents store strip mall, this place doesn't look so hot from the outside, but it's nicer inside, and there are plenty of signs about surveillance and security cameras to enforce the safety message. They havefour single rooms and one couple's room; bars on the ceiling allow for walking massages, if you so choose.

What to expect: You strip down to nothing and slip under the thin sheet, face down. They'll start with your feet and calves, working up to the back of your legs with their hands, and then, if you like, walk on you. Though we'd asked for traditional Thai massage, which doesn't use oil, our therapist got out the oil anyway. We suspect a few reasons for this. First, oil helps to enhance the benefits of massage on very tight muscles; if the therapist feels knots under your skin, oil helps her do a better job of relaxing them. Second, most people prefer Swedish massage. It's like non-Thais ordering super-spicy food at a Thai restaurant—they don't believe you can handle it. So an authentic oil-free massage? They think you won't like it! Finally, since Swedish has become the standard by which other massages are judged, you'll see a lot of "combo" treatments. It keeps a foot in both worlds and provides a nice experience for the customer. Indeed, we had a great massage here. After treatment, the therapist gave us bottled water and a cup of hot tea.

Services offered: Thai, Swedish, combo, deep-tissue and hot-stone massage, plus body scrub.

Parking: Plenty of free spots.

Why we like it: Once inside, it's a pleasant place, and Joy is a powerful little masseuse.

Taya's Body Works
17804 Chatsworth St., Granada Hills 91344
(At Lindley)
818.360.7852, tayathaimassage.com

Hours: Daily 10 a.m.–10 p.m.

Facilities: Don't turn away from this storefront spot—it's immaculately clean inside, and the staff is friendly and professional. There are five rooms with either a massage mat on the floor or a massage table. Call ahead and make a reservation with your preference.

What to expect: An authentic Thai massage! Starting at your feet and working up your body, the therapists rub, knead, stretch and walk on you (if you wish). Always checking if the pressure is too much or not enough, they are well trained, attentive and concerned about your experience.

Services offered: Thai, Swedish, sports and deep-tissue massage, plus a Thai foot massage and a couple's massage.

Parking: Lot in back or street parking.

Why we like it: This family-run establishment prides itself on your comfort and care. It's spotless and attractively decorated.

LONG BEACH

Enchantment Salon & Spa
5353 E. 2nd St., Ste. D, Long Beach 90803
(Between Argonne & Nieto)
562.434.9200

Hours: Mon.–Sat. 9 a.m.–7 p.m.; Sun. 10 a.m.–5 p.m.

Facilities: Primarily a hair and nail salon, there are two rooms in the back for massage. They are not the largest rooms, but the tables fit just fine on the diagonal. Robust colors and scented candles add interest.

What to expect: We couldn't possibly review every nail salon that does massage, but in five years of getting massages (for "research"), we've had two of the best Thai massages here. Seriously. We went in not expecting much (after all, this is really a hair and nail place), but left with our mouths open, like we'd seen a UFO. That's some serious relaxation.

Services offered: Primarily hair, nails and hair removal, but also Thai, Swedish, deep-tissue and sports massage.

Parking: In public lots or side streets.

Why we like it: See the comments above. If you live in Long Beach or anywhere close, make an appointment soon. You won't be sorry.

THAI

Hudavi Wellness Spa
5550 E. 7th St., Long Beach 90804
(Corner Ultimo)
562.433.2177, hudavispa.com

Hours: Daily 9 a.m.–9 p.m.

Facilities: This large facility has a more western spa feel, though it offers a range of ethnic massages. The large, warm waiting room and reception desk have lots of skin-care products and candles; beyond those areas are massage rooms and a communal reflexology room with four chairs. A comfortable relaxation room is off the reception area with warm towels, hot tea or cold lemon water. The space is also available for events.

What to expect: The Thai massage was a good one. Working on an authentic floor mattress, the masseuse worked her magic on the pressure points, from head to toe, followed by significant stretching. It felt great.

Services offered: Thai, chair, shiatsu, deep-tissue and pregnancy massage, foot reflexology, foot scrub, couple's massage and treatments, facials, waxing, ear candling, colon hydrotherapy and chiropractic care. Massage add-ons include cupping, scalp massage, body polish and reflexology.

Parking: Private lot in front.

Why we like it: It's not really a Thai place, but it's the service we got that determined its location in the book. It's a great place for Long Beach locals to try a variety of ethnic therapies without having to go into L.A. Ask for Rebecca.

LOS ANGELES
(HOLLYWOOD, SILVER LAKE, WEHO, CENTRAL L.A.)

The Barai Day Spa
2316 Hyperion Ave., Ste. A, Los Angeles 90027
(Silver Lake)
323.644.1051, thebaraispa.com

Hours: Daily 10:30 a.m.–8:30 p.m.

Facilities: Located right on busy Hyperion Avenue, where parking is a challenge, this spa is worth the trouble. Its ten rooms, each with mattresses on the floor, are separated by thin curtains.

What to expect: Pay for your service first. Take off your shoes and go to your room to change into a pair of loose pants. Leave a T-shirt on if you want, or remove your top. Once you change, lie face down on the mat, cover yourself with a towel and wait for the masseuse. One of us got the Thai herbal ball, and it was hot! Apparently they use the microwave, so beware—although it does feel incredibly good eventually. We also had some inventive therapists who hoisted us over their bodies like a tabletop. After all the stretching and pounding, they give you a mug of hot tea and a pretty arrangement of sliced oranges and apples. Service charge for credit-card payments.

Services offered: Thai, Thai herbal ball, Swedish, deep-tissue and pregnancy massage, plus reflexology.

Parking: Small lot on the side, but it's hard to back out onto Hyperion, so try to get street metered parking.

Why we like it: The facility is clean and attractive, the staff is hospitable, and we like the extra touches, like the little pillows and the tea with fruit after your treatment.

THAI

Let's Relax
5001 Wilshire Blvd., Los Angeles 90036
(Hancock Park, at Highland)
323.933.2039, letsrelaxmassage.com

Hours: Daily 10 a.m.–10 p.m.

Facilities: Located upstairs, this place has rooms in front with mats on the floor and rooms in back with massage tables. All rooms have curtains for doors. Make an appointment to reserve the room of your choice.

What to expect: A good traditional Thai massage—stretching, walking on your back and legs, and lots of hard pressure. You can wear your clothes or take them all off, whichever you like. We leave on our underwear due to the yoga-style positions that we get folded into. Service charge for credit-card payments.

Services offered: Thai, Swedish, combination and facial massage.

Parking: Private lot.

Why we like it: It's a nice, clean place that, although it has partial walls and curtains for doors, allows for a good sense of privacy as you're being stretched and pulled.

Another Let's Relax location: 15030 Ventura Blvd., Sherman Oaks 91403, 818.783.0999.

Pho-Siam
1525 Pizarro St., Los Angeles 90026
(Westlake, off Glendale)
213.484.8484, phosiam.com

Hours: Daily 9 a.m.–10:30 p.m.

Facilities: If you want a good and inexpensive Thai massage, this is the place. Pho-Siam is a huge operation with several employees who do nothing but take reservations. It's also a cash-only business, which explains the two ATMs on-site. Flat-screen TVs are also plentiful in the reception area and two waiting rooms. The building has a few wings, each with 16 rooms down long hallways; the halls and rooms are done up with draped fabrics and soft lights.

What to expect: The vibe is quite different here from all the mom-and-pop massage places—you could say this is the In-N-Out of Thai massages. Your therapist will call your number and take you to your massage room, where you'll change into loose shorts and no top. All massages are done on a mat. Once your treatment is complete, you're given a Pho-Siam bottle of water. We also like the facials; try the multi-vitamin facial—you'll be glowing afterward.

Services offered: Thai massage, Pho-Siam special, foot reflexology and facials.

Parking: Private lot on both sides inside a wrought-iron gate and some street parking.

Why we like it: If you have a large group of friends and want to plan a massage outing, this is the place.

Pho-Siam

The Raven
2910 Rowena Ave., Los Angeles 90039
(Silver Lake, off Hyperion)
323.644.0240, theravenspa.com

Hours: Daily 10 a.m.–9 p.m.

Facilities: A popular yoga studio (check out the schedule online), this place also does a variety of body treatments. You know a place is going to be something special visually when its website mentions its availability for photo and film shoots. And it is, in a rustic, laid-back, tropical-retreat sense. Large doors off the sidewalk open to a long, narrow gauntlet that serves as an outdoor relaxation and waiting area, with rattan chairs, side tables, large palm trees, umbrellas, latticework and, depending on the time of year, greenery and flowers. This definately sets the mood for what's to come.

What to expect: You're greeted warmly at the small reception area. A locker is provided, as well as a loose cotton shirt and fisherman pants. The main area has a small fountain and curtained partitions that define the massage areas. Massages are performed on traditional Thai mattresses on the floor. You'll hear the fountain and Thai music in the background. Off this main room are a couple of other rooms for private massage, yoga and other services. We got the Thai massage and found it true to tradition. You get a cup of hot tea and a little plate of seasonal fruit when your treatment is completed.

Services offered: Thai, Thai herbal ball, Swedish, deep-tissue, pregnancy, hot-stone, couple's and custom massages, with both male and female masseuses, as well as interesting facials, acupuncture and Reiki. Gift certificates available.

Parking: Definitely a challenge. There's metered (free on Sundays) and free street parking, but allow extra time for the hunt, and don't be surprised if you end up blocks away.

Why we like it: You can rent out the Raven for a special occasion, and we're trying to think of one right now. Check out the events page for some cool happenings. It's a good place for authentic treatments where English is spoken.

Serene Thai Massage
3959 Wilshire Blvd., B27, Los Angeles 90010
(Corner of Gramercy in the Wilshire Gramercy Mall)
213.739.9990

Hours: Daily 9:30 a.m.–10 p.m.

Facilities: Upstairs in a little strip mall, Serene has a large room with five big red reclining chairs and six small private rooms with curtains for doors.

What to expect: Pay for your service first and bring cash. You'll be given a pair of loose-fitting shorts but no top.

Change into the shorts, lie face down and get ready for a traditional Thai massage, starting at your feet. The rooms are clean, and the place smells good.

Services offered: Thai, deep-tissue and Swedish massage and foot reflexology.

Parking: Lot in front.

Why we like it: You and a few friends can experience both a traditional Thai massage and foot reflexology all together in the same place.

Serenity Thai Massage
2815 W. Sunset Blvd., Ste. 104, Los Angeles 90026
(Silver Lake, near Silverlake Blvd.)
213.484.4222, serenitythaimassge.com

Hours: Daily 10 a.m.–10 p.m.

Facilities: This mini-mall gem is very pretty and tidy inside, with dim lighting and gentle music. Choose between a massage table or a mat on the floor. There are five rooms, including one for couples; they have walls and heavy green curtains for doors.

What to expect: A classic Thai massage. You'll be given shorts and a vest-style top to change into. They offered oil, too.

Services offered: Thai massage.

Parking: Lot with tight parking or street meters.

Why we like it: A nice little enclave right off busy Sunset Boulevard. It smells good inside, and the setting is soothing.

While you're there: Right next door is Cowboys and Turbans, a hip place with outdoor dining, a fantastic ambience and delicious food. It's perfect for an after-massage treat.

Tranquility Body Spa
9925 Venice Blvd., Los Angeles 90034
(Palms, near Hughes)
310.842.9561, tranquilitybodyspa.com

Hours: Daily 9:30 a.m.–9:30 p.m.; last appointment 8:30 p.m.

Facilities: In this nice little storefront on busy Venice Boulevard you'll find eight curtained massage rooms, one with a table and the other with floor mats.

What to expect: Make an appointment, especially if you want your massage on a table, since there's only one. We've tried two therapists, and both were pretty skilled, giving similar massages. If you want to raise your head and neck off the mat so it doesn't get cramped, ask for an extra towel to roll up and rest your head on during the face-down part of the massage.

Services offered: Thai, Swedish and combination massages, plus skin care and waxing.

Parking: On the street; the meters on Venice Boulevard are one-hour, but there are two-hour meters on Dunn Street.

Why we like it: It's super clean, it smells good, and the décor is nice. The staff loves to take care of you; while you're there, you might want to try a facial or waxing.

Wilshire Massage
5474 Wilshire Blvd., Los Angeles 90036
(At Dunsmuir)
323.634.0835, wilshiremassage.com

Hours: Daily 10 a.m.–9 p.m.

Facilities: In this Wilshire storefront are seven private rooms divided by walls that are open to the ceiling. Massages are given on tables.

What to expect: You'll be shown to a private room and asked to take off your clothes; we left our underwear on, given the stretching aspect of the massage. They say they offer a classic Thai massage, but what we received was really more of a combination Thai-Swedish-deep-tissue treatment, perhaps because it was given on a raised table. The therapists were still able to get in some good stretches.

Services offered: Thai, Swedish, deep-tissue and pregnancy massage, plus reflexology.

Parking: Street or lot behind.

Why we like it: They have clean rooms and a professional staff. Try their Wednesday special and remember Wilshire massage on your birthday for another discount.

While you're there: Check out India's Tandoori (5468 Wilshire)—yummy veggie samosas, saag paneer and naan bread, to eat in or take home after your massage.

MANHATTAN BEACH

Busaba Thai Massage
1751 Artesia Blvd., Manhattan Beach 90278
(Near Aviation)
310.379.8899 or 310.379.8811, busabathaimassage.com

Hours: Daily 10 a.m.–9 p.m.

Facilities: This small, well-decorated facility has five generous massage rooms, all with tables.

What to expect: Therapists here give a fairly traditional Thai massage, except we didn't get the initial wipe-down of our feet. The massage did start at the feet, however, and from there followed standard protocol. The move we love is when they kneel on the butt and legs and "walk" in place a bit. From this perch the masseuse can better grab hold of your shoulders and neck, which usually need the most work. Therapists here also sometimes break tradition by using a little oil when massaging the neck, which we appreciated. It includes lots of stretching, and once you're on your back the therapist will put a dry washcloth over your eyes while she tends to your shoulders, arms and hands. To conclude, your whole body is wiped down with a scented cloth—an awesome way to end a massage.

Services offered: Thai, Swedish, combo, hot oil aromatherapy, deep-tissue, sports, four hands and Thai herbal ball massage, plus Thai herbal body scrub.

Parking: In the mini-mall lot on the corner.

Why we like it: The large rooms, the concluding wipe-down and the generous early-bird discounts (from 10 a.m.–2 p.m.). Ask for Koonie.

See also: Another location at 1106 Crenshaw Blvd., Torrance 90501, 310.212.5241, 310.212.5243.

Oasis Thai Massage & Spa
2709 N. Sepulveda Blvd., Manhattan Beach 90266
(Between Marine & Rosecrans)
310.802.1999, oasisthaimassage.com

Hours: Daily 10 a.m.–10 p.m.

Facilities: Oasis has one room dedicated to facials, a massage room with a mattress on the floor, two rooms with tables and one couple's room with two tables. (There's also a very cool bathroom.) Piano music plays, and the lighting is soft.

What to expect: Strip down and slip under the sheet. The therapist will start by wiping your feet with a wet washcloth, then massaging her way up to your head, with detours to the arms and hands. But not for long. Then it's back to your back from a different vantage point. Don't be surprised if she kneels on your butt to better work the upper back and shoulders—it's common in Thai massage. You'll also get a good leg stretching, followed by a gentle rub with a scented washcloth. At the end, she'll place your arms behind your neck, hook her arms in yours, and slowly twist you to one side and then another. We loved it! A cup of hot tea afterward adds to the relaxation.

Services offered: Thai, Thai herbal ball, Swedish, combo, deep-tissue, pregnancy and sports massage, plus body scrubs, facials and waxing. Thai herbal ball is available only with an appointment.

Parking: Private lot on the side.

Why we like it: It was a great massage, and we love the scented washcloths. Pure heaven! Ask for Linda if you want some different stretches.

Marico Massage
4280 Lincoln Blvd., 2nd Floor, Marina del Rey 90292
(Marina Centers, corner Maxella)
310.823.7705, maricomassage.com

Hours: Daily 10 a.m.–10 p.m.

Facilities: This turned out to be a much nicer place than we expected, but then again, it is on the westside. The large reception room is stocked with glossy magazines, and there are five private massage rooms, one facial room and communal rooms for reflexology.

What to expect: We both had traditional Thai massages on massage tables. They didn't provide clothing, so we just slipped out of our clothes and kept our underwear on. We appreciated being in a truly private room while they stretched and pulled us in all different directions.

Services offered: Thai, Thai herbal ball, shiatsu, Swedish, deep-tissue, hot-stone, couple's and pregnancy massage, plus foot reflexology, waxing, eyelash/eyebrow tinting, facials and other skin care.

Parking: In the shopping center or underground.

Why we like it: It's close enough to the beach to smell and see the ocean, which has therapeutic benefits of its own. When you call for an appointment, ask if there are any house specials.

THAI

NORTH HOLLYWOOD

Nu Thai Spa Therapy
4856 Lankershim Blvd., N. Hollywood 91601
(Between Magnolia & Camarillo)
818.763.9449 or 818.448.9077, numassage.com

Hours: Daily 10 a.m.–10 p.m.

Facilities: A small, warm place with four rooms with mattresses on a raised floor and three rooms with tables, as well as a room for facials. Walls separate the rooms but are open at the top; curtains give some privacy from the main hallway.

What to expect: The traditional Thai massage followed protocol and included some new variations of stretches, along with some light massaging on the head and face. They give you a bottle of water when it's finished.

Services offered: Thai, Swedish, combo, pregnancy and deep-tissue massage, as well as body steam, back scrub, facials and waxing. Gift certificates available.

Parking: Metered parking on street or park in the back.

Why we like it: It's a pleasant, clean place that gives an excellent massage.

Pretty Body Work
11421 Moorpark St., North Hollywood 91602
(At Tujunga)
818.763.8803

Hours: Sun.–Fri. 10 a.m.–10 p.m.; Sat. noon–10 p.m.

Facilities: Behind a little storefront nail salon are four private massage rooms.

Plai-Fah

What to expect: A nice Thai massage on a comfortable table. There's a service charge for credit-card payments.

Services offered: Thai Swedish, deep-tissue and stomach massage.

Parking: Street-metered or in the back.

Why we like it: A welcoming and friendly spot for a massage.

NORTHRIDGE

Baipoo Thai Spa
8902 Reseda Blvd., Northridge 91324
(Near Rayen)
818.626.9101

Hours: Daily 10:30 a.m.–10:30 p.m.

Facilities: We weren't sure about this place from the outside, but as massage junkies, we've learned to not judge a book

THAI

by its cover, so we ventured in and were surprised to find four attractive rooms, two with mattresses on the floor and two with tables. Walls are painted a beautiful shade of purple, and scented candles set a mood of relaxation.

What to expect: At Baipoo, they put more focus on massage than on stretching. Personally, we love the stretching, but if it's your least favorite part of a Thai massage, this will be your new favorite place. There's a service charge for credit-card payments.

Services offered: Thai, Thai herbal ball, deep-tissue, hot-stone, foot, head and shoulder massages as well as Thai facials.

Parking: On the street.

Why we like it: Where most frequent-buyer cards require ten massages for a freebie, here you get one after just five. Ask for Natalie.

Montha Thai Massage
8559 Reseda Blvd., Northridge 91324
(Between Lindley & Wilbur, south of Parthenia)
818.727.1424, monthathai-simplyrelax.weebly.com

Hours: Daily 10 a.m.–9 p.m.

Facilities: A quaint studio with six rooms, five of which have decorative mats on a raised floor; one has a massage table.

What to expect: A traditional Thai massage given on firm, clean mats; you can take off or leave on clothing as you prefer. We asked them to make a raised head rest from a towel. There's a $2 service charge for credit-card payments.

Services offered: Thai and Swedish-Thai combo massage.

Parking: Lot.

Why we like it: Traditionally decorated, clean and cool—a much-needed escape from the Valley heat!

Plai-Fah
8363 Reseda Blvd., Unit 14, Northridge 91324
(Royal Plaza, north of Roscoe)
818.709.4051, plai-fah.com

Hours: Daily 10 a.m.–9 p.m.

Facilities: A true find in Northridge! Although small, the five main rooms are equipped with massage tables, and another room, with two beautiful floor mats, is used for couples. All have curtains for doors.

What to expect: Many say a therapist cannot give a traditional Thai massage on a table, but this place proves that it can indeed be done. We had a classic treatment with all sorts of stretching moves that we didn't even think possible on a table. Take a look at the website for great photos of the stretches you'll experience here. There's a $1 service charge for credit-card payments.

Services offered: Thai, Swedish and deep-tissue massage, facials.

Parking: Lot in front.

Why we like it: A clean, quiet, good-smelling place with great stretching massages. Ask for Rose and she'll do what we call "the Thai table." Give it a try!

While you're there: Next door is Bonanos, an amazing Peruvian restaurant, so plan to have a meal after your massage if you can: chicken, lomo saltado, french fries with the traditional Peruvian sauces, garlic-infused rice, and of course *chichi morada*, a sweet drink made from purple corn. It's all delicious.

Pattaya Healing Massage

Pattaya Healing Massage
1525 E. Colorado Blvd., Pasadena 91106
(Across from Pasadena City College)
626.568.9570, pattayahealing.com

Hours: Daily 10 a.m.–9 p.m.

Facilities: Located behind Pattaya Café, this quaint place offers a lovely Thai massage in a plain but squeaky-clean facility.

What to expect: Most curtained "rooms" are equipped with a firm mat on the floor, but one has a table. You'll be given pajama-style bottoms, and you remove all your other clothes. They keep you covered, so don't worry about being exposed. The "Pattaya Healing Massage" is their version of a Thai massage. Focusing on your body's pressure points, the therapist uses her open palm, thumbs, elbows and arms to give you a deep, satisfying massage. It concludes with some stretches; don't forget to breathe. The only drawback is that the woman who makes the reservations is also a therapist and sometimes has to play double duty during your massage to answer the phone.

Services offered: Thai, Swedish, deep-tissue and four-hands massage, as well as reflexology and acupressure.

Parking: In the lot behind the restaurant.

Why we like it: No TV blaring, just affordable traditional Thai massage by kind women in a super-clean facility.

THAI

POMONA

Ayodhya
1455 Indian Hill Blvd., Pomona 91767
(Near Elmcroft)
909.624.5747

Hours: Daily 10 a.m.–9 p.m.

Facilities: Occupying a sweet little house, this Thai place is simply lovely, with hardwood floors, warm colors and pretty fabrics. The main room doubles as an instructional area for yoga, complete with mattresses on the floor. There are a couple of wooden benches off the cushioned floor where you wait for your treatment.

What to expect: The massage room has mattresses on a raised floor and drapes for privacy. They provide you with shorts and a loose shirt to wear. The massage follows the typical protocol, beginning with the wipe-down of the feet and continuing with compressions, massage and stretching. We love the setting, and our massages have not disappointed.

Services offered: Thai massage, acupuncture and acupressure.

Parking: Private lot.

Why we like it: Our massage experience was perfect, and the house is lovely. We'd gladly move in tomorrow if we could.

SANTA MONICA

Bangkok Thai Massage
3131 Lincoln Blvd., Santa Monica 90405
(At Navy)
310.450.3141, bangkokthaispa.com

Hours: Daily 10 a.m.–9 p.m.

Facilities: This place might lack the ambience of other spas, but it compensates by providing an authentic Thai massage. The five rooms (one for couples) have beds low to the ground topped with mats.

What to expect: When you arrive, they'll ask you to fill out a confidential information and health history form. You'll then be taken to a private room, where you undress and lie face down on the mat. We enjoyed a true Thai massage with all the stretches and moves. If you forget to bring cash, there's an ATM.

Services offered: Thai, deep-tissue and Swedish massage, plus Thai herbal body scrub. There's a full shower to rinse off after the scrub or an exceptionally sweaty massage.

Parking: Street or lot in the back.

Why we like it: Traditional Thai massage on the westside.

Thai Yoga Massage
2222 Lincoln Blvd., Santa Monica 90405
(Between Pacific & Strand, next to Ameci's)
310.450.8325, thaiyogamassageonline.com

Hours: Daily 9 a.m.–9 p.m.; last appointment 8 p.m.

Facilities: One of four locations, this marvelous mini-mall place is beyond compare. Outside it's generic, but inside the décor is lovely, the staff friendly, and the rooms stunning, with dark, flowing curtains and four-poster wood beds.

What to expect: They'll give you a two-piece outfit to change into. We had the traditional Thai massage and we were glad we did. Starting at your feet and working their way up, these therapists are skilled and strong. We were stretched and massaged to perfection.

Services offered: Thai, deep-tissue and Swedish (with oil) massage.

Parking: Lot or on the street.

Why we like it: All the locations are stunning and exotic, with friendly employees; you really feel like you've gone to Thailand. Plus they sell wonderful arts and crafts.

See also: Thai Yoga Massage below and at 2548 Lincoln Blvd., Venice 90291, 310.577.6760, and 10720 Washington Blvd., Culver City 90230, 310.559.5881.

Thai Yoga Massage
3020 Wilshire Blvd., Santa Monica 90403
(Between Yale & Berkeley)
310.998.8700, thaiyogamassageonline.com

Hours: Daily 9 a.m.–9 p.m.

Facilities: The mood is set by a lush, tropical entry with potted plants, wooden statues and stone pieces. Take your time browsing the shop, filled with Thai home décor items. The four massage beds, on platforms on the floor, are down a long hallway, in rooms separated by thin cotton curtains.

What to expect: After paying in advance, you'll be led to a room and given loose shorts. We found the Thai massage

to be very traditional, beginning and ending with the feet. Compressions were slow and firm, up the feet, calves, thighs and butt. On the back, the compressions morphed into serious muscle massage that moved to the shoulders, neck and arms. Stretching of the back and legs followed, then we turned over and it began again: compression, muscle manipulation and that awesome feeling that all was right with the world. In that moment in time, it was.

Services offered: Thai, Swedish, deep-tissue and back massage. They also sell home décor, Thai silk items and orchids and other plants.

Parking: Small lot off Wilshire or metered street parking.

Why we like it: A wonderful shop and another great, affordable, authentic massage. Check out the website for the promotions at each location.

See also: Thai Yoga Massage above and at 2548 Lincoln Blvd., Venice 90291, 310.577.6760, and 10720 Washington Blvd., Culver City 90230, 310.559.5881.

SHERMAN OAKS

Amazing Thai Swedish Massage
13521 W. Ventura Blvd., Sherman Oaks 91423
(Near Sunnyslope)
818.986.2931, amazingthaiswedishmassage.com

Hours: Daily 10 a.m.–9 p.m.

Facilities: A small corner space with only three rooms, each with a padded mat on the floor.

What to expect: A true Thai massage. Wear loose and comfortable clothes. You'll be stretched and pulled and will walk out feeling great.

Heaven Massage & Wellness Center

Services offered: Thai and Swedish massage.

Parking: Street meter or behind the building.

Why we like it: A great first-time place if you want to try traditional Thai massage on a mat. Clean, pretty and intimate.

Heaven Massage & Wellness Center
13509 Ventura Blvd., Sherman Oaks 91423
(Corner Sunnyslope)
818.783.1995, heavenmassageandwellness.com

Hours: Daily 10 a.m.–10 p.m.

Facilities: A little slice of heaven on Ventura Boulevard, this is a lovely two-story place whose walls are painted a calming blue. You'll find five beautifully appointed rooms downstairs and six more upstairs. All have massage tables.

What to expect: If it's your first visit, they'll ask you to fill out an intake form; be sure to list any past or present injuries, as your therapist will discuss these with you before your massage. She'll take you to a private room and let you undress; it's up to you if you want to leave your underwear on. Crawl under the sheet on the table, which is warmed with a heating pad (they'll adjust the temperature as you like). Then relax and enjoy a remarkable massage.

Services offered: Thai, deep-tissue, Swedish, hot-stone, pregnancy, sports and foot massage, plus reflexology.

Parking: Meters in front, free side-street parking and spots in the alley in back.

Why we like it: The therapists in this immaculate, well-run place take the time to find out what you want. Good ambience and a nice extra touch of serving tea before and after your treatment.

Thai Lotus Spa
13908 ½ Ventura Blvd., Sherman Oaks 91423
(Between Stern & Colbath)
818.789.3452, thailotusspa.com

Hours: Daily 10 a.m.–10 p.m.; last appointment at 9 p.m.

Facilities: Six rooms have massage mats on the floor and shoji screens as separators; other rooms are used for facials and body scrubs. This is an eco-friendly place, with organic sheets and natural spa products.

What to expect: Nice ambience, soothing colors, dim lighting. You strip down to your panties and slide under a sheet. We've had really great massages here, with a lot of kneading with feet, palms and elbows.

Services offered: Thai, foot and couple's massages.

Parking: Street.

Why we like it: This is the perfect remedy for a long day of shopping at Sherman Oaks Fashion Square; just make sure to call for an appointment.

SIGNAL HILL

Body Balance Chiropractic Spa
1830 Redondo Ave., Ste. F, Signal Hill 90755
(Between E. 19th & PCH)
562.986.6358, bbcspa.us

Hours: Daily 10 a.m.–9 p.m.

Facilities: Another looks-can-be-deceiving place, with a cheerful reception area and welcoming staff.

What to expect: We found the Thai massage wonderfully authentic, starting and ending with the feet. It was soothing and relaxing, with only minimal stretching at the end. Sometimes that's all we want.

Services offered: Thai, Swedish, combo, deep-tissue and pregnancy massage, plus body scrub and chiropractic treatments; Thai herbal ball can be added on. Gift certificates available.

Parking: In front in the strip mall.

Why we like it: We love discovering great places that others shy away from because of the exterior appearance or location. This is one of those places, with good rooms and an authentic massage at a low price.

STUDIO CITY

Bangkok Thai Massage
12436 Ventura Blvd., Studio City 91604
(Near Whitsett)
818.754.0334

Hours: Daily 7 a.m.–10 p.m.

Facilities: Enter from the front or rear; at both entrances, there's a little cubby to leave your shoes. Inside are eleven rooms separated by thin wood walls and draperies; one is a couple's room. They have both mattresses on the floors and massage tables.

What to expect: You'll be given a top that opens in the back and some unusual tie-less fisherman shorts—we had to be shown how to gather up the excess at the waist and knot it together. It's kind of bulky, but it doesn't get in the way of the massage. The massage began with the standard foot wipe-down, followed by pressure to the feet and up the legs to the back and neck. Once we were warmed up, the therapist walked on our butt and legs. It may sound weird, but it feels great. She asked us to untie the pant knot and pulled the pants down to just below the butt, à la the old Coppertone ad. (We thought you might want to know this was coming.) Oil is slathered on and combined with a slightly heavier cream, and all that gets massaged into the skin. She used a hot towel to wipe down any traces of oil not absorbed. You then pull up your pants and turn over for more of the same on your front side. We enjoyed awesome stretches to our legs, arms, neck and head. At the end, we sat up for more stretching of the neck, sides and back, some accomplished with the masseuse's feet. Karate chops to the back usually signal the end of the treatment, but once one of us got a terrific staccato foot slap. Each therapist has her signature move.

Services offered: Thai, Swedish, shiatsu, deep-tissue and foot massage.

Parking: On the street or behind the facility.

Why we like it: It was a great massage, and we loved the warm, scented towel used for the wipe-down. Check the website for discount coupons, and ask for Sarah if you'd like to be foot-slapped.

See also: Bangkok Thai Massage in Encino.

Oasis Thai Massage
4411 Laurel Canyon Blvd., Studio City 91604
(Between Moorpark & Landale)
818.766.7979, studiocitythaimassage.com

Hours: Daily 10 a.m.–9:30 p.m.

Facilities: Helen Keller couldn't miss this place, thanks to the huge signs for both parking and the massage center.

A brightly lit nail salon is in the front of the shop; behind a glass door is the massage, facial and tanning area. Four rooms have massage tables, and six have mattresses on a raised floor; walls separate each room, but they're open at the top. Nice background music plays throughout.

What to expect: This isn't the first place we've found that has a prominently displayed ATM machine (hint: cash only). We requested the Thai massage, stripped down and got under the thin sheet, face down. The therapist used tiger balm and some oil on the neck and shoulders. Otherwise, the massage was pretty true to tradition, and it ended with a heavenly wipe-down with a warm, scented towel. No complaints here.

Services offered: Thai, Swedish, combo and deep-tissue massage, as well as mani-pedicures, tanning, teeth whitening, facials and waxing.

Parking: Private lot off Laurel Canyon. You can't miss the sign.

Why we like it: It's a good massage at a great price. Rainy is a master at blasting out shoulder knots. We can't say there won't be painful moments, but if you can bite your lip and count to ten, she'll work her magic and you'll be on the other side of the pain.

Siam Thai Massage & Spa
11390 Ventura Blvd., 6A, Studio City 91604
(Near Tujunga)
818.506.4927 or 818.506.7126, siamthaimassagela.com

Hours: Daily 9:30 a.m.–10:30 p.m.

Facilities: Located on the second floor of a shopping center, this place has five very quiet rooms and both male and female therapists; licenses and permits are posted prominently.

What to expect: The massage was indeed traditional, beginning with a wipe-down of the feet, followed by massage on the feet, working up to the calves, thighs, butt, back, shoulders and neck. A little walking tour of our backsides followed, then the therapist used her arms and hands to apply some light oil and work it into the skin. After this wake-up call, it was back to the tight areas, which got a good pummeling. Not all Thai massages are the same, because if masseuses are doing their job, they respond to your body, working areas that need work. While we were still on our stomachs, our therapist splayed our legs one at a time, leading to some incredible stretches. After turning over, we were oiled, massaged and stretched again. After arranging our legs straight out in front of us, she pressed her feet on our back to help lay our chest on top of our legs, a move we haven't done since high school. In that seated position, we then got karate chops to the back, along with more neck massage and stretching. Slapping of the back meant it was over, and all too soon. There's a $2 charge for credit-card payment.

Services offered: Thai, Swedish, combo, deep-tissue and foot massage.

Parking: In the strip mall out front.

Why we like it: Already a steal, Siam is an even better bargain if you schedule your massage before noon. Ask for Yo-yo.

See also: Another location at 13215 Ventura Blvd., Studio City 91604, 818.788.4979.

Top Thai Massage
4344 Laurel Canyon Blvd., #10, Studio City 91604
(South of Moorpark)
818.508.5462, topthaimassage.com

Hours: Daily 10 a.m.–9 p.m.

Facilities: It's a sketchy-looking building from the outside but nice inside. The five curtain-separated rooms have mattresses on a raised floor.

What to expect: You'll be provided with boxer shorts. This was the first place we got our feet wiped down with a cool paper towel, but the rest of the massage was traditional and very thorough.

Services: Thai, Swedish, combo, deep-tissue and hand-foot massage. Gift certificates available.

Parking: On Laurel Canyon.

Why we like it: It's a bargain, especially if you get your massage before 3 p.m. Ask for Pon.

See also: Top Thai Massage in Los Angeles (Hollywood).

TOLUCA LAKE

Orchid Thai Massage
10910 Riverside Dr., Toluca Lake 91602
(Between Lankershim & Vineland)
818.754.0396, orchidroyalspa.com

Hours: Daily 10 a.m.–10 p.m.

Facilities: This place has been around a while, and it's not exactly in tip-top shape, but it's clean and quiet. There are six private rooms and one couple's room, all with massage tables.

What to expect: A good, strong Thai massage, at times even a bit unforgiving. Since therapists give the massage on a table, they'll balance and work on your back more than usual. Bars on the ceiling allow them to walk on your back if you want.

Services offered: Thai, Swedish, deep-tissue and couple's massage.

Parking: Street and lot behind building.

Why we like it: You must make an appointment, and you'll be glad you did. As long as they know you're coming, they are gracious and accommodating.

TORRANCE

Thai Body Works
4429 Torrance Blvd., Torrance 90503
(Between Hawthorne & Anza)
310.742.7345, thaibodyworks.net

Hours: Daily 10 a.m.–9 p.m.

Facilities: Your basic fugly, mini-mall-with-a-liquor-store place, but inside it's appealing, with spacious, peaceful and private (real doors!) single rooms and a couple's room. Large mattresses are on the floors, and a low altar sits at the back of the rooms.

What to expect: We enjoyed good Thai massages here, with an extra treat of a face and head massage. While on our backs, our legs were bent frog-style, and the masseuse used her body weight to pull and push, resulting in some excellent stretching. It never gets old.

Services offered: Thai, Swedish, combo and deep-tissue massage.

Parking: In the corner strip mall.

Why we like it: A good Thai massage in Torrance, with two more branches in Orange County.

VENICE

Island Yoga & Spa
1418 Abbot Kinney Blvd., 2nd floor, Venice 90291
(Corner of California)
310.396.7575, Islandyogaandspa.com

Hours: Daily 8 a.m.–10 p.m.

Facilities: A small, six-room studio with a little shop up front selling balm, fisherman pants and Thai tops. Some rooms are private and some separated by curtains.

What to expect: Bring cash and pay first for your service. They'll give you Thai fisherman pants and a loose top; you change in your room. The beds are heated, which feels great, especially if it's a chilly beach day. The massage starts at your feet and ends with great stretches.

Services offered: Thai and foot massage.

Parking: Street or in the alley.

Why we like it: The firm, heated massage beds in an intimate place that is fresh and clean.

THAI

Lamai Thai Massage
1350 Abbot Kinney Blvd., Venice 90291
(Between Milwood & California)
310.399.7953, lamaithaimassage.com

Hours: Daily 7 a.m.–10 p.m.

Facilities: This two-story studio has a dozen "rooms" separated by thin curtains, with mattress beds on the floor. This design is pretty standard and is not bothersome unless you have a particularly loud neighbor. You'll fill out a questionnaire, where you can mention problem areas and indicate your preferences for the type of pressure and the use of tiger balm. The mature women who work here speak pretty good English; you should have no difficulty communicating.

What to expect: You'll be given fisherman pants and a halter top. Our massage began face down, with a little on the feet and then the head. From the head, the therapist proceeded to the back, where 90 percent of the massage was focused. The emphasis on the back, along with the lack of stretching, differentiated this treatment from traditional Thai massage, though the technique was certainly Thai. We're not saying this is bad—maybe she was responding to what we needed at the time. After we turned over, she worked on the head as well as the calves and tops of the feet, then sat on a small stool to finish up the back, neck and head.

Services offered: Thai, couple's, baby and pregnancy massage. Gift certificates available, as well as yoga supplies.

Parking: Free parking in back.

Why we like it: Having a massage at Lamai Thai gives you a good excuse to visit all the indie shops along Abbot Kinney. Its website has a short but comprehensive video of what you can expect of the stretches and positions we write about. Ask for June or Nancy.

WEST COVINA

Ancient Thai Massage
2550 E. Amar Rd., A-3A, West Covina 91792
(Canyon Center)
626.810.7111, ancientthaispamassage.com

Hours: Daily 9 a.m.–8:30 p.m.

Facilities: We love this little place! Located in a shopping center, it has eight rooms with massage tables. They aren't large, but there's enough room for the masseuses to get around.

What to expect: Strip down to your level of comfort, slip under a thin sheet, and enjoy a traditional Thai massage. If you have any areas that need to be worked, ask for tiger balm and oil, which will facilitate the movement of the tissues and increase blood flow. They serve hot tea and a Thai biscuit afterward.

Services: Thai massage. Gift certificates available.

Parking: Plenty in the shopping-center lot.

Why We Like It: You gotta love a place that specializes in a single service and does it well. Ask for Susie—she worked magic on an arthritic joint.

Destiny Chiropractic & Thai Massage
21408 Ventura Blvd., Woodland Hills 91364
(Between Topanga Canyon & Canoga)
818.887.8244, destinychiromassage.com

Hours: Daily 9 a.m.–9 p.m.

Facilities: Greg Jukes, the owner and chiropractor, greets you at the bright reception area. His therapists are all Thai, and they wear embroidered pastel polo shirts. Off the reception and waiting area is a hallway that leads to seven massage areas, all with mattresses on the floor, and all separated by rich drapes.

What to expect: We received lovely Thai massages that followed the normal progression up the body from the feet. We welcomed a short walk on our backs and legs.

Services offered: Thai massage, chiropractic care and foot reflexology.

Parking: Off Ventura Boulevard or on side streets.

Why we like it: Bright, clean and true to its roots. Watch for specials on the website.

THAI

Chapter 3 – **Korean**

Beverly Hot Springs

THE BODY SCRUB

The Koreans take body care seriously. Korean massage follows the tradition of a healing art, where massage is used to relieve pain and induce relaxation by facilitating the flow of energy through channels of the body called meridians. Renowned for their body scrubs, Koreans often go once a week to the spa to steam, sweat, soak and get scrubbed with brightly colored mitts.

Let's say it up front: The Korean spa is not for the modest. You'll be naked for all your treatments, and you won't see anyone clutching wraps or towels while traveling to and from the pools and saunas. Bathing suits usually are not allowed, although we have seen some people getting scrubs with their underwear on. If you're really uncomfortable about being naked, take your towel wherever you go. Also, during the body scrub, the therapists are good about covering you up if you ask. The women who perform body scrubs all dress alike, in black bras and sturdy matching panties.

The Korean body scrub takes place in a same-sex, usually open, damp area. You lie on a plastic-covered massage table, and the therapist dips a large bowl into a tub of warm water and splashes it over your body, ensuring that every part of you gets wet. Once you're soaked, she puts on exfoliating mitts with some soap and scrubs vigorously all over your body, starting with one foot, up your leg, to your back and arms, and then moving to the other side. All over, top to bottom and back to front. Every part is scrubbed, and we mean *every* part. The treatment lasts 30 to 40 minutes, and throughout the process, the therapist throws on more warm water to rinse off dead skin cells.

Sometimes you can get a massage with your scrub. This is done on the same massage table and is a deep, slow-pressure massage. Some therapists use oil; others use just their hands, arms and elbows. The Korean body scrub also includes a thorough hair wash, sometimes a final body rinse with milk, and a mask of freshly grated cucumber, which acts as an astringent.

59

Whether you make an appointment for a scrub or go just to enjoy the sauna, the service fee usually includes towels, a pair of shorts and a T-shirt or a robe. If the sauna is a family sauna, you'll find a central, communal relaxation area called *jim jil bang*. Put on your T-shirt and shorts and remove your shoes before you enter the *jim jil bang* area. Usually the floor is heated and laid with mats, on which you can lie down and watch TV (usually a Korean soap opera or the Korean news).

Korean spas have a variety of sauna rooms. Some are located in the jim jil bang, where you wear your T-shirt and shorts. In the others, on the women's or men's sides, you'll find people in various states of dress and undress. Many people stretch and meditate in the saunas. We have experienced the following types of saunas:

Bulgama Room: Affectionately known as the kiln sauna, because it's heated to 235 degrees F, this is the hottest sauna we've ever experienced. Only a few Korean spas have them. Consider yourself a piece of clay that's being fired in the kiln.

Coral Room: Heated to about 140 degrees F, this sauna is said to help the eyesight and has the power to ease stress. The coral room also is known to restore harmony and to alleviate nutritional deficiencies, depression and lethargy.

Hwangto Room: Heated to 130 degrees F, this sauna, also known as the yellow ochre room, is equipped with heated yellow ochre (loess, a loose, yellow soil that contains potassium chloride and calcium) imported from Korea. This is said to promote blood circulation and metabolism while eliminating toxins from your body. The hwangto also is noted for soothing sore muscles and body aches, relieving stress and relaxing the mind through purification.

Salt Room: Heated to about 130 degrees F, this sauna has its walls coated with salt and minerals that cleanse your pores, allowing your skin to breathe and feel refreshed. Most rooms of this type use Himalayan salt.

Germanium or Clay Room: Heated to130 degrees F, this sauna uses on its walls a mineral mud that is believed to have healthful properties that affect the electrical current in the body and enhance the immune system. The clay room promotes oxygenation, which allows your entire body to breathe.

Gemstone or Jade Room: Heated to 115 degrees F, this room features walls covered in jade and gemstones (crystals). When heated, they are said to neutralize toxic elements, including heavy metals and chemical wastes in the body, and they also are known for improving skin and providing relief from fatigue. This room also professes to help women with hormonal imbalances.

Onyx Room or Jim Jil Bang: Heated to 95-100 degrees F, jim jil bangs usually have onyx tiles on the floor and sometimes on the walls. The floors and walls are heated. Grab a mat, lie down and feel the warmth rise into your body. You'll be surprised how fast you'll fall asleep.

Ice Room: Cooled to somewhere between 42 and 63 degrees F, the ice room causes the pores to close and helps the body re-acclimate to a normal temperature. It is recommended that you spend a few minutes here when you have finished using any of the saunas.

Loess Soil Room: A hot, dry room that smells of soil and herbs. This room is particularly soothing and is said to promote circulation, relieve stress and ease pain from arthritis.

STEPS IN VISITING KOREAN SPAS

1. Make an appointment for a body scrub
2. Pay in advance
3. Get a towel, robe, T-shirt, shorts and locker key
4. Usually your locker number is the number they call when they are ready to perform your service
5. Remove your shoes before entering the locker room. may find a shoe locker room before entering the womens locker room
6. Change into towel or robe if getting a treatment or using the women's sauna
7. Shower before doing anything
8. To warm and relax the skin before a scrub, soak in the warm-water whirlpool or take a sauna
9. Put on the T-shirt and shorts if you go to the jim jil bang

A FEW WORDS IN KOREAN

ENGLISH	KOREAN PRONUNCIATION
Hello	an-nyoung-ha-sae-yoh
Good-bye	ahn-nyeong-hee guh-sae-yoh
Yes	Ye
No	ah-nee-yoh
Thank you	gam-sa-ham-ni-da
Hurts	a-ppa-yoh

KOREATOWN

While it's boundaries are not formally set, Koreatown occupies much of the area of the Wilshire Center and is found between Arlington Avenue and Wilton Place on the west, Melrose Avenue on the north, Hoover Street on the east, and Pico Boulevard on the south.

HISTORY

In the first half of the 20th century, Wilshire Center was a wealthy commercial and residential district. As Los Angeles decentralized along newly constructed freeway corridors, Wilshire Boulevard and the areas surrounding it went into a lengthy decline. With property values drastically diminished, the area saw a heavy influx of Koreans in the late 1960s, after restrictions on immigration to the United States from East Asia were lifted in 1965.

In the 1970s, the Heavy-Chemical Industry Drive initiated by South Korean dictator Park Chung Hee, which displaced

Koreatown

much of Korea's petty bourgeoisie, resulted in even more Koreans settling in Wilshire Center, which was soon christened Koreatown. The name had more to do with the predominance of Korean-owned businesses on the community's major boulevards than with the demographics of the residents, as large parts of the area were heavily Latino throughout the 1970s and 1980s.

The early 2000s saw a revitalization of the area, with many Korean-Americans returning, seeking a more urban lifestyle than could be found in Korean-heavy suburbs such as Cerritos and Irvine. The neighborhood has become invigorated with the arrival of a new generation of middle-class immigrants from Korea, seeking better positions than are generally available in South Korea's stagnant economy. Koreatown also has become a somewhat chic destination for hipsters priced out of Los Feliz, West Hollywood and Park La Brea.

Koreatown now brims with vibrant nightlife and commerce, and the construction of mid-level to high-end residential buildings and shopping centers continues to attract new residents.

In the fall, Koreatown has the marvelous Los Angeles Korean Festival at Seoul International Park, with lots of activities for the family, food, vendors, music, dance and a parade. To find out more, visit koreatown.com or lakoreanfestival.com (be sure to click on the English version in the top right).

Koreatown is well known for its nightlife, which includes exclusive clubs, numerous bars and late-night restaurants. It's not unusual to see a hot spot on every block. Some of the Korean nightclubs include Karnak, Velvet Room and Express. Every club caters to an age group, ranging from the early 20s to late 50s. Koreatown is known for Korean barbecue, tofu houses, noodle shops and several 24-hour restaurants.

Bathing spas and saunas are another tradition imported from the homeland to Koreatown, and, of course, we feel that they should not be missed.

KOREAN MASSAGE IN KOREATOWN & ENVIRONS

Aroma Wilshire Center
3680 Wilshire Blvd., Ste. B01, Los Angeles 90010
(Near Serrano)
213.387.2111, aromaresort.com

Hours: Mon.–Fri. 6 a.m.–10 p.m.

Facilities: Designed more for the sports enthusiast who enjoys spa treatments after working out, this is a full-service sports club, with the emphasis on club—some areas are just for members. If you're a guest of a member, you can buy a one-day pass to enter the facilities accompanied by the member; you can also use the fitness center and saunas if you buy a spa treatment. The golf range (L.A.'s largest indoor/outdoor driving range, with four decks) is open to the public. The women's sauna has cold, warm and hot tubs, a dry sauna, a wet steam and mist sauna, a jade room and a hwangto room.

What to expect: You must purchase a service to gain entrance to the spa, waiving the entrance fee. Aroma is located on the third floor of a sizable complex. When you get off the elevator, you'll be greeted by large decorative doors and a marble reception area. After you pay for your treatment, you'll be given a towel and robe. Before you enter the locker rooms, remove your shoes. You can wear spa sandals, but barefoot is the norm.

Aroma Wilshire Center

Services offered: Body scrub, massage, skin care, mani-pedi and waxing.

Parking: Plenty in the large garage behind the facility. Aroma validates.

Why we like it: The shopping complex has lots of shops to explore. And if it's hard to get your BF to go for a massage, you might be able to entice him with some time at the driving range while you spa.

Beverly Hot Springs
308 N. Oxford Ave., Los Angeles 90004
(At Beverly)
323.734.7000, beverlyhotsprings.com

   $$ *(entrance fee)* *(services)*

Hours: Daily 9 a.m.–9 p.m.

Facilities: This is the only spa in L.A. that boasts truly natural, thermal water, which gushes from an artesian well 2,200 feet beneath the earth's surface. Warmed by geothermal heat, the water contains minerals and elements that are believed to have healing properties and health benefits. If you don't want a treatment, you can buy a day pass to simply enjoy the sauna, steam room and pools.

What to expect: The women's spa area, on the first floor, is separate from the men's, on the second. Lockers allow you to set your own combination, so you don't have to carry around a key. The hot spring comes up into a large pool shaped like a figure eight, and walls made to look like a cave surround it. The large Zen garden is equipped with a Buddha and lots of plants. Also on site are a cold pool, sauna and steam room. Showers are both sit down (traditional Korean) or stand up. You can bring your own scrub equipment or make an appointment to have one done. This consists of a full body scrub followed by a cleansing with warm milk, a hair wash and a fresh cucumber mask.

Services offered: Traditional Korean body scrub, sugar scrub, conventional massage (Swedish and shiatsu) and a unique bamboo-fusion massage that uses a warmed bamboo stick, rather than hands, to apply pressure.

Parking: Free parking behind and to the side of the entrance.

Why we like it: The one thing we can say for sure is that our skin felt wonderful afterward.

Century Sports & Day Spa
4120 W. Olympic Blvd., Los Angeles 90019
(One block east of Crenshaw)
323.954.1020, centurydayspa.com

    (entrance fee) **$$** *(services)*

Hours: Mon.–Fri. 6 a.m.–10 p.m.; Sat. & Sun. 7 a.m.–10 p.m.

Facilities: Quite the large facility, Century Day Spa has a women's spa on the second floor and a men's spa on the first.

What to expect: Showering, in either a standing or seated shower, is mandatory before entering any of the pools. On site are a mugwort hot bath, cold and hot pools, a eucalyptus steam room and dry saunas. Massage and body scrub areas are sectioned off from the main pool areas.

Services offered: Deep-tissue, sports and Swedish massage, as well as foot reflexology, acupressure, body scrubs and facials.

Parking: In the lot off Bronson Avenue.

Why we like it: Not one but two quiet rooms, one with clay floors and the other with marble. Since they are said to have different healing properties, you'll have to try them both.

Beverly Hot Springs

Crystal Spa
3500 W. 6th St. #321, Los Angeles 90020
(City Center, corner Alexandria)
213.487.5600, crystalspala.com

 (entrance) *(services & food)*

Hours: Sun.–Thurs. 6 a.m.–midnight; Fri. & Sat. 24 hours.

Facilities: This third-floor spa in the City Center mall has a modern, clean and soothing décor. The front desk doubles as a retail area for skin and hair products. As usual, there are separate men's and women's locker rooms, but the shared areas include the salt, ice, wood charcoal and mud clay rooms; each holds a dozen or so people. There's a large TV in the communal room and a WiFi area with three computers, for those who just can't leave the world behind. The women's spa has raised areas with hot and cold tubs leading to the six body-scrub tables.

What to expect: While there's definitely a buzz in the shopping center, you can get away from it all here. After we paid, we were given tops and long shorts to change into. We hung out in all the areas except the cold room. We particularly liked the wood charcoal room, which has a wonderfully rich, earthy smell. It was the first place we saw sand hourglasses next to the floor mats, and we dutifully observed the time limit. We don't know how long it was, but it was all we could manage anyway.

Services offered: Acupressure, a variety of body scrubs and massages, facials and other skin-care treatments.

Parking: Marked spots for Crystal Spa inside City Center on the second level.

Why we like it: We got a little tour before we committed, but we think they'll have you at "Welcome." Watch the website for specials and downloadable coupons.

Daengki Spa
4245 W. 3rd St., Los Angeles 90020
(Corner Serrano)
213.381.3780, daengkispa.com

  (entrance fee) *(services)*

Hours: Daily 7 a.m.–11 p.m.

Facilities: This is a traditional Korean bath house, on the small side but perfect for those not comfortable being part of the naked parade. Flanking the small hot and cold pools are six tables for scrubs, three on each side of the pools. A row of seated showers and shower stalls are off to the side. Steam and sauna rooms are on the other side.

What to expect: After you pay, turn in your shoes for a locker key and basket with a seersucker robe and two towels, one for hair and the other for body. Change in the locker room and head off to the mud and salt room, the relaxation area or the jade room, which has a heated floor. We found a dozen cartons of eggs stacked in the mud and salt rooms—ever practical, the staff was cooking their eggs the easy way.

Services offered: Traditional Korean scrub and massage, deep-tissue massage, aromatherapy and a feminine herbal steam, which is supposed to be helpful for those trying to conceive or who suffer from bad cramps.

Parking: A few spots in this small corner strip mall or on Serrano.

Why we like it: In addition to the customary wooden blocks, the spa provided rattan wedges for our heads, which were more comfortable than the usual wooden blocks. The entrance fee is a bargain, and you'll get to see the eggs cooking in the sauna to boot.

Dream Sauna & Spa
612 N. Vermont Ave., Los Angeles 90004
(Corner Clinton)
323.662.6767, dreamspala.com
    (entrance fee)  *(services)*

Hours: Daily 8 a.m.–10 p.m.; closed certain holidays.

Facilities: There are separate entrances for the women's and men's sauna and no central common area. The spa consists of small hot and cold tubs, a steam room and three heavenly sauna rooms: mineral salt, pure mud and jade stone. Be sure to try them all.

What to expect: Pay your admission fee (for spa only) or service fee (for a treatment) up front. You'll be given a towel, a robe and a locker key, and your locker number will be the call for your appointment. If you'd like, the helpful staff will show you around. Spa sandals are provided. The scrub room has five beds, all out in the open. The scrub starts with you lying face down, then you turn over and they scrub your sides. Not an inch of skin is missed. If you are ticklish, beware. The scrub includes a cucumber mask and a shampoo; these feel fantastic at the end of the scrub.

Services offered: Most scrub packages include body scrub, massage, cucumber mask and shampoo. Add on a unique body wrap of seaweed, mud or aroma oil.

Parking: Lot in front.

Why we like it: This is an intimate and authentic spa with a friendly staff; ask for Helen, who gives an awesome scrub and facial. Don't forget to add on a body wrap—it's well worth the price. If you want to get away from the über spas, this is a place for you.

Gahin Sauna
4003 Wilshire Blvd., #K, Los Angeles 90010
(Corner Wilton)
213.387.6112, gahinsauna.com
   (entrance fee) **$$** *(services)*

Hours: Mon.–Sat. 8 a.m.–8 p.m.; Sun. 9 a.m.–7 p.m.

Facilities: Petite and cute, this is a great find in the corner of a mini-mall. We had the place to ourselves, which was a good thing, because it doesn't appear to hold more than five people. The blue-tiled spa has showers, a dry sauna, a steam room, hot and cold pools, two scrub tables and three massage beds.

What to expect: This is for women only, so when you walk in, you'll see the changing area and lockers right away—less need for privacy. The sauna is in the back, and the massage area is on the side in a closed-off room. They'll give you a towel and robe to wear during your visit. You can go just into the sauna or get a service; we tried the body-line point massage, which felt magnificent.

Gahin Sauna

KOREAN

Services offered: Body-line point massage, body scrubs and facials.

Parking: Lot or street metered parking

Why we like it: Tiny and private. If you want to try the naked experience without people around, make an appointment for a scrub and the place will be practically all yours.

Grand Spa
2999 W. 6th St., Los Angeles 90020
(Koreatown, corner S. Virgil)
213.380.8889 for the women's side or
213.380.8887 for the men's, grandspala.com

   (entrance fee) *(services)*

Hours: Daily 24 hours.

Facilities: Women go to the third floor, men to the second, and there's no communal area. While waiting for our scrubs, we heard a big commotion and walked toward the source of the noise, which was a huge TV tunedto a Korean game show that was visible from the elevated hot and cold pools. On the backside was a second TV, visible from inside the dry sauna. That was a first.

What to expect: After you check in, you get a key to your locker that has a towel and robe. Plan to lounge a bit in the pools before having a treatment. Someone will call your locker number and take you to the area for body scrubs. The scrub area is one of the most private we've found to date, with doors and stalls like public bathrooms. The therapists follow the traditional scrub recipe, with a thorough back, front and side scrub, rinse, and oil

Grand Spa

massage, then a shampoo, cucumber facial and final milk rinse. If you don't want a treatment, you can try the Finnish sauna, heated from 158 to 212 degrees F; the hwangto sauna room, with hwangto clay brought from Korea and a lower temperature; the sauna room; a jade stone room; steam and mist sauna rooms; a relaxation room; and the ubiquitous cold, warm and hot pools.

Services offered: Korean body scrub, scrub and massage combo, acupressure, foot reflexology, facials, mani-pedis, hair services and tanning.

Parking: Private lot off the entrance.

Why we like it: The 24/7 schedule, plus separate stalls for the body scrub. For a great scrub, ask for Cho.

Hankook Sauna
3121 W. Olympic Blvd., Los Angeles 90006
(Koreatown, between Harvard & Kingsley)
213.388.8899, hankooksaunaspa.com

Hours: Mon.–Sat. 7 a.m.–11 p.m.; Sun. 7 a.m.–9 p.m.

Facilities: This medium-size, women-only facility has an open floor plan with a dry sauna and a wet herb steam room, a hot whirlpool, a warm mineral pool, two small individual whirlpools and a large cold pool. The shower area has three stand-up stalls and seven sitting ones. On one side of the spa is a long rectangular tiled basin that contains mineral water for bathing and rinsing. The open scrub room has seven beds and no partitions. In the dry area is a mineral mud therapy room, a Himalayan salt room, a rest area with a warmed jade-tile floor, and an ice room.

What to expect: After you pay, you'll get a locker key, body and hair towels and a robe. Take off your shoes before entering the locker room and shower before entering the pools. Plan on relaxing in any of the specialty rooms prior to or after your scrub. The scrub is traditional Korean, performed by ladies in black bras and panties, who go over every inch of you with exfoliating mitts. After rinsing, they begin the process again. You'll also receive a briskly cool cucumber facial while getting your hair washed, both before the milk body rinse that signals the end of your treatment.

Services offered: Body scrubs, oil, mineral and aroma massages, acupressure and skin, nail and hair care.

Parking: Plenty in front and on the side of the building.

Why we like it: An older, smaller Korean spa, Hankook has an appealing intimacy. While it's not for you and 20 of your close friends, it is a good place to share with two to three friends who enjoy a spa adventure.

Natura Sports Health Club
3240 Wilshire Blvd., Los Angeles 90010
(Wilshire Galleria, between Vermont & New Hampshire)
213.381.2288, natura-spa.com

Hours: Mon.–Thurs. 6 a.m.–10 p.m.; Fri.–Sat. 6 a.m.–11 p.m.; Sun. 7 a.m.–10 p.m.

Facilities: Natura, a member-preferred facility, is located in the basement of the building. Men's and women's facilities are separate and different. The women's spa has a yellow clay room, a jade stone room, a sleeping room, hot and cold pools, a lounge with TV and a skin-care center.

What to expect: We went for the body scrub and found a traditional experience. And we're so in love with all the rooms, which are simply beautiful.

Services offered: For women, body scrub, massage, acupressure, foot massage, skin care, mani-pedi and tanning; men can have everything except mani-pedi and tanning.

Parking: Plenty behind the Galleria.

Why we like it: We'd never seen complimentary gym apparel at a spa before. We had no excuse to skip a workout, but we did anyway, choosing instead to relax and enjoy our scrubs in this peaceful facility.

Olympic Spa
3915 W. Olympic Blvd., Los Angeles 90019
(Koreatown, between S. Bronson & S. Norton)
323.857.0666, olympicspala.com

Hours: Daily 9 a.m.–10 p.m.; closed Dec. 25 & Jan. 1.

Facilities: This is a mid-size facility that attracts fans from as far away as Pasadena and the Palisades. The spa has a warm mineral pool, hot mugwort tea pool, cold pool, jade steam sauna, clay dry sauna and charcoal therapy rooms.

What to expect: You must check in at least 30 minutes before your reservation for a treatment, which is just barely enough time to take a shower and explore the rooms and pools. When you arrive, you're given a locker key, towels and a robe, though those wearing robes are few and far between. The heated jade floor kept calling to us, and we lay there, awaiting the call to our scrubs. The body scrub follows the traditional protocol, and we marveled at the results. And where better to stare at our new skin than back on that jade floor? We had to indulge one last time before heading home.

Olympic Spa

Services offered: Body scrubs, acupressure, shiatsu, reflexology, milk soak and other body treatments and facials. A skin-care line is sold in the lobby. Gift certificates available.

Parking: Complimentary valet parking behind the spa, off Norton.

Why we like it: We love the heated jade floor, which was littered with women's bodies. After your service, try some homemade noodles in the restaurant.

Wi Spa
2700 Wilshire Blvd., Los Angeles 90057
(Corner Rampart)
213.487.2700, wispausa.com

   (entrance fee) (services & food)

Hours: Daily 24 hours.

Facilities: It's huge, with a women-only floor (capacity 235), men-only floor and co-ed floor. Each area has hot and cold whirlpool tubs, dry and steam saunas and a body-scrub area. The co-ed jim jil bang is spacious, with five sauna rooms: clay, salt, jade, ice and bulgama. Also in the jim jil bang is a large common area for relaxing, with a kid zone (off to the side), computer area, WiFi, comic-book area (Korean books) and full-service restaurant. There's also a rooftop terrace. The women's area also has a shop, nail salon, eight stand-up showers and 32 Korean-style sit-down showers and a sleeping area. The dry sauna is kept at 190 degrees F, and the wet sauna is kept at 126 degrees F.

What to expect: Arrive at least 30 minutes before your treatment. When you pay for your services, they'll give you a towel, T-shirt and wristwatch locker key. (Take our word for it: Put the key on your wrist immediately, because the

Wi Spa

locker has an automatic lock, and you'll be sorry if you lock your watch-key inside.) The front desk will give you a robe and a pair of shorts (they come in all sizes). Take off your shoes, enter the locker room, change, grab a towel and hit one of the 40 showers before entering any of the pools or rooms or before a treatment. If you're having a body scrub, wait by that enclosed area a few minutes before your treatment and the therapist will call your number. Once inside, most of the beds are separated by partitions, but some are not—your bra-and-panty-clad therapist, however, will keep your personal parts covered. Other staff members wear T-shirts that say, "Can I get you a towel?" on the back, and, in fact, you'll see clean towels everywhere you look. After your treatment, change into the T-shirt and shorts and head upstairs to the jim jil bang to try one or more of the five saunas, and consider a bite at the restaurant. Any extra costs (like food) will be charged to your locker number, and you pay when you check out. Don't forget to try the bulgama sauna—it's one of the few and the hottest in Koreatown.

Services offered: Body scrub, massage, facials, full salon services, fitness gym and yoga.

Parking: Lot behind building; use the valet if the lot is full or try the street metered parking.

Why we like it: This spa has it all, and 24/7. It's a great place for first-timers to the Korean spa experience because it's done a fantastic job mixing the ancient Korean bath house with the modern amenities of a luxury western spa. Make sure you try the bulgama sauna and sign up for a yoga class in the jim jil bang.

Wilshire Spa
3442 Wilshire Blvd., #100, Los Angeles 90010
(One block east of Normandie, enter on Mariposa)
213.387.0281, wilshirespa.com

Hours: Daily 24 hours.

Facilities: Located behind the 3440 building, this spa is a little gem. The entrance is on the first floor, and the modern, clean and spacious spa is downstairs. The sauna is designed to allow for privacy in every area. Eight stand-up showers line the wall, while 12 sit-down showers hide behind a half-wall partition. The dry sauna has large, clear windows and a TV (on mute but with Korean closed caption), and the whirlpools are located in the center. The body-scrub area is separate, with eight tables in two rooms. There are three sauna rooms: mineral salt, hwangto and onyx.

What to expect: After you pay for your services, they'll give you a plastic basket with two towels (one for your body, one for your hair) and a robe, all neatly folded. Walk downstairs to the spa, which has a soothing fountain at the locker-room entrance. Change out of your clothes and take a shower; don't forget to keep your locker key on your wrist or ankle. You'll find clean spa sandals by the showers. Wait for someone to call your locker number for your treatment. After that's finished, take some time to relax in any of the three sauna rooms: mineral salt, which regulates blood pressure; hwangto (yellow ochre), which helps eliminate toxins from your body; and the heated onyx room, a perfect place to relax on the floor. In the spacious vanity area you can blow-dry your hair and put on makeup.

Services offered: Body scrubs, massages, facials.

Parking: Pay lot behind building, and the spa validates; enter on Mariposa.

Why we like it: A great place for those who want to try a Korean spa but need a little assistance. The helpful staff will walk you through the whole place to get you oriented. The facility is incredibly clean, spacious and up-to-date. Because it's women-only and there's no common area, you can more easily focus on just pampering yourself for the day.

BEYOND KOREATOWN

CITY OF INDUSTRY

Spa Renaissance
17980 Castleton St., City of Industry 91748
(Corner Stoner Creek)
626.820.0588, sparenaissance.com

 (entrance fee) **$$** *(services)*

Hours: Mon.–Thurs. & Sun. 8:30 a.m.–11p.m.; Fri.–Sat. 8:30 a.m.–midnight.

Facilities: A gracious curved reception area welcomes you. Beyond the locker room is the spa, with five body-scrub tables, standing and seated shower stalls, and steam and sauna rooms. Outside is a communal lounge with a huge flat-screen TV. Off to the side is a food bar with fruit and vegetable juices and Chinese and Korean food. The Himalayan salt and red clay rooms are co-ed, too.

What to expect: We purchased a combo spa visit with a foot massage at the place next door—the reflexology place is a separate business, but they smartly have a package deal to promote both businesses. With the purchase of a one-hour foot reflexology treatment, you'll get a discount on the spa entrance fee. They speak English at the

reception desk, but it's limited inside the spa. You'll be given an oversize T-shirt and knee-length cotton shorts to wear, and you'll see many women with their children, because this is very much a family place.

One note: When you enter the women's locker room, you'll see a wall of small lockers. This was one of our first Korean spa experiences, and we were trying to cram all our clothes in them before someone walked in and stopped us. They are just for shoes.

Services offered: Body scrub, acupressure, salt-scrub Swedish and stone massage, facials and other skin care, mani-pedi and waxing.

Parking: Plenty in the large lot in front.

Why we like it: Just off the women's locker room is the quiet room. There's not much to say about a bare room where you lie on the floor, but we loved the concept and the experience.

GARDENA

Gardena Women Sauna
15435 S. Western Ave., Gardena 90249
(Gardena Village Mall, one block north of
Redondo Beach)
310.538.2229, gardenawomensauna.com

   (spa only) **$$** *(services)*

Hours: Daily 8 a.m.–10 p.m.

Facilities: This small, simple spa is a great place to hang out and relax. Downstairs are dry and wet saunas, warm, hot and cold whirlpools and a salt pool. Stall showers and Korean sit-down showers are on one side of the spa; the body-scrub room is on the other side. Upstairs is a rock salt sauna and a warm sleeping room, plus a deli that serves noodles, dumplings and soups.

What to expect: Pay for your service in advance, and you'll get towels, a robe and a locker key. Remove your shoes before entering the locker room and shower before entering the pools. The body-scrub area is open, so it's not for the excessively modest. The scrub itself is great and includes a cucumber mask, a hair wash and a final body rinse with milk.

Services offered: Traditional Korean body scrub, oil massage, wraps and facial.

Parking: Lot in front or side of building.

Why we like it: A peaceful, basic Korean spa where Korean and Japanese women of all ages come to relax and be taken care of.

While you're there: Check out Marukai (1620 W. Redondo Beach Blvd., Gardena). Everything about this supermarket is super. You'll want to try something, taste something, smell something or buy something from every aisle. Aside from the amazing array of food, it has bizarre yet useful cooking gadgets and fun, sometimes stunning plates, tea services and tableware.

HACIENDA HEIGHTS

Hacienda Joy Spa
2020 S. Hacienda Blvd., Hacienda Heights 91745
(Vons Shopping Center, corner Halliburton & Newton)
626.855.1877, haciendajoysauna.com

   (entrance fee) **$$** *(services)*

Hours: Daily 8 a.m.–10 p.m.

Facilities: While this place could use a facelift, it's cozy and easy to use. The women's spa is on the left and the men's on the right; they do not share a common area. Inside each are dry and wet saunas, warm, hot and cold whirlpools,

Aroma Wilshire Center

and stand-up and sit-down showers. The body-scrub area is partitioned to allow for privacy.

What to expect: Once inside, you take off your shoes and clothes and store them in a locker. They'll give you towels and a robe; we bring our own spa sandals, and you may wish to do the same. Make sure to use the warm, appealing mineral jade room and the salt rooms.

Services offered: Body scrub, aroma-oil massage, salt massage, facial.

Parking: Lot in front.

Why we like it: There's no pressure to get a service—in fact, we brought our own shampoo and felt right at home. The mineral room and the jade room are heated perfectly, and in them you can work up a therapeutic sweat.

Royal Health Spa
1020 S. Hacienda Blvd., Hacienda Heights 91745
(Corner Gale, behind the Mobil station)
626.369.8484

    (entrance fee) **$$** *(services)*

Hours: Daily 8 a.m.–11 p.m.

Facilities: It may be ugly from the outside, but when you enter you'll be amazed at the transformation. This attractive mid-size spa focuses on your relaxation and enjoyment. Besides the men's and women's spas, it has a small fitness room with treadmills and other equipment, a body-massage area with four tables, and a foot spa with nine chairs.

What to expect: The spa is well equipped, with eight Korean sit-down showers, two stand-up showers, a dry sauna, wet sauna, and cold, warm and hot whirlpools. Three scrub tables have a partition in front for privacy. The jade room is small but cozy, and there's a pleasant open space in which to cool down and rest on a warm floor. As at all Korean spas, you must remove your shoes before you enter and shower before you partake of any services, sit in any baths or relax in any sauna. They'll provide you with a robe, towels and spa sandals.

Services offered: Body scrub, massage, facial, foot massage.

Parking: Lot in front or on the side.

Why we like it: This is a find. The amazingly friendly and helpful staff takes pride in their spa and makes sure you know about all the amenities. The place was empty when we visited; the location and ugly façade may deter folks, but don't let that stop you.

NORTHRIDGE

CJ Grand Health Spa
10211 Balboa Blvd., Northridge 91325
(Between Devonshire & Mayall)
818.407.9000, cjgrandspa.com

  $ *(entrance fee)* **$$** *(services)*

Hours: Daily 8 a.m.–11 p.m.

Facilities: Located down an alley, this large, two-story family spa is hard to see from the street. Enter on the first floor and pay for your entry or services. The women's spa is on the left and the men's on the right. Upstairs is the communal room with a small food-service area. We sat on the floor and enjoyed some traditional Korean food before heading into the sauna rooms on this floor: a jade room, loess soil room, mineral salt room and ice room. The treatment areahas seven completely private scrub rooms, which look like large bathroom stalls. You'll also find the usual stand-up and sit-down showers and three pools (warm, hot and cold). In the common areas are a fitness room and two large sleeping/relaxing rooms.

KOREAN

What to expect: The front desk will give you two towels (one for your hair, the other for your body), long pink shorts, an oversize T-shirt and an electronic locker key. Remove your shoes before entering the locker room, which is the dividing area between the treatment room and the spa. The scrubs are performed in uncommon privacy. We had the seaweed massage with a green tea mask: It was wonderful. Once you're done with the spa and your treatment(s), change into the T-shirt and shorts and head upstairs for time in the spacious saunas, which have gorgeous stone and tile work. The salt sauna is lined with blocks of salt that are lit from behind, reminiscent of stained glass; it looks like a holy place. The loess soil room smells of herbs and rich earth, which has a relaxing effect. Be sure to try them all.

Services: Body scrub; acupressure; Swedish, oil, seaweed, foot and deep-tissue massage; facials and other skin-care services. Check the website for promotions.

Parking: Lots in front, side and behind.

Why we like it: If you don't want to go to Koreatown for an authentic body scrub, have it here. The private rooms make it a great place for folks who don't like the idea of being scrubbed naked in public.

NORWALK

Pioneer Spa
16511 Pioneer Blvd., #108, Norwalk 90650
(Pioneer Plaza, corner 166th & two blocks
north of the 91 Fwy.)
562.924.6678

   _(entrance fee)_ _(services)_

Hours: Sun.–Fri. 8 a.m.–11 p.m.; Fri.–Sat. 24 hours.

Facilities: This full-service spa has a men's section, a women's section and a _jim jil bang_ (a common area), plus

CJ Grand Spa

multiple rooms for relaxing: coral room, salt room, clay room, gemstone room, and ice room. There are the standard cold-water and hot-water whirlpools, a dry and wet sauna, stand-up or sit-down showers and three body-scrub tables. Overall, the place is clean and lively but not too noisy—sure, there are TVs in the common area, but they're not blaring.

What to expect: Pay first and get your towels, T-shirt, shorts and toothbrush (!). Enter the spa and remove your shoes. The key for the locker is electronic, and you wear it on your wrist or ankle. After you partake of the sauna, put on the T-shirt and shorts and walk over to the common area. The sauna rooms are found on the perimeter of the common area and include a jade room, heated to 115 degrees F, which is said to help women with hormonal imbalances. The clay room, heated to 130 degrees F, has mud rich in minerals, which promotes healthy breathing. The 130-degree salt room contains salt and minerals that cleanse your pores. The 140-degree coral room is said to help with eyesight as well as decrease stress and restore harmony. Finally, the ice room, cooled to 63 degrees, feels great after all that heat.

Services: Body scrubs and massages, including wet body, acupressure and foot massage.

Parking: Lot in front.

Why we like it: Korean families and friends get together here to rest and relax. We particularly love the unique sauna rooms. The food is tasty, especially the refreshing shaved ice with red bean and fruit.

RESEDA

Valley Day Spa
19255 Vanowen St., Reseda 91335
(Corner Tampa)
818.757.7088, valley-day-spa.com

   $$ *(entrance fee)* **$$** *(services)*

Hours: Daily 9:30 a.m.–9:30 p.m.

Facilities: Deceptive from the outside, this two-story building is home to separate spas for men and women, which are located downstairs. All dry treatments are performed upstairs in one of the fifteen rooms.

What to expect: When you pay up front, you'll get two large towels and a waffle-weave robe. Enter the spa, remove your shoes and head to the curtained-off locker room. If you're comfortable, undress completely, although bathing suits are allowed. Remember to shower before entering any sauna or the whirlpool tub. The best way to enjoy this spa is to get a service first; there's a variety of massage packages to choose from. If you don't get a massage upstairs, you can get a body scrub downstairs in the spa, which has a small, three-table body-scrub area, a whirlpool, dry sauna and wet sauna, as well as three private showers with curtains and three open-air showers.

Services offered: Massages, body scrubs, body wraps, facials.

Parking: Huge lot in front.

Why we like it: The spa is cozy and clean, and the staff is super friendly and accommodating. The great lounge is a fun place to meet friends and bring in food or just relax and drink tea.

ROWLAND HEIGHTS

Diamond Family Spa
1140 Coiner Ct., Rowland Heights 91748
(North of the 60 Fwy. between Fullerton & Nogales)
626.581.0304, diamondfamilyspa.com

   **$** *(entrance fee)* **$$** *(services)*

Hours: Mon.–Thurs. & Sun. 8 a.m.–11 p.m.; Fri.-Sat. 24 hours.

Facilities: In an area full of bland industrial buildings, you'll find one of the largest Korean spas in Southern California. The women's and men's spas are separate, and the jim jil bang has a small restaurant, juice bar, reading area and computer area. The jim jil bang also has co-ed saunas: Himalayan salt, yellow earth, charcoal, the "dome" sauna (a hot bulgama) and ice room. In the spas are four whirlpool tubs—warm, hot, cold and the "event spa" (warm water and herbs that tint the water green)—as well as plenty of stand-up and sit-down showers. Each spa also contains a wet and dry sauna.

What to expect: When you check in you'll be given towels, T-shirt, shorts and an electronic locker key. When you enter the locker room, put your shoes in the space that corresponds with your key number. In the locker room, change out of your clothes and head to the showers to rinse off before using any of the tubs or getting a service.

If you're getting a treatment, wait until your number is called. The body-scrub area has opaque glass partitions between the tables, allowing for some sense of privacy.

Services offered: Body scrubs and massages (oil, aroma, wet or foot).

Parking: Ample parking in the lot.

Why we like it: This is a popular, family-oriented spa, especially on the weekends. If you want to experience a Korean family outing with your friends and family, come here. We especially like finding the eggs cooking in the bulgama. If you're not adventurous enough to try the food here, head to the Tea Station around the corner. We shared some fried tofu and sweet potato and taro balls. And as you would expect, it has a great tea selection.

TORRANCE

Palace Health Club
21210 Hawthorne Blvd., Torrance 90503
(Corner Torrance)
310.316.3393, torrancenaturalspa.com

    (entrance fee) *(services)*

Hours: Mon.–Sat. 9 a.m.–10 p.m.; Sun. 10 a.m.–10 p.m.

Facilities: The men's and women's saunas are on separate sides, mirroring each other, and they share access to a few of the treatment rooms. Each has its own locker room and small gemstone dry sauna and steam sauna rooms. On the women's side are a body-scrub shower (with a table), a standing rinse shower room and a couple's massage room.

What to expect: The reception area is ample, so the small steam and sauna rooms came as a surprise. When we first visited, the place was bustling, but on our next visit, we were the only ones on the women's side. If you time it

Riviera Health Spa

right, you could very well have the place to yourself. Don't make this your first Korean sauna experience—it needs a little repair and updating. We found cracks in the ceiling and floors of the dry sauna.

Services offered: Body scrub and body wash, as well as shiatsu, Swedish and deep-tissue massage.

Parking: In the Robbins Bros. lot.

Why we like it: If a handful of cosmetic issues are addressed, we'd recommend this as a cozy, intimate spa.

Riviera Health Spa
3601 Lomita Blvd., Torrance 90505
(Near corner Hawthorne)
310.375.5600, rivierahealthspa.com

    (entrance fee) *(services)*

Hours: Daily 8 a.m.-midnight.

Facilities: The 30,000 square feet of this facility are spread out over two floors. Separate men's and women's locker rooms, with their own hot and cold pools, warm Jacuzzis and hair salons, are on the first floor; the second floor is co-ed, complete with an exercise room, game room and four saunas: salt, clay, jade and ice. The *jim jil bang*, the large communal area, in the middle has heated floors, perfect for hanging out with something to nibble from the restaurant or smoothie bar.

What to expect: A gracious entry greets you, and after checking in you'll get a two-toned T-shirt, long shorts and towels. Once you head into the locker room, you'll find large and beautiful rooms. We hung out all afternoon in the jade, clay, and salt saunas, then rinsed and washed in the women's spa, enjoying dips in the heated pools before calling it a glorious day.

Services offered: Body-scrub, shiatsu, Swedish and combo massages, skin care and salon services. Gift certificates available.

Parking: Plenty in the facility lot, but choose an end spot as the spaces are narrow.

Why we like it: Massages until midnight seven days a week, including holidays.

While you're there: Stop by the Mitsuwa Market (21515 S. Western Ave., Torrance, 310.782.0335). If you're hungry after your spa experience head to the market's food court, where you'll find sushi, ramen, tonkatsu, curry, cakes and much more. Mitsuwa has a vast selection of Japanese groceries and products.

Chapter 4 – **Russian**

MORE THAN A MASSAGE: *THE BANYA EXPERIENCE*

The Russia *banya*, or steam bath, has been a part of Eastern European culture for centuries. In the past, banyas in private homes were heated once a week for bathing and at other times for special occasions and rituals—for example, the nights before and after a wedding, both bride and groom would enjoy separate ceremonial banyas.

The traditional banya ritual is simple and can be repeated several times throughout a visit to the spa. After taking a quick shower, you step inside the banya (either the wet steam room or the dry sauna) and sit or lie on one of the lower benches; the higher you sit, the more intense the heat. After a good sweat, rinse off in the shower and repeat.

After you repeat this process a few times, you'll be ready for the most important element of the Russian massage: the *platza*. This is a rigorous massage performed with the *venik*, a leafy, fragrant bundle of oak, birch or eucalyptus soaked in warm water. The massage therapist, also known as the platza master, warms and relaxes the skin by rhythmic stroking and tapping with the venik. This generates heat over the body while releasing the essential oils from the leaves. The platza is said to draw out impurities, improve circulation, prevent premature aging of the skin, improve metabolism and refresh the spirit, and we won't quibble with any of those claims. Leave it to a country with such intense winters to make being slapped with leaves an enjoyable experience!

The beauty of the banya experience doesn't end there. After being tapped vigorously with the venik, you run outside the banya and dive into an exceptionally icy pool. While it seems like torture, it really is the best feeling imaginable.

After your plunge into the cold pool, you can repeat the whole process. Some go through the cycle five to ten times in a couple of hours, but we recommend that only for the most seasoned of banya goers.

Vôda Spa; photo by Edward Duarte

A FEW WORDS IN RUSSIAN

ENGLISH	RUSSIAN PRONUNCIATION
Hello	*zdrah*-stvooy-tee
Good-bye	duh-svee-dah-nee-ya
Yes	das
No	nyet
Thank you	spah-*see*-buh

WEST HOLLYWOOD

While Russians have been immigrating to the United States since the 18th century, West Hollywood saw its large wave of immigrants arrive when the Soviet Union was dissolved in 1991. Packed with Russian mom-and-pop grocery stores, bakeries and shops, Santa Monica Boulevard in West Hollywood is rich with the tastes and smells of the Old Country.

It will add to your spa experience to visit this neighborhood and sample the Russian delicacies, either in-house (some offer café dining) or take out. Look for borscht, marinated mushrooms, pickled tomatoes, *olivieh* (think potato salad with minced meat) and, of course, blini and caviar. And absolutely explore the fantastic bakeries. Instead of trying the frou-frou desserts, indulge in the quintessentially Russian dark rye bread (great with butter and caviar), *piroshki* (savory or sweet baked buns) and *vatrushka* (pastry filled with sweet cheese).

If you make the effort to say thank you—that's *spah-see-buh* in Russian—you'll surely get a smile.

RUSSIAN SPAS

City Spa
5325 W. Pico Blvd., Los Angeles 90019
(Corner Burnside)
323.933.5954, lacityspa.com

Hours: Men only on Tues., Thurs. & Fri. 10 a.m.–10 p.m., Sun. 7 a.m.–6 p.m.; co-ed days are Mon. & Sat. 2 p.m.–10 p.m., Wed. 10 a.m.–10 p.m.

Facilities: Similar to New York's legendary bathhouses, this Russian spa is a men's club that allows women only three days a week. It boasts a multi-level Russian rock sauna that's heated to a marvelous 200 degrees. Other features: indoor swimming pool, whirlpool, cold plunge pool, steam room, dry sauna, exercise equipment, café, TV room and "sun deck" upstairs, where you can bring your food and, in proper Russian style, smoking is permitted.

What to expect: If you want a massage or platza treatment, you must have an appointment, but if you just want to use the sauna, you can walk in. First-timers are asked to fill out a health questionnaire and show identification. They'll give you keys to a safe deposit box for your valuables and a locker. The guy behind the front desk is a little curt, but don't let him ruin your mood—everyone else is friendly and helpful. If you're a woman, your therapist will take you upstairs to the women's locker room. Bring your bathing suit and a pair of spa sandals or flip flops, and they'll give you two towels and a poncho-like sheet, which is great to wear in the sauna—it slips easily over your head and keeps you covered but is lightweight.

We had a massage first and then used the sauna. You can do it either way, and there's no time limit on your stay.

RUSSIAN

Vōda Spa; photo by Edward Duarte

Each massage therapist has his or her own room upstairs, and you can request whatever type of massage you like, with or without oil. After your massage, head down to the sauna; just remember to shower before entering any pool, sauna or steam room.

Services offered: Platza, deep-tissue, Swedish and sports massage, as well as body scrubs and wraps.

Parking: Some spots on the street, and there's a lot next door at the lumber store with a nominal charge (they do watch the lot).

Why we like it: City Spa welcomes newcomers and is brimming with cultural pride and friendliness. If you bring your own venik, someone will probably offer to tap you with it. Don't mind the "No Spitting" sign in the sauna—it is, after all, just a suggestion!

Vōda Spa
**7700 Santa Monica Blvd., West Hollywood 90046
(Corner Stanley)
323.654.4411, vodaspa.com**

Hours: Facility open Mon.–Fri. 9 a.m.–midnight, Sat.–Sun. 7 a.m.–midnight; treatments daily 10 a.m.–10 p.m.; Wed., women-only in the sauna, banya & pool.

Facilities: Vōda is a über-chic contemporary Russian spa that beautifully mixes Old World charm with modern flair. Downstairs in the clean, courant spa proper are a large lap pool, a whirlpool, a very cold plunge pool and showers. Always shower before you enter any pool or room. Also there are the traditional Russian banya, a dry-hot (200 degrees F) sauna, a Turkish steam room, a cooler Finnish dry sauna and rooms for body scrubs and wraps. Upstairs are quiet massage rooms and areas for facials, nail and hair care and waxing. Vōda Café serves delicious Russian dishes, salads and California cuisine, while the V Room serves cocktails; you can also get a smoothie poolside. It's almost a resort.

What to expect: When you arrive, you'll be asked to fill out a health history and liability release form (to save time, you can download them in advance from the website). We recommend putting your valuables in the safe-deposit box supervised by the management. Next you'll be escorted upstairs to the locker room, where you choose a locker and enter a self-selected combination. Vōda provides rubber sandals and a waffle-weave robe. After you change into your swimsuit and put on your robe, head back downstairs to the spa and rinse off in a shower.

For treatments, the platza is demanding but worth a try— unless you're particularly sensitive to heat. The intense temperature of the sauna turns your skin red, and you can get dizzy, although we were told this is a desirable outcome.

The platza is an Old World massage done in a 200-degree dry sauna and administered with *venik*, small branches of oak, birch or eucalyptus that have been bundled together like a large, loose bouquet and soaked in warm water. A therapist strokes your body with these branches, releasing their natural essential oils onto your skin. As nice as this sounds, you probably won't last long in the sauna (seriously, we're talking minutes), after which you'll run out and plunge into the cold pool. Don't try to set any records here, either. You may have experienced the hot-cold phenomenon before, but the Vōda experience is particularly intense.

Once you go through the process a few times, and take the time to relax and cool down, you should feel immensely invigorated. And we slept like babies that night!

If you're feeling up to it, try a salt scrub or Russian Bear massage, but schedule either of these services for after the platza.

Services offered: Platza, Russian Bear, deep-flow, Swedish, hot-stone, four-hand, prenatal, couple's and foot massages, plus aromatherapy, scrubs, waxing, facials and hair care.

Parking: In the pay lot down the street or right behind the spa.

Why we like it: Russian tradition intertwined with contemporary California style and comfort. If you're a woman, try to go on a women-only Wednesday— we did, and we practically had the place to ourselves.

Vōda Spa, photo by Edward Duarte

Chapter 5 – **Japanese**

JAPANESE SHIATSU

A word created from *shi* (finger) and *atsu* (pressure), shiatsu is a traditional, hands-on massage therapy that originated in Japan. It consists of a finger-pressure technique that uses the traditional acupuncture points of Asian healing. Similar to acupressure and also considered to be a holistic, healing form of bodywork, shiatsu concentrates on unblocking the flow of energy, known as *chi*, in the body and restoring the balance in the various meridians. The belief revolves around the concept that everyday stressful events and challenges negatively affect our body and our internal energy flow. Shiatsu massage attempts to reduce tension to facilitate the flow of blood and energy, which in turn increases the body's healing powers. It is a pleasant and powerful treatment, designed to help people achieve a state of balance and harmony.

THE SHIATSU MASSAGE

For shiatsu massage, you lie down, usually on a mat (*tatami*) on the floor. The therapist applies pressure with his or her fingers, thumbs, palms, elbows and/or knees to specific zones on your skin that are located along the energy meridians. Shiatsu involves 838 pressure points (*atten*), and it never uses oils or lotions. Since the neck and shoulders hold the most tension in the body, the therapist concentrates first on these areas, continuing to the forearms and slowly moving down the back. All areas of the body are worked. You'll typically remain fully clothed for this treatment, either in loose pants and a top provided or in your street clothes. You may also be covered with a towel or thin sheet during the procedure.

AFTER YOUR SHIATSU MASSAGE

The benefits after a shiatsu massage are the same ones you will find in other forms of bodywork: deep relaxation, stress relief, improved flexibility and increased energy and stamina. But because shiatsu balances the systems in the body, its effects can be more comprehensive and can last longer.

A FEW WORDS IN JAPANESE

ENGLISH	JAPANESE PRONUNCIATION
Hello	kon-ee-chee-wa
Good-bye	sah-yoh-nah-rah
Yes	hah-ee

LITTLE TOKYO

Little Tokyo is a Japanese-American district in downtown Los Angeles, one of three official Japantowns remaining in the United States. Founded around the beginning of the 20th century, the area, sometimes called Lil' Tokyo, J-Town or Shō-tokyo, is a cultural center for the Japanese-Americans of Southern California. At its peak, Little Tokyo had some 30,000 Japanese-Americans living in and around the area, but these days Japanese-Americans are no longer as segregated, and Gardena and Torrance have become more popular residential hubs; only about 1,000 mostly elderly Japanese-Americans live in Little Tokyo. These days it is an increasingly popular entertainment district, known for the Japanese American National Museum and a thriving restaurant scene.

The remnants of the original Little Tokyo occupy a few large city blocks that are bounded on the west by Broadway, on the east by Alameda, on the south by 3rd and on the north by Temple. More broadly, the neighborhood is bordered by the Los Angeles River to the east, Downtown to the west, City Hall and Parker Center to the north, and the recently named Arts District (home to galleries and live-work lofts in former warehouses) to the south.

One of the best events in Little Tokyo is the Nisei Week Japanese Festival, which hosts exhibits, entertainment, food, games, arts and crafts, traditional celebrations, a street fair, music, dance, vendors, a parade, a car show, sumo and martial arts demonstrations and contests. For more information go to niseiweek.org.

SHIATSU IN LITTLE TOKYO

E-Z Shiatsu
Honda Plaza, 400 E. 2nd St., Ste. 205, Los Angeles 90012
(2nd & Central)
213.680.4970

Hours: Mon.–Sat. 10 a.m.–6 p.m.

Facilities: Located on the second floor of Honda Plaza, this place justifiably prides itself in providing shiatsu massage for more than 25 years. Mr. Metoki, the current owner, was trained in Japan and worked for various local spas until he took this place over. With just two massage tables and one floor mat, this intimate yet functional space provides the peace and balance that should accompany a shiatsu massage.

What to expect: You must make an appointment. When you arrive, call in to the office and someone will buzz open the door; you will take the stairs or elevator to the second floor. You remove your shoes, leave your clothes on and place your belongings in a plastic bucket, which is neatly stored beneath your massage table. The therapist will ask if you have any problem areas. Don't be shy—let him or her know. The massage starts face down and ends with you lying on your back. Although you keep on your clothes, care is taken to always keep a sheet or towel between the therapist's hands and your skin. The comprehensive massage covers your entire body.

Services offered: Shiatsu massage.

Parking: Validated parking in Honda Plaza.

Why we like it: We received focused attention and constant checking-in from our therapist. He asked if the pressure was just right or too much. He reminded us to breathe and made sure we were comfortable. This is a professional operation with an extremely courteous staff.

While you're there: Directly downstairs is Frances Bakery & Coffee, owned and operated by a Japanese-American baker in the true French spirit. Cakes are moist and not too sweet. The flaky croissants and pain au chocolat remind us of the bakeries of Paris.

Miyako Spa
Miyako Hotel, 328 E. 1st St., Los Angeles 90012
(Between Central & San Pedro)
213.617.0004, miyakoinn.com

Hours: Daily 3 p.m.–midnight; last appointment at 10 p.m. Appointment required for massage; walk-ins accepted for spa.

Facilities: On the third floor of the Miyako Hotel, this spa caters primarily to hotel guests but makes a pleasant getaway for locals. A recent upgrade of the hotel bypassed the spa, which could use a touch-up. Nonetheless, it is quaint. The largest room is the warmly lit massage room, with eight beds. Even at capacity, it doesn't feel crowded, thanks to the separate men's and women's rest areas.

What to expect: The spa will provide you with a robe, towels and sandals. The shiatsu massage is given on a table in an open room that holds seven other tables. If you're uncomfortable about being uncovered, ask for a pair of disposable boxers. The treatment starts face down, and ends face up. Let your therapist know if there are areas

you'd like her to work more and she will. If not, you'll get a full massage from head to toe.

Services offered: Shiatsu massage, sauna, hot tub, cold tub, exercise room, showers and vanity area. The hot tub fits two people max, and the saunas (dry and steam) accommodate three comfortably.

Parking: On the street or in the hotel, although the latter is a bit pricey.

Why we like it: After a long day of exploring Little Tokyo and the Japanese American Museum, you can pop into the Miyako, relax in a clean, quiet spa and let the shiatsu settle your nerves and relax your mind.

Tokyo Spa
211 S. Central Ave., Los Angeles 90012
(Near 2nd)
213.617.1234

Hours: Daily 11 a.m.–10 p.m.

Facilities: Located across from Honda Plaza, this tiny, no-frills spa offers a nice shiatsu massage. Extras include a Jacuzzi that seats four, two shower stalls and a small dry sauna. The main massage room has six tables.

What to expect: The shiatsu massage is done on a table in an open room. You'll be given a nightgown-type top and a pair of shorts. The massage is done with your spa clothes on and usually a sheet over you. Even though you're in the room with other people, once the massage begins, you forget them and begin to relax.

Services offered: Shiatsu massage, hot tub and sauna.

Parking: Street or in Honda Plaza.

Why we like it: We like to get a massage after work, before going to one of the many fine nearby restaurants for dinner. Because of its central location, Tokyo Spa is convenient for many Angelenos, and it's clean. Women and seniors get a ten percent discount on Wednesdays.

While you're there: Try our favorite shabu-shabu restaurant, Kagaya, which is known for its exceptional ingredients, including Kobe and Wagyu beef. The best part of the meal comes when you finish eating all the meat, fish and veggies; they take the pot back into the kitchen and turn the rich broth into a thick soup with your choice of rice or udon. Save room for this part—it's divine!

BEYOND LITTLE TOKYO

DOWNEY

Japan Shiatsu Massage Center
8641 Firestone Blvd., Downey 90241
(West of Lakewood Blvd.)
562.862.5111, japanshiatsu.com

Hours: Mon.–Fri. 10 a.m.–8 p.m.; Sat. 10 a.m.–6 p.m.; Sun. 10 a.m.–5 p.m.

Facilities: Established in 1977, this spa specializes in finger shiatsu. Most of the technicians were trained at the first Shiatsu Institute in Japan and have been practicing the technique for many years. Their keen sense of touch enables them to sense your body's tender and unhealthy areas.

What to expect: When you arrive at the front desk, you'll be given a robe and towels and directed to the appropriate locker room, where you'll change into a pair of boxers and the robe. You can make use of the dry sauna, wet sauna and whirlpool tub; just make sure to shower before entering these areas. Sandals are not provided; you should bring your own. Once you've warmed up, put on your robe and head to the main waiting room until you're summoned. The massage will be in a large room partitioned by curtains. The tatami mats and mattresses are on platforms that you step up onto; remove your shoes and enter. The massage starts with you lying on your side. You keep your robe and boxers on throughout. The therapist uses a thin cotton cloth on any exposed areas; his fingers never touch your skin. Lying on your side, you place you head on a buckwheat pillow, and you'll be given other pillows to hold and for your legs. The massage starts at your head and neck and works down to your legs and feet. Then you turn over to your other side and the same process happens again. After your sides are massaged, you'll lie face down, and the massage will continue from your head to your toes. It concludes with you lying on your back.

Services offered: Shiatsu massage, plus dry and wet sauna, whirlpool tub, showers, vanity and lockers.

Rolling Hills Shiatsu Center

Parking: Parking lot in front.

Why we like it: This was one of the best shiatsu massages we've ever had! The center is clean and authentic, the staff is nice and respectful, and the massage area is quiet and calming. The attention to detail makes the experience delightful—you can tell you're in the hands of a master shiatsu therapist. Come at least 30 minutes early to enjoy the sauna.

GARDENA

Hide's Shiatsu
Gateway Plaza, 1425 W. Artesia Blvd., #31, Gardena 90248
(At S. Normandie)
310.538.3959

Hours: Daily 10 a.m.–11 p.m.

Facilities: Located in a large mall, Hide's offers walk-in shiatsu massage on a massage table. White curtains separate the six beds, allowing for some privacy.

What to expect: Keep on your clothes, take off your shoes, put your belongings in a little plastic box and lie down on the table. The therapist will cover you with a thin white sheet and massage whatever part of your body needs attention.

Services offered: Shiatsu massage.

Parking: Big lot in front.

Why we like it: You can walk in without an appointment and get a nice, quick massage for 15, 30 or 60 minutes. Very clean, and the staff is professional.

Quick Massage
15484 S. Western Ave., Gardena 90249
(At Redondo Beach Blvd.)
310.527.4332, quickmassage.us

Hours: Daily 9 a.m.–midnight; no treatments after 11 p.m. Walk-ins accepted.

Facilities: Located in Tozai Plaza, this facility is primarily one large, open room with good natural lighting. When you walk in, you'll see seven cot-size raised beds on the diagonal, and the nice green and white décor. One room is curtained to allow for a more private massage.

What to expect: You remain fully clothed, taking off only your shoes. You begin face down, head cradled in the head rest. You'll be covered with a sheet that the therapist works through. After the back side is complete, you'll be asked to turn over for the remainder of your treatment.

Services offered: Shiatsu massage treatments that range from 15 minutes to two hours. Ask about the discount coupons for multiple visits. Gift certificates available.

Parking: Ample free parking in Tozai Plaza.

Why we like it: Another great shiatsu center; the 15-minute massage affords a great way to try shiatsu if you haven't before.

LOS ANGELES

LA Shiatsu
3807 W. 8th St., Los Angeles 90005
(Koreatown, corner Western)
213.387.5555

Hours: Daily 10 a.m.–10 p.m.

Facilities: Originally a Japanese establishment, LA Shiatsu is now run by Koreans, and they've modified the shiatsu massage to include hot oil. The place is in an old building that could use some sprucing up, but the staff is friendly, and the interior is clean.

What to expect: We were asked to pay first, which is not unusual. There are six rooms with massage tables. You'll be given a light robe to slip into and can either leave your undergarments on or take them off. The beds are heated, and the massage lasts 50 minutes.

Services: LA Shiatsu offers one type of service: a 50-minute massage that consists of 30 minutes of acupressure and 20 minutes of hot oil. If you want hard pressure, the therapist will walk on your back.

Parking: Lot in back with plenty of parking.

Why we like it: The massage therapists were very professional and asked us constantly about the pressure and if we were okay. The hot oil was a nice addition.

TORRANCE

Rolling Hills Shiatsu Center
Rolling Hills Plaza, 2505 Pacific Coast Hwy.,
Torrance 90505
(Near Anza)
310.325.7756, happyshiatsu.com

Hours: Daily 10 a.m.–7 p.m.

Facilities: This small storefront has three separate rooms, sectioned off by drapes. Large charts of the body's pressure points are on the walls. The owner is a shiatsu master.

What to expect: You can change into the center's pants and top or keep on your own clothes. We've done the latter. The massage starts on your side with a pillow between your knees. Your body and head are covered with a thin towel. Finger pressure is applied in a systematic manner, at specific points, to unblock energy and release toxins. The massage starts with the head and neck and progresses to the feet. Once the feet are done, you roll over to the other side and repeat.

Services: Japanese shiatsu and chair massage.

Parking: Plenty in the shopping center lot.

Why we like it: It's a cozy place with a neighborhood feel and lots of regulars, which is a testament to the effectiveness of shiatsu.

Spa Relaken
Miyako Hybrid Hotel, 21381 S. Western Ave.,
Torrance 90501
(At 213th)
310.212.6408, relaken.com

Hours: Daily 10 a.m.–9 p.m.

Facilities: Located on the first floor of the Miyako Hybrid Hotel, it caters to guests but is open to the public. This is a beautifully decorated spa with thoughtful touches. The décor and accents set the tone for what's to come. There are separate men's and women's dressing areas; only the hot-stone room is co-ed. It features six generously sized massage rooms and one couple's room, all with plushly padded bed-like tables. The focus on hospitality is palpable.

Spa Relaken

What to expect: Take some time to rest in the waiting room, and sip some hot tea to start the relaxation process. They'll give you a top and long shorts and lockers in which to store your clothes. Take advantage of the *ganban-yoku*, the hot-stone spa, a half-hour before your treatment, but be sure to drink water every 15 minutes or so. Large glass dispensers of lemon water are in the hallway just outside, so staying hydrated is easy. Your therapist will come get you (or awaken you, if needed) for your massage. We had a classic shiatsu massage. It was fabulous!

The *ganban-yoku* is a Japanese ritual that involves bathing without water, by lying on heated stones in a sauna-like room. The room is kept at high humidity to encourage sweating. It is deeply soothing.

Services: Shiatsu, deep-tissue and Swedish massage, plus reflexology and Reiki. Purchase of a massage treatment entitles you to use the hot-stone spa. You may opt to pay the entrance fee to use the Jacuzzi and sauna and forgo a body treatment, but it won't get you into the *ganban-yoku*—and you shouldn't miss it. It also offers specialized aroma treatments, including one with essential oils, a Balinese aroma, and Thai herbal ball treatment, as well as facials. All spa amenities (shampoo, conditioner, blow dryer, body lotion, and more) are provided. A membership deal brings discount privileges. It's worth it if you, like us, want to try everything.

Parking: Plenty in the hotel's lot.

Why we like it: It's just such a gorgeous place—you feel better simply by sitting in the lobby. The spa has package deals that include a bento-box-style healthy lunch with your treatment. What a great idea! Be sure to pop in the Japanese market just behind on Western Avenue while you're in the neighborhood.

Chapter 6 – **Chinese**

CHINESE TORTURE TREATMENTS

Upon entering a communal foot-reflexology room, we passed a Chinese woman on her way out. She moaned and said, "Chinese torture treatment," spurring an epiphanic, "*Ah-ha*" kind of moment. Between her groans, this woman hit the nail on the head, providing the perfect description for what most call a rather "rigorous" massage.

We've read the complaints online—people are shocked when arms and legs are picked up and dropped, when backs, heels, legs and butts are slapped mercilessly, and when fingers are stuck in ears, followed by two-fisted karate chops to the head. By Swedish massage standards, this is rough and invasive treatment. Knowing that foot reflexology and body massage are done fully clothed provides little solace.

The Chinese have an affection for pain. At Dana Foot Massage, Mr. Lee said, "Pain? Pain is good!" We got the message. "Pain" is one word you won't have to learn in Chinese. The Chinese communicate it through action. Remember, this is a therapeutic massage used to treat a problem; it is not intended to be a soothing experience to lull you to sleep.

In general, much more thought is put into the treatment than to the ambience. The Chinese aesthetic demands that the facilities be set up for efficiency, with plain, sterile, communal spaces meant to maximize the number of patrons treated. Nevertheless, Chinese massage is an ancient healing art. Keep reading to rid yourself of negative preconceptions and worries about this adventurous experience.

CHINESE MASSAGE

Traditional Chinese therapeutic massage, called *tui na*, is based on the body systems of Chinese medicine. As with acupuncture, tui na utilizes the meridian system, or channels, through which energy flows through the body. This system comprises two meridians following the midline of the body as well as symmetrical meridians on both sides of the body, each related to a specific organ. The Chinese have identified many pressure points along each meridian.

The philosophical approach suggests that disease disrupts the body's flow of energy, so meridians become congested and imbalanced. This is manifested by pain and/or weakness. Meridians may be unblocked and restored to balance through pressure stimulation with acupuncture, acupressure and/or massage.

Tui na means "pushing-grasping," hinting at the masseuse's inclination to brush, knead, roll, stretch, pull, press, tap and rub the area along acupressure points, meridians and between joints to stimulate the flow of blood and energy and to promote healing. These techniques are particularly useful in alleviating muscle, joint and bone pain. It's a great massage for those seeking a focused therapy to treat chronic problem areas, such as the lower back and the shoulders. Stimulation of acupuncture points balances internal organs, so this therapy is also effective for those with digestive problems and insomnia. Chinese massage may be used in conjunction with acupuncture, cupping, compresses and Chinese herbs. There are several different methods or schools of tui na massage, so no two tui na massages will be alike.

You can tell a Chinese reflexology place by the foot reflexology picture in the window. Throughout this chapter are examples of the sort of signs you may see.

Although the charts detail the area of the body and the corresponding internal organs, it's more complex than that. For example, eye problems are often associated with poor kidney and liver functions, and pressure points control the various systems of the body, such as circulatory, reproductive, lymphatic and nervous systems.

CHINESE FOOT MASSAGE: REFLEXOLOGY

The best place to start your Chinese massage experience is with foot reflexology. Reflexology isn't much of a full-body massage, because there isn't any rubbing until the end of the treatment. The focus is on the pressure or reflex points of the feet, hands, face and ears. Based on an ancient Chinese system, reflexology is grounded in the notion that the nerve endings in these areas correspond to all muscles and organs in the body. Whereas massage is applied to the muscles and soft tissues of the body, reflexology focuses on the nerve endings. This technique affects the reflexes, not

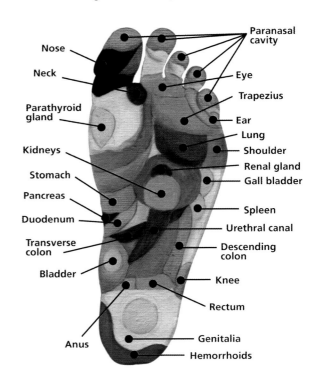

just the surface of the skin. Therefore, reflexology of these pressure points is said to stimulate the internal organs and improve circulation, contributing to healing. Some of the benefits of reflexology are instantaneous; others may take several treatments to achieve.

Before the treatment, the therapist will soak your feet in a bucket filled with hot water or a tea bath of Chinese herbs. You will remain fully clothed but need to dress appropriately in loose clothing like pants that can be rolled up over your knees. Because your legs get bent and moved about, a skirt or dress is a regrettable choice. You might sit on an ottoman as your feet soak while the therapist massages your neck and shoulders. Or you might recline in a large chair and receive a face and head massage while your feet soak. Or they might simply cover you with towels and allow you to rest, undisturbed. After your feet soak for about ten minutes, the therapist removes the soaking bucket and towels. A traditional Chinese reflexology treatment is usually dry, with no lubricant, but we've seen many using lotions ranging from slick baby oil to thicker creams, probably to make the treatment more palatable. The pressure is firm and done in sweeping movements on the various points of the feet. This includes between the toes, on the tops of the feet and around the ankles. Tools of a reflexology therapist are thumbs, fingers, knuckles and often a wooden or plastic implement with rounded ends. Some therapists wear thin latex gloves.

While this can be a relaxing treatment, it is not a typical first response. According to Chinese reflexology, if you don't feel any sharp pain, you're healthy. But if you do feel some pain, the painful spots correspond to illnesses in corresponding parts of the body. You also might find that you have pain on only one side of the body. This is an indication of imbalance. Don't be surprised if a spot or two on the bottom of your feet makes you jump. Because of the firmness of the treatment, the ticklish don't usually suffer.

Foot reflexology includes some body massage, but the time spent on your body versus your feet can vary. And you can expect your face, head, ears, neck, shoulders, arms, backs and fronts of legs and your butt (yes, your butt) to be massaged. Whether you are getting foot reflexology or a full-body massage, you are fully clothed and covered with a towel at all times.

THE BODY MASSAGE

You are typically (although not always) fully clothed for this, and it may be performed in the same large, reclining foot-reflexology chair or in a raised bed in another room. Thin white towels or sheets cover your body, and, surprisingly, the masseuse is able to work effectively through them. Massaging the meridians releases muscle tension and promotes healing by improving the flow of energy. There is slapping, light hitting and karate chopping of just about every body part. The best advice we can give is to know what's coming and keep a slack jaw.

Cupping: Cupping, sometimes called fire cupping, is an ancient method of applying acupressure. It involves using small cups to create suction on the body by generating a vacuum. Typically a match is extinguished inside the glass, plastic or bamboo cup, and immediately thereafter the practitioner places the cup on your back along the meridians. This forms an air-tight seal, causing the blood to rise to the surface of the skin.

The process opens the meridians and allows the internal energy to move freely throughout the body. If the cups are left alone, an even stronger suction is created, which pulls your skin into the cup. Our favorite practice involves a little oil used on the back before the cups are put in place. This way, the therapist can move the cups around, creating a pleasant-feeling suction. Cupping may also be used on your neck, shoulders and the backs of the upper arms. After the cups are removed, you'll be left with telltale dark red circles, reminiscent of a hickey, but on your back. The longer the cup stays in one place, the more intense the coloring. These will last a couple of weeks, which is why you might choose this therapy during the winter months. Any backless, strapless, halter-top or even short-sleeve shirt will reveal your cupping experience and have people talking. The treatment should not be painful, but you may feel a minor discomfort as skin is pulled into each cup. Talk a friend into doing this with you; it really is worth experiencing and something you'll be talking about for a long time.

Scraping: Also known as *gua sha*, this treatment involves scraping the body (back, shoulders, chest, inner elbow, inner knee) with a smooth, hard object, traditionally a porcelain spoon or large coin, but nowadays often a plastic rectangle about the size of a credit card. Although the result is often large, nasty-looking bruises, it usually does not hurt, and the bruises signify the release of toxins. The principle is similar to acupuncture—the scraping stimulates critical points in the body and is supposed to treat everything from sunstroke and food poisoning to measles. It's also used in regular therapeutic massage, although it's not seen nearly as often as cupping and acupuncture.

A FEW WORDS IN MANDARIN

ENGLISH	MANDARIN PRONUNCIATION
Hello	nee hao
Good-bye	zai jie-an
Yes	shrr
No	boo shrr
Thank you	shey shey
Pain	tong

CHINATOWN

Chinatown is located north of downtown Los Angeles, just north of the 101 freeway and just east of the 110 freeway. It's bordered by Hill Street on the west, Cesar Chavez Avenue on the south, and Olvera Street on the east. The main streets are Broadway, Spring and Hill. The Gold Line rail station at Chinatown Metro efficiently transports to and from this community.

HISTORY

Chinatown is one of the oldest ethnic communities in Los Angeles. In 1880, its original location was around Alameda and Macy, where Union Station is today. At its peak in the late 1890s until 1910, Chinatown had 15 streets and 200 buildings. During that time, despite heavy discrimination, Chinese immigrants dominated the laundry and produce industries, and they also worked as gardeners, ranch hands and day laborers. At that time laws prohibited their citizenship, which eliminated such rights as owning property and voting. After 1910 Chinatown began a gradual decline, fueled by crime and corruption, and eventually was demolished to make way for Union Station.

Present-day Chinatown was constructed 1938, largely through the efforts of Peter Soo Hoo, Sr., a Chinese-American community leader. He led the collective effort to design, fund and establish a new Chinatown. The project was bolstered by Central Plaza, the first mall to be owned and operated by Chinese. You can see Chinese architectural design elements and symbols throughout the complex. In the 1980s, Chinatown expanded, adding several shopping centers.

Its dramatic architecture makes Chinatown a popular location for film crews. Jackie Chan's movie *Rush Hour* was filmed there, as well as the concluding scenes of the film *Chinatown*, which were shot on Spring Street.

Today, older enterprises from the 1930s and 1940s and businesses built in the 1980s share the neighborhood, and you see a wider variety of ethnic groups. Some of the newer immigrants include Cambodians, Cantonese, Taishanese (a dialect of one of the southern provinces in China) and Vietnamese.

Chinatown is a worthwhile destination with an abundance of notable landmarks. Whether you have company in town or want to do a solo walk around the neighborhood, you'll enjoy the experience. While Central Plaza was the first shopping center in this area, there are several others: Far East Plaza on North Broadway, West Plaza, Chinatown Plaza and Mandarin Plaza on Bernard Street. Great architecture, authentic restaurants, art galleries, herbal stores, tea shops, grocery stores and bakeries only surmount the tip of the cultural iceberg when exploring the nooks and crannies of this still-evolving community.

You can experience Chinatown in all its finery by attending the Chinese Lantern Festival. Also known as the Spring Festival, this happening ends the 15-day celebration of Chinese New Year and is celebrated the night of the first full moon of the lunar New Year. The date changes every year, because it's based on the Chinese calendar, a complex combination of solar and lunar calendars. During this two-week period, people make a fresh start, hoping to carry purity and luck into the upcoming year. It is a time for family honor, reconciliation, atonement and gratitude. Many practices commemorate this new beginning, from cleaning house to wearing brand-new clothes. Eating *tang yuan*, round balls of sticky rice flour stuffed with different fillings, is a big part of the Lantern Festival celebration. This treat symbolizes the key values memorialized through this celebration: family unity, reconciliation and good fortune. It's a great time to experience a traditional Chinese village street fair, complete with displays, performances, books, arts and crafts and, of course, delicious food.

For information on monthly tours of Chinatown (the first Saturday of the month) as well as other interesting cultural events, go to chinatownla.com.

SAN GABRIEL VALLEY

The largest concentration of Chinese now live in the San Gabriel Valley, the 30-mile strip that parallels the 10 and 60 freeways, extending from Monterey Park to Diamond Bar. Packed with restaurants, bakeries, dumpling houses and tea shops, it's known as the Chinese food capital of America, so it's no surprise that it houses hundreds of foot-reflexology and body-massage places. Many of the workers seem to be employed in both industries, and we've found it common that when there's a good Chinese restaurant, there's usually a massage facility nearby. Staffing is frequently flexible, and a quick call can bring in a rush of massage therapists on a particularly busy day. This doesn't mean they are not trained; we've found quite the opposite to be true.

You'll find a plethora of Chinese restaurants, jewelry stores, hair salons, small businesses and clothing and home furnishing shops along Valley Boulevard in the city of San Gabriel and on the main streets of neighboring Alhambra. Any shopping center likely will have at least one massage business. The cars on Valley Boulevard are packed like sardines on Friday nights (they don't call it Chinese Disneyland for nothing). Our advice is to get there early and plan on making right turns only.

CHINESE MASSAGE IN THE SAN GABRIEL VALLEY

ALHAMBRA

Ajenn Spa
600 W. Main St., Ste. 108, Alhambra 91801
(Corner 6th, east of Atlantic)
626.281.3486 or 626.284.8822

Hours: Mon.–Fri. 10 a.m.–10 p.m.; Sat.–Sun. noon–10 p.m.

Facilities: A small place with just two rooms, used strictly for massage.

What to expect: A heavy-handed, intense massage with hard-hitting strokes on your legs and back. They'll charge you $4 extra if you pay by credit card.

Services offered: Foot massage, herbal treatment, Swedish massage.

Parking: Lot behind.

Why we like it: It's perfect for the more masochistic of massage-goers.

Anthony's Asian Massage Therapy
429 S. Garfield Ave., Alhambra 91801
(Between Main & Mission)
626.289.7428, anthonysmedspa.com

Hours: Mon.–Fri. 10 a.m.–10 p.m.; Sat.–Sun. noon–10 p.m.

Facilities: What this locale lacks in outward beauty it makes up for in privacy. The reception area is dimly lit, as are the massage rooms.

What to expect: Completely disrobe or undress in accordance to your comfort level. The masseuse will cover you with a thin sheet, leaving only the areas of focus bare. For the full-body acupressure massage, pressure was rhythmically applied along the body's meridians. Although we did not request the combo massage, which includes an oiled-up Swedish massage, she did it anyway. We went with it, but be sure to insist on specifics if you care. The masseuse, it turned out, knew best: We found the massage (combo and all) so incredibly relaxing that we asked for an extended session.

Services offered: Full-body acupressure, Swedish, combo and deep-tissue massage, facials and waxing.

Parking: In back, off Garfield.

Why we like it: Do what the locals do: Ask for Eileen.

ARCADIA

Arcadia Spa
28 E. Duarte Rd., Arcadia 91006
(At Santa Anita)
626.445.4800, bestarcadiaspa.com

Hours: Daily 9:30 a.m.–9 p.m.

Facilities: An intimate setting: four private rooms with massage tables and curtains for doors, plus two big recliners for foot massage.

What to expect: We had the table massage, and it was a delight. Spacious, private rooms and an attentive therapist provide a fantastic experience.

Services offered: Reflexology, deep-tissue and Swedish massage, ear candling, sea-salt scrub.

Parking: Lot.

Why we like it: The staff really knows how to maintain a spotless spa and professional work ethic.

Happy Day Spa
308 S. 1st Ave., #C, Arcadia 91006
(Corner of California)
626.254.8519

Hours: Daily 10 a.m.–9 p.m.

Facilities: This relatively new place offers Chinese body massage on a table. It has just five rooms, all made private with curtains.

What to expect: Take off your clothes and slip under the sheet in your quiet, private room. The therapists are adept at a variety of massage techniques. You can also take a refreshing shower after your massage.

Services offered: Chinese massage, facials, waxing.

Parking: On the street.

Why we like it: We love Connie and Sherie, two truly talented masseuses.

Happy Day Spa

Magic Hands Spa
145 E. Duarte Rd., Arcadia 91006
(Between 1st & 2nd)
626.254.8839, magichandsspa.com

Hours: Daily 10 a.m.–9 p.m.

Facilities: In a little strip mall, this combination spa and skin-care salon is a true find.

What to expect: Not as intense as many Chinese massages, this one is exceptional. You'll be asked to take off your clothes and lie face-down under a sheet.

Services offered: Foot and hot-oil massage, deep-tissue, Swedish, plus waxing and skin treatments.

Parking: Lot in front.

Why we like it: Amanda, the owner, may well be the most skilled therapist we've ever had. Her massage proved unbelievable as she maneuvered herself with the assistance of the bars in the ceiling. We don't know if it was her feet or her hands doing the work, and we don't care. It was a fantastic, mind-bending experience.

Orient Retreat
1007 S. Baldwin Ave., Arcadia 91006
(At Duarte Rd.)
626.254.9588, orientretreat.com

Hours: Daily 9 a.m.–8 p.m.

Facilities: This small, women-only spa and boutique has a eucalyptus steam room, a sauna sans Jacuzzi, white couches in the lounge, and private massage rooms.

What to expect: The immaculate, brightly lit lounge area is a perfect place to snack on refreshments before or after your treatment. We had body massages in private rooms. The staff escorts you to your treatment room, showing you around the spa and making sure you're comfortable. The

Orient Retreat

rooms are warm and cozy. We liked the thoughtful extras, like the cold facial towels in the refrigerator.

Services offered: Massage, salt scrub, stone therapy, facials, skin care.

Parking: Lot in front.

Why we like it: A true oasis with a focus on relaxation done right. We loved the atmosphere and the luxurious pampering; we can't wait to return.

While you're there: A great place for lunch or dinner is Bean Sprouts (103 E. Huntington Dr., 626.254.8708), an excellent vegetarian restaurant. Try the pan-fried radish patties (extra crispy) and the noodles with curry sauce.

HACIENDA HEIGHTS

Dynasty Foot Spa
17110-F Colima Rd., Hacienda Heights 91745
(Bixby Hacienda Plaza, corner Azusa)
626.965.2319

Hours: Daily 10 a.m.–11 p.m.

Facilities: Located in a mall, this foot reflexology spa has ten reclining chairs and six massage tables located in the back, all partitioned by curtains.

What to expect: Your typical Chinese foot spa, with piping-hot foot soaks and unwinding foot rubs.

Services offered: Foot soaks and foot and body massages.

Parking: Lot in front.

Why we like it: A fantastically inexpensive opportunity to take a load off and brush up on your Mandarin.

Heavenly Soaking Foot Massage
3148 Colima Rd., Hacienda Heights 91745
(Between Hacienda & Avalo)
626.968.0022

Hours: Sun.–Thurs. 10 a.m.–10 p.m.;
Fri.–Sat. 10 a.m.–11 p.m.

Facilities: Ten chairs in the communal area and two private rooms in the back. Also in the back are three specialty chairs for back massage only. Although the lights are dim, you can still see the big-screen TV on the wall; when we visited, thankfully, the sound was on mute.

What to expect: The staff uses hand sanitizers before the massage. We chose the foot-body combo and received a traditional service. No complaints whatsoever. It was a great massage at a bargain price.

Services offered: Reflexology and full-body and combo massages.

Parking: Plenty in the shopping center.

Why we like it: Signs posted ask patrons to silence cell phones, which fulfilled our desire for a silent, calm environment. For a good massage without an appointment, request Vincent.

JCS Foot Massage
1669 S. Azusa Ave., Hacienda Heights 91745
(Corner Colima, south of the 60 Fwy.)
626.839.8888 or 626.322.8313

Hours: Daily 9 a.m.–11 p.m.

Facilities: Located in the 99 Ranch Market mall, this is a large place with a light and breezy interior. Curtains partition the space to accommodate 11 reclining chairs and six tables.

What to expect: It's a lovely setting for a foot or full-body massage. You can remove your clothes or keep them on for the body massage.

Services offered: Foot, body and combination massages.

Parking: Lot in front.

Why we like it: It's roomy, and the massage chairs have lots of space between them, so you feel like you're in your own private space. It's very clean, and the staff is professional.

Royal Health Spa
1020 S. Hacienda Blvd., Hacienda Heights 91745
(At Gale, behind the Mobil station)
626.369.8484

Hours: Daily 8 a.m.–11 p.m.

Facilities: Ugly from the outside, it's quite attractive inside. It's a mostly Korean spa, complete with sit-down showers, saunas, hot and cold tubs, and body-scrub tables, but there's also a large area for Chinese foot massages, which is what we're addressing here. (See the Korean chapter for details on the other stuff.)

What to expect: The foot-massage area is located on one end of the facility, with nine big reclining chairs. The foot soak is divine, because the area is spacious, and there's no TV. The massage focuses primarily on the feet, but the therapist will briefly loosen up the rest of your body. You'll remain fully clothed for this massage, but if you opt for the Korean body scrub, of course, you'll have to strip.

Services offered: Foot and body massage, facials, body scrubs.

Parking: Lot in front or on the side.

Why we like it: Despite the eyesore of a building, the place is very clean and the staff are very helpful and professional, and treatments are often a bargain.

Sun Fa's Room
15865 E. Gale Ave., D & E, Hacienda Heights 91745
(Between Hacienda & Stimson)
626.968.7890, haciendafootmassage.com

Hours: Daily 10 a.m.–9:30 p.m.

Facilities: In a communal room off the small reception area are nine chairs in three rows, all facing a wall with a large-screen TV flanked by two big red Chinese lanterns. The TV is on but muted. Two private rooms have massage tables.

What to expect: We had the foot and body massage in the comfortable communal area, where the chairs aren't too close to one another. One of our massages followed the Chinese conventions, except at the end. We had a masseuse who must be a drummer on the side. He had an unusual syncopation going on that was quite musical. If you have to get slapped at the end of a massage, you might as well get slapped in rhythm. It was the most dramatic finish we've ever had.

Services offered: Foot reflexology and body massage.

Parking: A half-dozen spots out front.

Why we like it: Check the website for discount coupons, but even the regular prices make us feel like we're stealing. Ask for Charlie if you like a big, drummer-style finish.

MONROVIA

Relax Station Foot Massage
414 W. Foothill Blvd., Monrovia 91016
(In the 7-11 center)
626.357.3898, relaxationstationfootmassage.com

Hours: Daily 10 a.m.–10 p.m.

Facilities: There's good signage from the street, and inside the communal room is nicely laid out with two rows of chairs. The place also has a treatment room and a doctor's office.

What to expect: Since it's in our neighborhood, we came here for a last-minute, midweek massage, and it did not disappoint. The treatment was authentic and followed standard protocol—nothing out of the ordinary, but a good one.

Services offered: Reflexology and foot and chair massage. Gift cards available.

Parking: In the 7-11 lot.

Why we like it: It's a nice neighborhood place and a great value, with easy parking and an authentic foot massage. Ask for Jerry.

MONTEREY PARK

Atlantic Beauty & Foot Spa
138 S. Atlantic Blvd., Monterey Park 91754
(Deerfield Plaza, corner Garvey)
626.293.1789

Hours: Daily 9 a.m.–11 p.m.

Facilities: The reception area separates two sides of this spa, which has 14 massage chairs. Inside the dark communal room is a big-screen TV, but it was turned off when we visited.

What to expect: You can expect a wonderful foot and body treatment here. They use unscented lotion for the face, neck and ear portion of the massage, and at our last visit, our therapist used gloves and gave us an exfoliating scrub on the feet and calves.

Services offered: Foot and body massage, Thai shampoo, facials, waxing and nails.

Parking: Plenty in Deerfield Plaza.

Why we like it: It's nice, clean and quiet. For a gentle, soothing, rhythmic massage, ask for Luna.

Huang's Healing Foot Massage
313 E. Garvey Ave., Monterey Park 91756
(Jade Plaza)
626.258.9848

Hours: Daily 11 a.m.–11 p.m.

Facilities: This mini-mall place is recognizable by the red lanterns hanging out front. It's nicely decorated inside, with dim lighting, nine chairs for reflexology in the communal room off the entry, and a private room with two massage tables. There is, alas, a large TV on the wall, but when we visited the sound was muted.

What to expect: Traditional foot reflexology that includes a good whole-body massage.

Services offered: Foot reflexology and full-body massage.

Parking: Plenty of space in Jade Plaza.

Huang's Healing Foot Massage

Why we like it: It's one of the rare Chinese massage facilities that is truly quiet inside. It's so relaxing that one patron at the other end of the room was snoring—always the sign of a good massage!

While you're there: Pop into Kee Wah Bakery, just down the street at 729 W. Garvey, and pick up some delicious pastries and bread.

PASADENA

A Beautiful Day Spa
965 E. Colorado Blvd., Pasadena 91106
(One block east of Lake)
626.578.9999, beautifuldayspa.com

Hours: Daily 10 a.m.–10 p.m.

Facilities: Four private rooms with massage tables and a small communal area between the rooms with three chairs for foot reflexology. It's clean and attractively decorated, with white patterned screens between the chairs.

What to expect: They can usually handle walk-ins. In the small reception room, you'll be asked to complete a brief intake form and to pay in advance.

Services offered: Foot reflexology, Swedish, deep-tissue and four-hands massage, acupuncture and facials. Gift cards available.

Parking: Free street parking on Mentor, Colorado and Catalina, but you might have to walk a bit.

Why we like it: It was a terrific massage in a pleasant setting at an amazing rate. Ask for Annie. It's on the same block as one of our favorite cheapie theaters, the Academy. Massage and a movie—now that's a great combo.

Body Healing Center
187 N. Hill St., Pasadena 91106
(Corner Walnut)
626.795.6670, bodyhealingcenter.com

Hours: Daily 10 a.m.–10 p.m.

Facilities: A corner spot with six private rooms, all with massage tables. The little steam sauna feels great before or after your massage.

What to expect: The therapists will do whatever type of massage you like. The place is clean, and the rooms are private. We walked in and got immediate service, although we always recommend making an appointment first just in case.

Services offered: Reflexology, acupressure and Swedish, deep-tissue, hot-oil and combination massages.

Parking: Lot on the side; enter from Hill Street.

Why we like it: The sauna is a nice extra.

Green Tree Massage Therapy
2525 Foothill Blvd., #3, Pasadena 91107
(Corner Altadena)
626.796.8854, greentreemassage.com

Hours: Daily 10 a.m.–10 p.m.

Facilities: This strip-mall place has five massage rooms, one couple's room and two showers, one with powerful dual shower heads and the other with a rain-style shower head.

What to expect: Pay first. If you wish, you can shower before your massage. After the shower, the therapist will show you into your room, where you'll undress and lie down on the table. The spa makes its own massage oil with olive oil; if you opt to have a hot olive oil massage (not a bad idea), you'll be wiped down afterward with a hot towel.

Services offered: Full-body and hot-oil massage, reflexology.

Parking: Lot in the mall, or behind the store through the alley (enter on Del Rey Avenue).

Why we like it: Of the massage places in East Pasadena, this is the cleanest and most professional. We also like the weekend specials; check the website for details.

Heart & Sole
163 W. Green St., Pasadena 91105
626.578.9933, heartandsolereflexology.com

Hours: Mon.–Thurs. 11 a.m.–11 p.m.; Fri.–Sun. 10 a.m.–midnight.

CHINESE

Facilities: Located in prime Old Town, this clean, modern space has large reclining chairs and a dark, quiet room with soothing music. No TV and no talking.

What to expect: A foot soak and a fully clothed, full-body massage, all while sitting/lying in a comfy chair. You can walk in at off hours, but if you want to come at the popular lunchtime and after-work hours, make an appointment.

Services offered: Foot soak, body massage, reflexology.

Parking: Street meters.

Why we like it: No TV, no talking and no cell phones, and the therapists focus on you and are not busy answering the phone or chatting among themselves. A surprisingly good value given the high-rent neighborhood.

ROSEMEAD

Alibaba Foot Spa
8518 Valley Blvd., #B106, Rosemead 91770
(New Valley Plaza, near Walnut Grove)
626.288.1230

Hours: Daily 10 a.m.–9 p.m.

Facilities: This large place seems to serve as a community center. It was bustling the day we visited, with lots of patrons and workers rushing around. We got in right away without an appointment and promptly reclined in one of the sixteen chairs in the common room.

What to expect: The full-body massage was traditional. While we sat on a stool and our feet soaked in a tea bath, the therapist worked on our head, neck and shoulders. Moving to the chair, we got prone and covered with a

towel. The massage proceeded through the towel on our backs and backsides. When we turned over, the therapist moved to the face, head, ears and hair, then to the arms and hands, and finally to the feet. Then she proceeded with some compression up the legs to the hip flexors, concluding with a final slapping and hitting on the legs.

Services offered: Foot and full-body massage.

Parking: In the shopping center lot.

Why we like it: A great massage at an excellent price.

While you're there: Check out a terrific Chinese vegetarian restaurant, New Happy Family (8632-E E. Valley Blvd., 626.288.5786). It has great vegetable and tofu dishes.

Franklyn Palace Massage
8450 E. Valley Blvd., Ste. 101, Rosemead 91770
(One block west of Walnut Grove)
626.571.1088

Hours: Daily 9 a.m.–9 p.m.

Facilities: Located in the back of a mall, this is quite a big place. The foot-massage area has 12 reclining chairs, and the body-massage area has seven private rooms with quarter-length curtains as doors.

What to expect: The guy who runs the reception is helpful and knowledgeable. We had a foot massage and a body massage, both of which were quite thorough and professionally executed. Signs throughout remind you that this is a professional massage place.

Services offered: Foot reflexology and body massage.

Parking: Lot in the mall.

Why we like it: It's an older place that could use some freshening, but the massage was great. For the price, you can't beat it.

ROWLAND HEIGHTS

Avant Rowland Heights Reflexology Center
1788 Sierra Leone Ave., #211, Rowland Heights 91748
(Ruby Plaza, off Jellick)
626.581.1868, avantrhts.com

Hours: Daily 11 a.m.–11 p.m.

Facilities: A great find in an upstairs corner of Ruby Plaza, Avant is stocked with 15 large reclining chairs for foot massages and five private rooms (one is a couple's double room) for full-body massages. Everything is clean and modern, the place is quiet, and the surroundings are lovely.

What to expect: You'll be greeted by the receptionist, who will call your therapist over, and he or she will escort you to either a chair (for a foot soak and massage) or a room (for a body massage). The staff members introduce themselves and are respectful and friendly. After your treatment, they'll give you a hot cup of tea, and you can relax a bit more before you leave. Note that there's a service charge for paying by credit card.

Services offered: Foot reflexology, full-body massage, ear-wax cleaning, cupping.

Parking: Lot in front.

Why we like it: Not your run-of-the-mill foot reflexology place. It's up-to-date, with accommodating therapists who keep quiet while working, and the price can't be beat. We can't wait to go back.

While you're there: Walk across the street to Hong Kong Plaza and head for the outdoor food court. At the end is Tofu King, where the house specialty is "stinky tofu": hunks of deep-fried tofu with garlic, chili and kim chee. You won't believe how good it is until you try it. And pop into H2K market to visit the tea shop in the center, with its beautiful teapot sets and loose-leaf teas.

Happy Feet Health Center
18931 A E. Colima Rd., Rowland Heights 91748
(Rowland Plaza, between Nogales & Fullerton)
626.839.3577, happyfeethealthcenter.com

Hours: Mon.–Thurs. & Sat. 10 a.m.–10 p.m.; Fri. 10:30 a.m.–10 p.m.; Sun. 1–10 p.m.

Facilities: You have to hunt for this place, which is hidden in a shopping center, but it's worth the effort. Up front are a dozen or so "bio beds," infrared thermotherapy pod-looking beds that you pass on the way to the ten reflexology chairs. Our curiosity was piqued—what are these pods? (Read on to learn.) The communal reflexology area is dark and quiet, with soft background music; the large TV is usually kept muted.

What to expect: We did the reflexology and full-body massage, performed in the large chairs. We remained fully clothed and, as per the norm, enjoyed a head massage as our feet soaked. After we moved into the chair and our feet were dried, the masseuses put on thin gloves and massaged our feet and calves, using an unscented light lotion. We then moved to another room with about six tables for the last ten minutes of the back massage. As for those thermal-pod beds: A one-hour reflexology treatment gets you 15 minutes on one of them. Woo-hoo! Well, not initially—at first, it feels like two people are slowly roller-blading down your back. But what starts out feeling weird and downright uncomfortable totally changes by the end of the session. If you can hang in there, you'll be as surprised as we were, and you'll want to go back and bring your friends.

Services offered: Reflexology and thermotherapy beds.

Parking: Free in Rowland Plaza.

Why we like it: The foot reflexology was excellent, but the thermotherapy bed experience is a trip. If you're anywhere near Rowland Heights, you have to check out both.

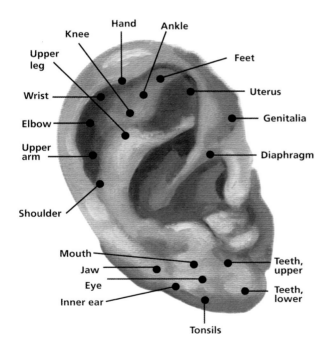

Kingdom of Reflexology
18435 E. Colima Rd., Rowland Heights 91748
(Corner Batson)
626.696.7699

Hours: Daily 10 a.m.–10 p.m.

Facilities: Kingdom is right. This is a big place, with more than a dozen massage chairs in a communal room. The room has low lights, and a TV takes center stage on the wall, but it's on mute.

What to expect: Hot green tea is provided as you soak your feet. We like having our tea during the massage, though this is rare.

Services offered: Foot reflexology, body and combo massages.

Parking: Shopping center parking is plentiful.

Why we like it: It's a popular neighborhood place that happens to be quite large. Tranquil pampering at an awesome price.

Tong Ren Tang Acupuncture
1722 Desire Ave., #203, Rowland Heights 91748
(Rowland Heights Plaza, at Colima)
626.964.1900, lisacupuncture.com

Hours: Mon.–Sat. 10 a.m.-10 p.m.; Sun. noon–10 p.m.

Facilities: The second-floor strip-mall space is really an acupuncture clinic that offers foot and body massage. The three rooms are very clean, and each contains a reclining chair and massage bed. There is an herbal medicine dispensary at the reception area.

What to expect: If you want a foot massage, you can sit in your own private room, soak your feet and stay in the chair for the foot massage. Or, if you want a body massage, you can lie down on the massage bed and just relax. Your choice.

Services offered: Reflexology, massage, acupressure, acupuncture and cupping.

Parking: Two-hour parking in Rowland Heights Plaza.

Why we like it: Off the beaten path, this little acupuncture clinic offers a great massage in your own room. The next time we visit, we'll make an appointment with Dr. Li to discuss medicinal herbs.

SAN GABRIEL

Beauty Foot Massage
828 E. Valley Blvd., San Gabriel 91776
(Corner Gladys, one block east of San Gabriel)
626.288.5400

   (on weekends)

Hours: Daily 10 a.m.–11 p.m.

Facilities: A rectangular room lined with 12 chairs, which fully recline and have a hole in the headpiece so it's comfortable to lie face-down. In the back of the room are four tables for body massage.

Services offered: Foot reflexology, body massage.

Parking: On the street.

Why we like it: Even though it's busy on the weekends, the wait is never too long, and while the TV is always on, it's usually on mute.

Chinese Ancient Foot Massage
529 E. Valley Blvd., 188A & 248B, San Gabriel 91776
(Sunny Plaza)
626.572.5191

Hours: Daily 9 a.m.–11 p.m.

Facilities: The downstairs location has ten reclining chairs for foot massage and two tables in the back for body massage. The upstairs location has 12 reclining chairs for foot massage and 20 tables in semi-private rooms separated by curtains.

What to expect: This is a bustling place—go upstairs if you want less commotion. It provides a foot soak, foot massage and fully clothed body massage in a chair.

Services offered: Foot reflexology, cupping, body massage.

Parking: Lot with spaces above and below ground.

Why we like it: With two locations so close, you can walk right in and always get a service. We prefer the upstairs location, because it's off the main walkway and a bit quieter.

While you're there: Pick up a tasty treat from Domies Bakery (at #118-B).

Empress Shiatsu Foot Massage
425 W. Valley Blvd., #105, San Gabriel 91776
(One block east of N. New)
626.282.5588

Hours: Daily 10 a.m.–9 p.m.

Facilities: Twelve large reclining chairs are found up front for foot soaks and massage. In the back are eight rooms for body massage.

CHINESE

Five Star Foot Spa

What to expect: Although the name says shiatsu, this is actually a Chinese reflexology place. We had the body massage and enjoyed every minute of it. The room was clean, and the massage bed was comfortable.

Services offered: Foot and body massage.

Parking: Private lot behind or street parking.

Why we like it: Nice, clean and spacious. Whether you get a foot or body massage, you won't feel like you're right on top of the person getting a service next to you.

Exotic Spa
702 W. Las Tunas Dr., San Gabriel 91776
(Between Mission & Santa Anita)
626.281.1730 or 626.905.0611

Hours: Daily 10 a.m.–11 p.m.

Facilities: The name might invoke other thoughts, but don't let that stop you. It's pretty dim when you walk in off the street, but natural light comes in from the back of the spa. It has ten chairs in two rows and two portable kneeling massage chairs.

What to expect: We got the full-body massage, keeping our street clothes on and starting with a foot soak in the big comfy chair. The rest of the massage was true to tradition. The place is small but offers an authentic massage.

Services offered: Foot and full-body massage.

Parking: Street in front or in back off Alanmay.

Why we like it: It's located on Las Tunas, which is less trafficky than Valley. You can count on a professional massage. Ask for Sam.

Five Star Foot Spa
140 W. Valley Blvd., #201B, San Gabriel 91776
(Focus Plaza with the 99 Ranch Market, two blocks west of Del Mar)
626.757.2054 or 626.272.6176

Hours: Daily 10 a.m.–midnight.

Facilities: Located upstairs in the busy Focus Plaza, this is a find. The room has 12 cush reclining chairs; in the back, partitioned off from the main room, are two massage tables. The TV is on but is muted, and the place is clean.

What to expect: Appointment or not, the staff will make every effort to take you in and get you going. They use medicinal herbs in the foot-soak basin, and the water is extra hot, so beware. They'll add some cold water if you ask.

Services: Foot soak and massage, body massage.

Parking: Lot in mall.

Why we like it: For several reasons: It's open late, it takes credit cards. It's clean, and the water for the foot soak is really hot. Plus it's near our favorite vegetarian restaurant (see below).

While you're there: Check out Gourmet Vegetarian at #222: We just love everything about this place. Outstanding Chinese vegetarian food.

Fu Sheng Foot Soak
301 W. Valley Blvd., #201, San Gabriel 91776
(Prospect Plaza, between New & Del Mar)
626.300.9188

Hours: Daily 10:30 a.m.–11:30 p.m.

Facilities: In an older, run-down plaza, Fu Sheng has a dozen or so chairs in the communal room; four chairs by the window are for the workers. It has good natural lighting, with fresh air coming in through the open door. There's a TV, but it's muted.

What to expect: The foot soak was toasty, and we enjoyed the work on our necks, backs and shoulders with the therapists' fingers, thumbs and forearms. They set us up with pillows for our knees and face; using the knee pillow helped us get a better stretch on the back. When we moved to the chairs, we laid face down and they covered us with towels and massaged shoulders, back, butt, thighs and calves, then we turned over for more of the same on arms and hands, thighs and feet. We sat up in the chair for the final karate chopping and felt good to go.

Services offered: Foot reflexology, full-body massage.

Parking: Free lot in the plaza or in the subterranean garage.

Why we like it: Ask for Nancy, she has a wonderful touch.

Happy Massage Spa
327 E. Valley Blvd., San Gabriel 91776
(Between Euclid & Walnut)
626.569.9069, perfectmassagespa.com

Hours: Daily 9:30 a.m.–11 p.m.

Facilities: This small spot has six reclining chairs for the foot soak and massage, and seven tables for body massages are in "rooms" created with curtains. Each has bars on the ceiling to aid therapists walk on clients' backs.

What to expect: The place is neat and clean, and we saw the therapists change the sheets after each massage. We had the body massage, which included the therapist walking on us. They add a fee if you pay by credit card.

Services offered: Foot soak, foot and body massage.

Parking: Lot in front, but it's tight.

Why we like it: The spa lights up red lanterns at night, which gives it a welcoming glow. The staff is friendly, and the place is well kept.

Harmony Day Spa
856 E. Valley Blvd., San Gabriel 91776
(Between Gladys & Charlotte)
626.288.2599

Hours: Daily 11 a.m.–midnight.

Facilities: The pleasant lobby introduces a generously sized spa. On one side is the foot-massage area, with 20 large reclining chairs. At busy times it gets noisy, even though folks try to keep quiet. The other side has 12 massage tables, all in private rooms with doors.

CHINESE

What to expect: Enter from the front and pay for your service. If you get a foot soak and massage they'll take you into a large, dimly lit room with a lot of chairs. The foot massage is traditional, including the soak and the clothes-on body massage. If you opt for a full-body massage, however, you'll go into a private room and strip down to your underwear, and the massage will be given on a table.

Services offered: Foot reflexology, body massage.

Parking: Lot in back.

Why we like it: It's a large place but you still feel like you're getting an intimate service. It's a good place to take a group of your friends.

While you're there: Check out Van's Bakery (860 E. Valley Blvd.), which specializes in Chinese, French and Vietnamese baked goods.

Joyful Spa
139 E. Las Tunas Dr., San Gabriel 91776
(Between Del Mar & San Gabriel)
626.309.1663

Hours: Daily 10 a.m.–11 p.m.

Facilities: The reception area is open, with a door leading to the communal foot massage area stocked with 11 chairs. Three private rooms have tables for full-body massage. The lighting is dim but not dark, and the atmosphere is professional.

What to expect: You can anticipate a calming massage and genuine customer service.

Services offered: Full-body, foot and combo foot and body massage, plus facials and teeth whitening.

Harmony Day Spa

Parking: Street spots in front or behind.

Why we like it: It seems like 95 percent of Chinese foot massage places are located on Valley Boulevard. If you don't want to face a lot of people (or all that traffic), come here for an authentic massage at a place that remembers your name. It gets a lot of loyal customers, and for good reason—Joyful deserves all the business it gets. Go, ask for Bryan, and see what we mean.

KM Beauty Spa
617 W. Las Tunas Dr., San Gabriel 91776
(Between Franklin & Sycamore)
626.872.2477, 626.652.9279

Hours: Daily 10 a.m.–11 p.m.

Facilities: The staff is friendly and welcoming at this clean place. Nine chairs for foot and body massage sit on one side of the room, and four tables for Thai hair washing are on the other. A separate area is used for blow-drying the hair after the Thai shampoo.

What to expect: In our travels around the county, we'd seen occasional signs for Thai shampoo and finally got a chance to check it out here. They give you a terrycloth strapless wrap that adheres with Velcro under your arms. The shampoo massage table is not as comfortable as the massage chairs or tables, but once the therapist starts scratching your head, you won't care. They use a hand sprayer to wet your hair and, of course, you get shampooed, but it's the scratching that will win you over. After the rinse, you'll be escorted to the back room for a blow-dry.

Services offered: Foot and body massage, skin care, Thai shampoo.

Five Star Foot Spa

Parking: Street spots on Las Tunas or behind.

Why we like it: If you love a good, long, scalp-stimulating hair-washing, try the Thai shampoo experience at KM, and ask for Michelle.

Kortry Foot Reflexology
1788 S. San Gabriel Blvd., Ste. 102, San Gabriel 91776
(South of Valley, before Dewey)
626.280.4488 or 626.280.2988

Hours: Daily 10 a.m.–10 p.m.

Facilities: The foot reflexology is part of Kortry Skin Care Center next door. If you enter from the back, you'll see the wide, long room for foot massage has 12 chairs. The room gets progressively darker toward the front, facing San Gabriel Boulevard. At our last visit, at 2 p.m. on a weekday, there were two other customers, and by the time we left, it was almost full. It's so popular that it's adding another area next door for hot-stone and deep-tissue massage. Sign us up!

What to expect: You'll get a standard foot and body massage, starting with a foot soak in a wooden bucket of warm water that's the color of blue Kool-Aid. While your tootsies soak, your back gets the attention, and when your feet are dry, you'll move from the ottoman to the chair, which is laid flat. As usual, the rest of the treatment includes a full-body massage in the chair, fully clothed. We left completely satisfied.

Services offered: Foot reflexology.

Parking: Private lot in the back off San Gabriel.

Why we like it: You should be able to walk in and get a service, and the people at reception speak a bit of English. Ask for Leo. Consider purchasing the package of a dozen massages—it'll make your hourly rate just barely into the double-digits. A heck of a deal.

LS Massage
301 W. Valley Blvd., #212-213, San Gabriel 91776
(Prospect Plaza, between New & Del Mar)
626.202.7632, lsacupuncture.net

Hours: Daily 11 a.m.–11 p.m.

Facilities: LS's official entry is at 213, but you'll walk through a shallow hallway to 212. It has seven rooms between the spaces, all done in a salmon color, with only partial walls but real doors—there's plenty of privacy.

What to expect: A very thorough treatment, under the supervision of a Chinese doctor.

Services offered: Acupressure, acupuncture and Chinese massage.

Parking: Free in the plaza lot or the subterranean garage.

Why we like it: The therapists are licensed and serious about what they do. Ask for Annie.

While you're there: Head down the street to our favorite vegetarian restaurant, Gourmet Vegetarian (140 W. Valley Blvd. #222).

Lucky Foot Spa
1039 E. Valley Blvd., B113, San Gabriel 91776
(Gold World Plaza)
626.572.0588

Hours: Daily 10 a.m.–10 p.m.

Facilities: Thin drapes separate the shallow, narrow reception area of this large spa from the bright, open communal room, which has 18 or so chairs for foot reflexology and body massage.

What to expect: The workers are professional and keep the talking to a minimum.

Services offered: Foot and body massage.

Parking: Plenty in the plaza.

Why we like it: It's a clean place with easy access. Ask for Sunny.

Mirage Reflexology
1237 S. San Gabriel Blvd., San Gabriel 91776
(Corner Wells, north of Valley)
626.292.7441

Hours: Mon.–Sat. 11 a.m.–9:30 p.m.

Facilities: A peaceful little place off the beaten Valley Boulevard path, with just four comfy, reclining chairs in the main room, and four massage tables separated by curtains in another room.

What to expect: The owner, Stephanie, has transformed Mirage into a women's sanctuary. They'll bring you a pot of tea of your choice while you soak your feet in the wooden tub. The space is lit with candles and soft lights. You can get your body massage in a chair or opt for the table. Appointments are mandatory.

Services offered: Foot soak, body and foot massage.

Parking: Two-hour street parking in front or spaces behind.

Why we like it: For the serenity and quiet—it's just right for drinking tea, soaking your feet in a warm tub and getting a stress-reducing massage.

Oasis Sauna
1617 S. Del Mar Ave., San Gabriel 91776
(Corner Valley)
626.571.1822 or 626.202.3128

Hours: Daily 10 a.m.–10 p.m.

Facilities: Oasis has a friendly, helpful reception and eight massage rooms, all with doors.

What to expect: A nice little spot with a sauna and classic Chinese treatments, plus a Korean-style body scrub. Small fee for credit-card usage.

Services offered: Foot and body massage, body scrub and sauna.

Parking: In the small shopping center.

Why we like it: A good, traditional Chinese massage.

Oriental Natural Treatment Center
Chinese Foot Massage
502 & 504 E. Valley Blvd., San Gabriel 91776
(Between Del Mar & Palm)
626.280.0069, orientalnaturaltreatment.com

Hours: Daily 10 a.m.–midnight.

Facilities: This is an established place you may have driven by for years, with its green awnings and large signage. Inside are eight chairs, as well as a couple's room and

Oriental Natural Treatment Center

another private room with one table. The stand-alone kneeling massage chair was in the back, calling our name.

What to expect: This was perhaps the most intense massage we've ever had. And we've had a LOT of massages. After we wrapped ourselves around the skeleton chair, we were covered with a towel. The massage began on the neck, back and shoulders. The therapist continued down the sides of the back and up again, and then more on the shoulders. We could see his legs and feel his arms pushing with all his body weight into our shoulders. We wanted to cry, we wanted to laugh, and we welcomed the relief when he moved to the arms and hands. And then he was back to the shoulders, full force. Just as foot reflexology isn't limited to the feet, neither is a portable chair massage limited to the upper body. He used his forearms on the hips, butt and down the legs, using a sort of walking compression. Karate chops all around, up and down, and it was over. We felt fantastic afterward.

Services offered: Foot reflexology, chair and full-body massage, acupuncture, acupressure, cupping and scraping.

Parking: Street or small side lot.

Why we like it: Hit me, baby, one more time. Ask for Jiao.

SF Beauty Salon & Foot Spa
720 E. Valley Blvd., San Gabriel 91776
(Corner San Gabriel)
626.288.8869

Hours: Daily 10 a.m.–midnight

Facilities: A large place on a busy corner, with eight recliner chairs for foot massage and four tables for the hair wash, plus two rooms for couple's chair massages.

What to expect: The hair wash is done lying down, face up on a massage/shampoo table. A little headrest lies over the sink. Your hair is washed twice with Kirkland shampoo, and then conditioner is applied. Our hair was literally squeaky clean. There's a little salon area for blow-drying. Full-body massages are done on tables in a little room. The foot soak has herbs, and the massage is conducted with you fully clothed in a recliner chair. Service charge for paying with a credit card.

Services offered: Foot soak and massage, hair wash, body massage, combination massage, shampoo and blow-dry.

Parking: Lot on side of building.

Why we like it: For a reasonably priced shampoo and massage all in one, and they can usually handle walk-ins.

Sole So Good
801 E. Valley Blvd., #102, San Gabriel 91776
(Minh Plaza, corner San Gabriel)
626.307.1788, SoleSoGood.com

Hours: Daily 10 a.m.–10 p.m.

Facilities: A smaller facility with six reclining chairs for the foot soak and massage. The chairs are close together, but the place is clean.

What to expect: A relaxing foot soak in warm water and a great foot massage, plus a few added touches, like the cool pack for your eyes and the warm pack for your stomach.

Services offered: Foot and body massage and reflexology.

Parking: Lot with spots both above and below ground.

Why we like it: They serve hot tea when you arrive, and during the massage, they'll place a cool pack on your eyes and heat packs on your tummy. Both feel divine. The place is dimly lit, which helps you relax.

Tibetan Herbal Feet Soak
227 W. Valley Blvd., Ste. 218A, San Gabriel 91778
(Hilton Plaza, between Del Mar & New)
626.968.9888or 626.588.2666

Hours: Daily 10 a.m.–9 p.m.

Facilities: It's a professional, comfortable place, with a bright-blue main room and therapists in matching uniforms. It has 12 large reclining chairs for the foot soak and massage.

What to expect: The foot soak is wonderful, but the water is extremely hot. They put a little wooden stool inside the bucket to place your feet on instead of directly in the water, and they cover the bucket with a towel, so you can "steam" your feet first. Be forewarned that the steam is almost as hot as the water. After about ten minutes of steaming, they pour cooler water into the bucket to bring the temperature down. Now you can soak your feet in the water, which is chock-full of fragrant medicinal herbs. The foot massage is thorough and relaxing. You can add on a body massage in a chair if you wish.

Services offered: Tibetan foot soak and reflexology foot massage.

Parking: Lot with surface and underground parking.

Why we like it: Did we mention that the water is really hot? We love the Tibetan method of steaming the feet first before soaking. Once you get used to the heat, your feet feel great.

Twin Jade Foot Massage
731 E. Valley Blvd., San Gabriel 91776
(Corner San Gabriel)
626.288.2345

Hours: Daily 10 a.m.–11 p.m.

Facilities: A charming, no-surprises establishment.

What to expect: Straight-up traditional foot soak and massage.

Services offered: Foot soak and foot massage.

Parking: Lot in front.

Why we like it: This place is a little lighter and brighter than most of the places on Valley. They serve tea before your treatment, and the price is right for a foot soak and full-body massage in a reclining chair.

While you're there: Check out Pho Ga (741 E. Valley Blvd., 626.288.3900) for a great bowl of noodle soup after your massage.

Vivid Spa
225 W. Valley Blvd., H228, San Gabriel 91776
(Inside the Hilton Hotel, 2nd floor)
626.308.2112 or 626.308.9188

Hours: Daily 10:30 a.m.–11 p.m.

Facilities: The Hilton has done a nice job with this big spa, which has 15 private rooms, another one for couples and a communal room with four chairs for the foot massage.

What to expect: A good full-body massage, given in a private room, so you can strip down to undies or embrace your naked self. The massage is performed through a sheet until the second round on your back. At that time, the therapist will expose your back and bring out the oil for the back and then legs, with a warm wipe-down before turning over. While on your back, your face, neck, head and finally arms and legs will be massaged.

Services offered: Body, Thai, foot and chair massage, as well as cupping, scraping and facials in a separate facility on the same floor.

Parking: Two hours free in the Hilton garage.

Why we like it: The hot-pink business card brought to mind a young, Hello Kitty sensibility, but it's really a mature clientele. And if you're thinking of exploring all the spas on Valley Boulevard, start with Vivid, which is the one farthest to the east.

Zhi Zhi Ba Foot Massage
250 W. Valley Blvd., Ste. H, San Gabriel 91776
(Life Plaza)
626.457.1789

Hours: Daily 10 a.m.–9 p.m.

Facilities: This branch of the two-store mini-chain has eight chairs in a communal room and five tables with thin curtains around them. The TV is prominently displayed for the workers to watch, though the volume is muted.

What to expect: We had an hour-long foot massage, which followed the typical Chinese protocol. The masseuse applied consistent, firm pressure. Remember to keep a slack jaw when the karate chops start coming.

Services offered: Foot and Chinese full-body massage.

Parking: In Life Plaza.

Why we like it: This was a great massage, traditional and thorough. Ask for Sunny. And always spend some time browsing (and eating) in the plazas that have foot and body massage businesses.

Another location: 534 W. Valley Blvd., #6, San Gabriel 91776, 626.288.2596

Happy Feet Massage
1118 Fair Oaks Ave., S. Pasadena 91030
(Between Oxley & Monterey)
626.799.3669, happyfeetmassage.com

Hours: Mon.–Sat. 10 a.m.–10 p.m.; Sun. 11 a.m.–9 p.m.

Facilities: With its wood floors, amber walls and large reception area, Happy Feet does its best to welcome you and set the tone for a relaxing experience. It has eight massage beds in the communal area, and though there's no curtain to separate them, they're spaced generously enough so you don't feel cramped. Drapery separates two chairs for a more private couple's treatment. Decorative Chinese screens separate the reception and waiting area from the rest of the massage room.

What to expect: You are fully clothed for this massage; just remove your shoes and you'll be covered with a white towel. The massage is done through the towel on the

Happy Feet Massage

meridians up and down your body. We're always amazed at how discerning the fingers of a trained masseuse can be. The massage was as we'd hoped, and we left feeling refreshed.

Services offered: Reflexology, acupressure and neck-and-shoulder and combo (the signature package) massages.

Parking: On the street or behind the store.

Why we like it: We liked the nice ambiance provided by the décor and soothing colors. They have great early-bird specials between 10 a.m. and 2 p.m.

Another location: 257 E. Colorado Blvd., Pasadena 91101, 626.796.9986

SP Asian Therapy & Spa
1008 ½ Fair Oaks Ave., S. Pasadena 91030
(Between Monterey & Mission)
626.441.6282

Hours: Daily 10 a.m.–11 p.m.

Facilities: Small place with four private rooms with massage tables. Jenny is the owner, and she has three full-time therapists on staff.

What to expect: A great body massage in a quiet and clean facility. Your therapist will work with you on sore or stressed points, with or without oil. The hot-stone massage is great for those hard-to-release areas.

Services offered: Body and hot-stone massage, body scrub.

Parking: Lot behind in the alley or street parking.

Why we like it: Buy six services and get one free. This is a clean place that pays attention to your needs.

CHINESE

WEST COVINA

Flora Day Spa
521 N. Azusa Ave., West Covina 91791
(Between Cortez & Walnut Creek)
626.315.5965 or 626.315.3268, floradayspa.com

Hours: Sun.–Fri. 10:30 a.m.–10:30 p.m.; Sat. 9 a.m.–9 p.m.

Facilities: Flora is known for hair, permanent makeup, facials and waxing, but it also has a separate Chinese foot-reflexology section. Even though there's an entrance to the reflexology area on Azusa, your fellow patrons would appreciate it if you'd enter from the back—when people walk in from the sidewalk, they bring with them glaring light that disrupts the dark, soothing setting. Seven chairs are situated around this small space. It gets crowded even midweek; on weekends you might want make an appointment.

What to expect: We got the full-body treatment and were happy with the massage. During the foot soak, you sit on the ottoman for a head, neck and shoulder massage. Moving to the chair, you're covered with a light blanket, and the masseuse proceeds with the massage after wiping off your feet. Service charge for paying by credit card.

Services offered: Foot reflexology, body massage, facials, waxing and salon services.

Parking: Lot in the back.

Why we like it: It's a one-stop beauty-shopping center. Owner Flora is known for restoring eyebrows by tattoo— she's a real artist. We're glad she added Chinese massage treatments. It's a great local place offering quality massage at a bargain price. Ask for Charlie.

BEYOND THE SAN GABRIEL VALLEY

ARTESIA

My Massage Place
11618 South St., Ste. 215, Artesia 90701
(Seaplace Market Plaza, at Jersey west of Pioneer)
562.860.5989

Hours: Daily 11 a.m.–10 p.m.

Facilities: Up a flight of stairs, this is a clean place with ten reclining chairs and one couple's room with two massage beds behind curtains.

What to expect: A seated foot-reflexology massage is the specialty. Soak your feet in the tub of warm water while the therapist massages your head and neck. Pull your feet out of the water, and the therapist works all your pressure points. Flip over, with your face down through the hole in the chair, and she'll finish up on your back. If you want the back massage done on the massage table, just ask.

Services offered: Foot reflexology and body massage.

Parking: Free lot in the mall with plenty of spaces.

Why we like it: A spotless space, and the professional staff take the sign "Sexual Solicitation Prohibited" seriously.

CHINESE

Asian Foot Reflexology
251 S. Robertson, #101, Beverly Hills 90211
(Between Burton & Wilshire)
310.358.9628

Hours: Daily 10:30 a.m.–10 p.m.

Facilities: This little storefront on Robertson has eight reclining chairs and one massage room in the back with a massage table.

What to expect: Traditional Chinese foot reflexology and full-body massage.

Services offered: Foot reflexology and body massage.

Parking: Street meter or in alley behind.

Why we like it: A convenient locale, a clean facility, authentic foot soaks and some truly splendid reflexologists.

Aurora Foot Spa
8324 Wilshire Blvd., Beverly Hills 90211
(Corner San Vicente)
310.866.1048, aurorafootspa.com

Hours: Daily 10 a.m.–10 p.m.

Facilities: A mini-mall (next to the Coffee Bean) setting, with 12 reclining chairs.

What to expect: Foot soaks and foot and body massage, all clothed and in the chair. Wear loose clothes so the therapist can roll up your pants.

Services offered: Chinese foot reflexology and body massage.

Parking: Two spaces in the front lot, as well as street parking.

Why we like it: The spa asks that you turn off your cell phone and speak only in whispers. Awesome. Lie back and enjoy in silence.

Bao Foot Spa
156 S. Beverly Dr., Beverly Hills 90212
(South of Wilshire)
310.777.7512, baofootspa.com

Hours: Daily 10 a.m.–10 p.m.

Facilities: This spa is just what you might expect in Beverly Hills, with a beautifully designed interior. It is not Chinese-owned, but all the therapists are Chinese. Screens separate the reception desk from the communal foot-reflexology area, where there are six comfy chairs. Straight through a beautifully arched doorway is the bathroom.

What to expect: The therapist massages your head and shoulders while you're on your back. When you turn over, you might feel a tug at your pant legs, pulling them down your hips enough to allow massage of the upper hips and waist. A couple of other places do the pant tug, too. Just expect it here and decide your course of action (that is, how low you'll allow them to pull).

Services offered: Half-hour foot reflexology or one-hour combo foot-body massage. The upgraded VIP treatment includes flowers in your foot soak, a choice of massage oils and lotions and facial mask. Gift cards available.

Parking: Two-hour free parking in city structure on Beverly.

Why we like it: On top of it being visually beautiful, the spa doesn't allow cell phone usage in either the reception or the treatment areas. Become a fan on Facebook to receive discounts.

Healthy Foot Massage
291 S. Robertson Blvd., Beverly Hills 90211
(Between Olympic & Gregory)
310.289.1979

Hours: Daily 10 a.m.–10 p.m.

Facilities: There are six massage chairs in the communal area with holes in the headrest for your face to rest comfortably when lying on your stomach. There are three private rooms in the back.

What to expect: You'll soak your feet in a tea bath while the upper body massage is taking place. The massage follows the typical procedure, and therapists are talented and detailed.

Services offered: Foot and body massage and combo.

Parking: On the street or behind the business.

Why we like it: It's a cozy little place where you can get an authentic, enjoyable Chinese massage, in Beverly Hills no less.

JB Natural Foot Massage
329 S. Robertson Blvd., Beverly Hills 90211
(Between Olympic & Gregory Way)
310.657.3888

Hours: Daily 10:30 a.m.–10 p.m.

Facilities: A small spot with six reclining chairs for foot and body massage.

What to expect: Make an appointment, because this place fills up quickly, and walking in does not guarantee prompt service. It's clean and the staff gives a great massage.

Services offered: Foot and body massage.

Parking: Street meter or lot in back.

Why we like it: It's an intimate place that pays attention to your needs. The TV displays nature shows with soothing music, instead of the typical Chinese movies.

BURBANK

Burbank Spa & Garden
2115 W. Magnolia Blvd., Burbank 91506
(Near Myers)
818.845.1251, burbankspa.com

Hours: Mon.–Sat. 9 a.m.–9 p.m.; Sun. 10 a.m.–9 p.m.

Facilities: The spa has a green awning that you can't miss from the street. As you pass through the gate, you'll see a lovely garden that divides the two buildings. On the left is a two-story building with 11 massage rooms. The building on the right is for facials, waxing and mani-pedi. We can't help but think it's the perfect place to take your mom or mother-in-law. This is a cozy place where you'll want to sit in the sun and enjoy the scenery. Separate facilities for men and women.

What to expect: The foot reflexology differs from a traditional Chinese reflexology in several ways. You are in a private room, on a raised mattress table with your pants off. There is a wonderful heating pad on the table that

CHINESE

will warm and relax you. The masseuse begins a soothing massage with lotion on your feet and legs up to the knee. After the massage, your legs are wiped down with a warm washcloth scented with peppermint oil. She then wraps them individually and does more massage through the cloth. After a couple of minutes, you can feel the tingling of the peppermint, and the aroma is pretty therapeutic, too.

Services offered: Swedish, deep-tissue, shiatsu, hot-stone and pregnancy massage, reflexology, sauna, facials, nails and waxing. Bundled spa services are available for both men and women, and gift certificates, too.

Parking: Street spots in front or on side streets.

Why we like it: Though it's not in a strict ethnic category, the reflexology massage is a good introduction. If you're a little timid about going to San Gabriel, Chinatown or Little Tokyo, go to Burbank Spa & Garden for your reflexology and shiatsu massage. Come early and use the Finnish sauna before your appointment. Ask for Renata.

CHATSWORTH

Jolly Foot
20533 Devonshire St., Chatsworth 91311
(Devon Plaza)
818.993.7515, jolly-foot.com

Hours: Mon.–Sat. 10:30 a.m.–10:30 p.m.; Sun. 1:30–10:30 p.m.

Facilities: There are 12 chairs in the communal room and two massage tables and a chair in a separate room. You move to the separate room for the full-body massage. We noticed the large TV in the communal room, but it was turned off, and Christian music was playing on the audio system.

What to expect: Per typical Chinese body massage, you remain clothed and are covered with a white towel. After the foot soak and reflexology, we moved into the separate room for the full-body portion of the massage. The therapist pulled up our shirt in the back, unhooked our bra and tried to pull the shirt up more, but we stopped them where it was comfortable. This may happen, and you can go with it or not. There's nothing sordid about it—it's just part of the full-body massage. After the oiling and massaging of the back, there was a wonderful warm wipe-down. Then the therapist re-hooked the bra, pulled the shirt down and worked some more on the back. All the therapist use six- and eight-inch stools during the treatments—that extra height gives them a lot more leverage and therefore more power to the massage. Two thumbs up.

Services offered: Foot reflexology, full-body or combo massage.

Parking: Plenty in Devon Plaza.

Why we like it: Stop in and pick up discount coupons, and ask for Sean when you book a massage. The shopping centers on each of the other three corners at this busy intersection are worth checking out, too.

Another location: 5160 Vineland Ave., #106, North Hollywood 91601, 818.763.1500

No.1 Foot Spa
9820-A Topanga Canyon Blvd., Chatsworth 91311
(Between Lassen & Marilla)
818.885.8538

Hours: Daily 10:30 a.m.–10:30 p.m.

Facilities: A large curtain at the entrance helps keep the light outside from coming in. Once you pass through that, you'll see eight reclining chairs spread out nicely, allowing some space, as well as one semi-private massage room.

What to expect: It was relatively empty when we arrived, so we decided to splurge on the 90-minute treatment, which was fantastic. First up is a foot soak and neck and shoulder massage. Then the therapist concentrates on foot reflexology for a good 30 minutes, then moves on to the body massage, which you can have in the chair or on the table.

Services offered: Foot soak and foot and body massage.

Parking: Lot.

Why we like it: If you're on your feet all day, you should be kind to your tootsies with a good foot massage, and this is the place to do it.

Super Relax
10160 Mason Ave., Chatsworth 91311
(Corner Devonshire in the Devonshire Mason Center)
818.886.8866, superrelaxshop.com

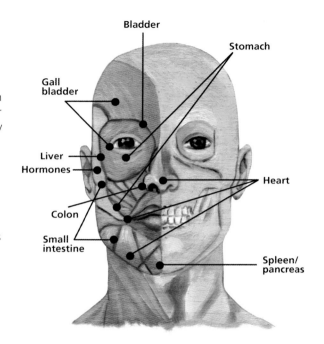

Hours: Daily 10:30 a.m.–10:30 p.m.

Facilities: A large place with two partitioned rooms with massage tables in the front and nine reclining chairs in the back. The staff is friendly.

What to expect: We had a foot massage with herb-infused water. The full-body massage after the foot soak and foot reflexology was just right. When you're done with your massage, they'll serve you a cup of tea, always a nice touch.

Services offered: Foot soak, foot massage with herbs, full-body massage, detox foot bath.

Parking: Lot in front.

Why we like it: This is a great place to go with a bunch of friends because it has plenty of therapists to accommodate a crowd. Just let them know in advance if you have a gang.

Another location: 14449 Ventura Blvd., Sherman Oaks 91423, 818.783.9999

CULVER CITY

Yaoqi Reflexology
10200 Venice Blvd., #205A, Culver City 90232
(Two blocks east of Motor, corner Jasmine)
310.558.1758

Hours: Daily 11 a.m.–9:30 p.m.

Facilities: This second-floor place occupies two storefronts. On one side are three foot massage chairs; on the other side are private massage rooms with tables.

What to expect: The foot soak is quite relaxing, and the therapist spends about 30 minutes on foot reflexology. The massage is provided in the reclining chair and covers your entire body.

Services offered: Foot reflexology and body massage.

Parking: Lot in front or on the side.

Why we like it: For a serious foot reflexology session, come here and get the 60-minute treatment plus the 30-minute body massage. Ask for Lili or Lisa.

Zen Reflexology
10808 Washington Blvd., Culver City 90232
(Corner Midway)
310.839.3608, zenreflexology.com

Hours: Daily 10 a.m.–10 p.m.

Facilities: On the first floor of a nondescript building, Zen has eight reclining chairs, separated in pairs by office-style cubicle partitions.

What to expect: Foot soak and reflexology with a body massage in a clean and quiet surrounding.

Services offered: Foot reflexology.

Parking: Behind the building or on the street.

Why we like it: Small, quiet and clean, Zen is a nice change from the larger foot spas. Ask for Li—she was quite the professional and got to all our tough spots.

DIAMOND BAR

6 Star Villa Foot Spa
21010 Golden Springs Dr., Diamond Bar 91789
(West of Brea Canyon)
English: 909.598.5828 or 626.814.5566,
Chinese: 909.569.3662

Hours: Daily 10 a.m.–10 p.m.

Facilities: There's no signage or name outside, but the outline of the soles of feet in lights and a reflexology map of the body in the window tip you off. The massage room is off the reception area, and it's equipped with 15 chairs in rows; around the corner is a communal room with five tables for the full-body portion of the treatment. It also has three private rooms.

What to expect: The foot reflexology was calling us this particular day. After settling into the comfy chairs and putting our feet in wooden buckets of hot water, the therapists wrapped plastic around our knees to steam the calves while our feet soaked. Then they massaged our faces, heads and necks with a little balm. They used a heavier lotion on our feet and legs, using the sides of their hand to pound us (lightly) up and down the legs.

They wiped off the remaining oil on our legs with a hot washcloth. The last ten minutes is for the full-body massage, and you move to the communal room with massage tables for that.

Services offered: Foot reflexology and full-body massage.

Parking: In the strip mall out front.

Why we like it: It's a great massage, and you can walk right in without an appointment.

iRelax Foot Spa
20627 Golden Springs Dr., #1-0, Diamond Bar 91765
(West of Lemon)
909.594.6888, irelaxfootspa.com

Hours: Daily 10 a.m.–10 p.m.

Facilities: This place is cozy and clean, with seven chairs in the communal room, two rooms with two beds and one private room with two chairs for couples. It's a well-run business whose focus is tending to your needs.

What to expect: The full-body massage is performed on a table and follows the typical protocol. The therapists are attentive and thorough, using every part of their hands, forearms and elbows to unblock meridians.

Services offered: Reflexology, foot and body massage.

Parking: In the shopping center.

Why we like it: Ask for Michael. One of his secret weapons is to work your butt with his elbow. Hurts so good!

Sakura Foot Massage
21343 Cold Spring Ln., Diamond Bar 91765
(Diamond Hills Plaza)
909.598.2829

Hours: Daily 10 a.m.–10 p.m.

Facilities: A new place that is clean and modern, with nine large, reclining chairs for foot soaks and massage and three massage tables in private rooms.

What to expect: A respectable reflexology session and foot massage. The staff dresses professionally and respects your space. Extra attention is paid to keeping things sanitary and making you comfortable.

Services offered: Foot soak, foot and body massage, cupping.

Parking: Lot.

Why we like it: This place is pristine, with a friendly staff and great services.

Shan Ya Massage
223499 Golden Springs Dr., Diamond Bar 91765
(Corner Diamond Bar)
909.860.8555

Hours: Daily 10 a.m.–10 p.m.

Facilities: Good storefront signage heralds this clean place, which has nine chairs in the communal setting and five private rooms with tables. It's minimally decorated but pleasant.

What to expect: The massage was traditional and pleasant, beginning with soaking our feet in a tea bath all the way to the slapping of our legs at the end. There is a small service charge for paying by credit card.

Services offered: Foot reflexology and body massage.

Parking: Plenty in the shopping center.

Why we like it: It's a quiet place with convenient parking. Ask for Tim.

ENCINO

J Song's Acupuncture
17130 Ventura Blvd., #100, Encino 91316
(Encino Town Center)
818.905.7575

Hours: Daily 10:30 a.m.–8 p.m.

Facilities: A Town Center place with two rows of three chairs in the communal room behind the reception desk. Two private rooms with massage tables are separated by light drapes. There wasn't a TV in sight.

What to expect: The foot reflexology is excellent—no bells and whistles, just an all-around great service.

Services offered: Foot reflexology, acupressure and sports, shiatsu and oil massage.

Parking: Private lot behind the shop; the entrance is back there anyway.

Why we like it: A licensed acupuncturist and a sports massage specialist are on staff. It's no surprise this establishment has a loyal following. We got frequent-buyer cards and continue to use them.

Phoenix Foot Spa
17336 Ventura Blvd., Encino 91316
(CVS Plaza)
818.788.3777

Hours: Daily 10 a.m.–10 p.m.

Facilities: Two thick, red drapes separate the reception desk from the eight chairs in the communal area. A private room is in the back. There's no TV; maybe that's an Encino thing. We suspect TVs are provided for the workers more than the guests, but it strikes us as the focal point in many a Chinese spa.

What to expect: While our tootsies soaked, we experienced a pleasant massage with an unscented lotion on our face, head and neck. Our heads were scratched like they do when your hairdresser is washing your hair, only there's no shampoo. Who doesn't want more of that? Next was shoulders, arms, hands and feet. That part was pretty standard, but as we turned over, our masseuses reached under our shirts to unhook our bras. (Just saying this could happen to you, and you can go along, as we did, or opt out, although the masseuse may not ask first.) This, of course, gives unrestricted access to the back, so the massage can continue smoothly, uninterrupted by pesky bra straps and hooks. We understood this better by the next move, which was to climb on top of us, gaining fuller access to work the connected muscles in our back. You may not even notice this, because the masseuse uses the arm rests to support her knees. You'll just know it feels great. After that, we were put back together, covered with a towel, and worked over in the butt, thighs and calves. Don't fear the butt massage until you've tried one.

Services offered: Foot reflexology and body massage.

Parking: Plenty in the CVS lot.

Why we like it: Ask for Nancy; she has a great knuckles technique for the soles of your feet.

While you're there: Head next door to the Mediterranean Grill—tasty food and great service.

Good Mood Foot Massage
16545 Ventura Blvd., #19, Encino 91436
(Rubio Plaza, between Rubio & Hayvenhurst)
818.788.4966

Hours: Daily 10 a.m.–10:30 p.m.

Facilities: An attractive little storefront massage place, with red walls and large Chinese wooden screens to block the outside light. Eight reclining chairs are angled to allow for space.

What to expect: Foot soak and foot massage, including work on your head, shoulders and back. Dress comfortably, sit back and relax.

Services offered: Foot soak and foot massage.

Parking: Two hours free in the lot in Rubio Plaza.

Why we like it: We didn't make an appointment, and even though they were busy, they did everything they could to get us in. The setting is clean and decorated in tasteful Chinese style.

Happy Feet Salon
17629 Ventura Blvd., Encino 91316
(Between White Oak & Balboa)
818.981.6288, happyfeetsalon.com

Hours: Daily 10 a.m.–10 p.m.

Facilities: For a foot massage place, this is pretty special. With a large water fountain in the middle, the room has 12 chairs facing the fountain and bamboo curtains between every two chairs to allow for some privacy. The lights are dim, and the music is soft and soothing.

What to expect: For the foot soak and massage, we sat on the ottoman and soaked our feet, while the therapist massaged our head, neck and arms. After you soak for about 15 minutes, then you lie down and enjoy the rest of your massage, starting with and focusing primarily on the feet. Eventually your entire body gets a good rubdown. Wear comfortable clothes.

Services offered: Foot soak and foot massage.

Parking: Lot in front.

Why we like it: A peaceful and serene ambience: no TV blaring, no talking, and all the clients turn off their cell phones. Just focus on the water falling in the fountain and you'll be transported.

GARDENA

Pacific Bay Retreat
1630 W. Redondo Beach Blvd., #16, Gardena 90247
(Pacific Square, one block east of Western)
310.323.0598

Hours: Daily 10 a.m.–10 p.m.

Facilities: When you walk in, everything is to the left: a large, open area with 15 reclining chairs (in a gold-on-gold print) and, in back, a couple's room with two tables and three private rooms with tables.

What to expect: Chinese foot reflexology—a foot soak first, then move to the table for the body massage portion. You can stay in the chair for the entire service if you wish.

Services offered: Foot reflexology.

Parking: Lot.

Why we like it: A perfect place to go after you a shopping trip Marukai Market in the same plaza.

While you're there: Try the yummy Peruvian restaurant for a change from Chinese food: El Pollo Inka, 1425 W. Artesia Blvd., 310.516.7378.

GRANADA HILLS

Sunny Q Wellness Center
17706 Chatsworth Blvd., Granada Hills 91344
818.522.5355

Hours: Daily 10 a.m.–10 p.m.

Facilities: Don't let the dreary storefront put you off—this place is clean, quiet and pleasingly decorated in a Chinese style, with eight chairs in the main room and two more in a private room. All services are performed in chairs. We added herbs to our foot soak, which was a delight.

What to expect: Foot soak and full-body massage sitting in the chair with your clothes on.

Services offered: Foot soak, body massage, reflexology, detox foot bath, additional herbs/scents for the foot soak

(sea salt, rose petal) and bath oils (milk, lavender, lemon, jasmine, Tibetan herbs).

Parking: On the street or behind the building.

Why we like it: No TV, calm and clean. The massage therapists' licenses and pictures are posted.

Sunshine Health Center
17027 Chatsworth St., Granada Hills 91344
(Near Balboa)
818.366.1618

Hours: Daily 10 a.m.–10 p.m.

Facilities: The storefront is run down, but inside it's not so bad. There are three private, sectioned-off areas, each with a single chair, and two other areas with two chairs each, offering much more privacy than the typical communal room.

What to expect: A great foot massage. The head and face massage was especially memorable, given while our feet soaked.

Services offered: Foot and body massage and combo massage.

Parking: Plenty in the mini-mall.

Why we like it: A good massage at a great value.

*While you're there: After your massage, go to Ali Baba right next door for authentic Persian food. Try the hot tea, the yogurt with cucumber and mint (*mast 'o khiar*) and the rice with dill, lima beans and herbs (*baghali polo*).*

LA MIRADA

Ava Foot Massage
13946 E. Imperial Hwy., La Mirada 90638
(Imperial Plaza, west of Valley View)
562.229.0743

Hours: Tues.–Sun. 11 a.m.–10 p.m.

Facilities: The main business is a hair salon, facing Imperial Highway, but on the east side you'll find a separate massage area. As you face the building, park on the left, and you'll see the entrance for massage. Inside there's soft lighting, soft music, and eight massage beds in a communal room.

What to expect: The full-body massage followed expectations; the only variance was some slapping of the calves with the tops of the masseuse's feet—which means it's one of those places where the masseuses climb on the chairs on top of you to get the job done. And we're glad they do. There's a small fee for using a credit card.

Services offered: Foot and body massage.

Parking: Large side lot.

Why we like it: It's another clean, quiet neighborhood place. You should be able to walk in without an appointment. Ask for Judy.

LONG BEACH

King & Queen Spa
5237 E. 2nd St., Long Beach 90803
(Belmont Shore, between Corona & Covina)
562.433.1200

Hours: Daily 10 a.m.-midnight.

Facilities: Sometimes you want to be off the beaten path and sometimes you want to be right in the mix of things. This place is for the latter, thanks to its location in the heart of Belmont Shore, a great destination to stroll, eat, shop and, thanks to several massage businesses, get a spa treatment. This place has a bay of eight fully reclining massage chairs separated by drapes.

What to expect: We made an appointment for body massages. Our technicians led us to our respective chairs and we removed most of our clothes, which we placed on little stools. They covered us with heavy towels and proceeded to massage every inch of our bodies. The massage incorporates hot stones, which felt fantastic. The place was busy, and you could hear people coming in and out. The massage was great, especially after a long day of strolling 2nd Street.

Services offered: Chinese, prenatal and scalp massage, plus hair washing, facials, waxing, threading, eyelash extensions.

Parking: On the street or in any of the public pay lots off 2nd Street.

Why we like it: All massages come with the complimentary hot stones. Ask for Kevin.

Foot-soaking buckets at Five Star Foot Spa

Rivini Foot Reflexology
4160 N. Viking Way, Long Beach 90808
(West of Bellflower)
562.420.1798

Hours: Daily 10 a.m.–10 p.m.

Facilities: One of the quaint Parkview Village shops, this spa is quiet and clean. The posted "Respect the Quiet" signs indicate a peaceful massage experience ahead, and the soft lighting adds to the effect. It has eight traditional chairs for Chinese massage in the communal room and two portable chairs.

What to expect: We opted for a classic foot reflexology session. A third of the time was spent on our upper body (head, neck, shoulders and arms) and two-thirds was spent on the foot and lower body massage.

Services offered: Foot reflexology, foot and body massage, facials and waxing.

Parking: On the street or in the Parkview Village lot off Viking Way.

Why we like it: A classic Chinese massage. If you want special attention paid to your arms, ask for Paul.

Skin Care & Chinese Therapy Center
238 Cherry Ave., Long Beach 90802
(Between Broadway & Appleton)
562.343.2633

Hours: Daily 10:30 a.m.–7:30 p.m.

Facilities: A storefront with a narrow hallway, a reception area, four massage rooms with tables and a skin-care area.

What to expect: The massage tables are warmed, which is lovely, because you take off your clothes for this massage and lie under a sheet. They offer a solid Chinese massage, and the masseuse will walk on you if you like. The 30-minute "body talk" massage focuses on specific tension-filled areas.

Services offered: "Body-talk" and Chinese reflexology massage, plus skin care.

Parking: Street parking.

Why we like it: It's unassuming but it delivers a great massage.

LOS ANGELES

Apple VIP Spa
5324 Wilshire Blvd., Los Angeles 90036
(Mid-Wilshire, at Detroit)
323.936.1309

Hours: Daily 11 a.m.–11 p.m.

Facilities: A Wilshire storefront with a welcoming receptionist. There are six private rooms with massage tables and curtains.

What to expect: The receptionist will introduce you to your therapist. Make sure you tell him if you do or do not want oil or hot stones. The rooms are decent in size, and the fountains in the hallway add soothing ambient sounds. You'll see notices everywhere asking you to turn off your cell phone and to not ask for sex—it's not that kind of place. The rooms have CD players—bring your own CD if you're picky, or get ready to listen to a lot of Karen Carpenter.

Services offered: Foot and body massage, with oil or hot stones.

Parking: A lot in the back or metered street parking,

Why we like it: Clean, professional and organized, and it can handle walk-ins—but try to make an appointment with CiCi or YoYo.

Spaahbulous & More
668 N. Spring St., Ste. 223, Los Angeles 90012
(Chinatown, between Cesar Chavez & Ord)
213.596.7421, spanmore.com

Hours: Daily 11 a.m.–8 p.m.

Facilities: It's easy to spot, thanks to good signage. In the massage area, the lighting is cave-like, which is an initial challenge, but once your feet hit the water to soak, you appreciate the dark. Seven chairs in the communal area are used for foot reflexology and body massage, and one massage table is sectioned off with sheer drapes.

What to expect: Schedule an appointment on the website (allow four-hour advance notice). You'll remain fully clothed except for rolling up your pants to the knee. Your feet soak in hot herbal water inside a plastic-lined wooden bucket. You sit on an ottoman as you soak, and the masseuse works on your neck, shoulders and back. You then move to a big comfy chair for the rest of your foot and body massage, while the masseuse takes your place on the ottoman. She'll cover you with a white towel. After your feet are dried, she'll use a lotion to facilitate the reflexology. We were ready for a nap when it was over. Was it the dim lighting or the heightened state of relaxation? We'll have to do more research.

Services offered: Foot reflexology and massage, full-body and deep-tissue massage, acupressure and skin care. Frequent-buyer cards and gift certificates available.

Parking: Plenty in the pay side lot off Spring.

Why we like it: TJ, one of the owners, said she doesn't book more than four or five people at a time, so the place doesn't get too busy or noisy, and everyone gets the attention they deserve.

While you're there: There's plenty of good shopping and eating in this Chinatown neighborhood, from seafood restaurants May Flower and CBS and the French-Vietnamese Linh's Bakery to Gin-Herb Corp, packed with herbs, teas, snacks and spices, and Asian E Shop, with beautiful (and inexpensive) silk jackets, pillowcases and gifts. Other eateries to try are Spring Street Smoke House (640 N. Spring St.), Philippe's for french dip sandwiches (1001 N. Alameda) and La Luz del Dia on Olvera Street.

Sunny Foot Care
5169 W. Sunset Blvd., Los Angeles 90027
(Kafco Plaza in East Hollywood, corner Kingsley)
323.662.5888, sunnyfootmassage.com

Hours: Daily 11 a.m.-11 p.m.

Facilities: A wee mini-mall place with eight reclining chairs for foot massages.

What to expect: A comforting foot soak and foot reflexology session.

Services offered: Foot reflexology and body massage.

Parking: Lot in the mall.

Why we like it: The pink chairs are a must see—plus it's open late.

Wellness Foot & Body Spa
5226 W. Sunset Blvd., Los Angeles 90027
(99 Cents Only Plaza in East Hollywood, at Hobart)
323.666.1216, wellnessfootandbodyspa.com

Hours: Daily 11 a.m.–11 p.m.

Facilities: Don't let the potholes in the parking lot deter you from coming here for a reflexology massage. It's a find, with nine reclining chairs in a spacious room and four separate massage rooms separated by curtains.

What to expect: A foot soak with medicinal herbs and massage to the neck, head, arms and back are included in the basic treatment; other body parts are worked over by request.

Services offered: Foot reflexology and body massage.

Parking: Lot in front.

Why we like it: Buy five treatments and get the sixth one free. They take pride in the services they offer, and it shows from the moment you enter. Check it out.

NORTH HOLLYWOOD

Himalayan Sen
10670 Riverside Dr., North Hollywood 91602
(Toluca Lake, near Cahuenga)
818.568.7671, himalayasen.com

Hours: Daily 11 a.m.–10 p.m.

Facilities: Lawrence, one of the owners, is Afghani, but all the therapists are Chinese. He's created a pleasant setting, with a green and white décor; serenity is ensured because he makes sure the masseuses aren't on their cell phones. The comfy reflexology chairs can lie completely flat for the body massage portion of the treatments.

What to expect: If you forgot to bring cash (like we did), an ATM machine is two doors down. Lawrence speaks English, but his staff, not so much, so you might need to dust off your charades gestures if you have something important to convey. While we soaked our feet, Carl worked on our upper body, moving down to the arms and hands and then reaching the feet. He does reflexology with lotion and his bare, magical hands. Finally he does a little more back massage, ending with slapping and karate chops—and big smiles on our faces.

Services offered: Foot and body massage.

Parking: Easy and free, in front of the store.

Why we like it: Great place, good price. Ask for Carl if you want an awesome, completely platonic butt massage.

Top Dragon Massage
10855 Magnolia Blvd., North Hollywood 91601
(Between Vineland & Cahuenga)
818.763.9060

Hours: Daily 10 a.m.–10 p.m.

Facilities: It doesn't look promising from the outside, but come in and you'll be pleasantly surprised. Open the door, pull back the red curtain and you'll enter a dimly lit room with four large leather recliners for foot massages. In the back are three massage tables for body massages.

What to expect: Pay first and take a seat in one of the recliners. Soak your feet while the therapist massages your

shoulders and neck. After the soak comes the massage for your feet, touching on all the reflexology points.

Services offered: Foot and body massage.

Parking: Lot in front.

Why we like it: Of all the places in the area, this one is the nicest: small, comfortable and clean, with a sharp attention to detail. There's no TV blasting, just soft Chinese music in the background.

NORTHRIDGE

Foot Massage
19520-2 Nordhoff St., Northridge 91324
(Near Shirley)
818.718.0088

Hours: Daily 10 a.m.–10 p.m.

Facilities: Pleasantly decorated with dark-red walls, large wooden screens as partitions and ten reclining chairs. The ambience is calm and soothing.

What to expect: A truly relaxing foot massage. They make an extra effort to refrain from talking during the massage. People respect your space, and they make sure you have a relaxing experience and leave in a good mood.

Services offered: Foot soak and foot and body massage.

Parking: Lot in front with ample space.

Why we like it: They whisper when checking in to see how you feel, and they pay special attention to your well-being. The fact that there's no TV says a lot about the mood they've created.

Panda Massage
8823 Reseda Blvd., Northridge 91324
(Between Parthenia & Nordhoff)
818.882.6268

Hours: Daily 10 a.m.–10 p.m.

Facilities: This is a small place with six reclining chairs, five curtained massage rooms with tables and one couple's room.

What to expect: If you choose a foot massage, it will be in one of the comfy large recliner chairs. If you opt for a body massage, you can have it in a private room on a table. They use oil for the body massage, so if you don't want it, let your therapist know. We walked in on a Saturday and were taken right away.

Services offered: Foot and body massage.

Parking: Lot in back or street parking.

Why we like it: Mina, the front-desk receptionist, is friendly and patient, translating what you want or don't want to your therapist. We didn't want oil with our massage, so we appreciated her help.

Soothing Ocean Chinese Foot Massage
9669 Reseda Blvd., Northridge 91324
(Boulevard Shops Center)
818.700.2866

Hours: Daily 10:30 a.m.–10:30 p.m.

Facilities: There are 12 chairs and one table in this typical communal room for foot and body massage. The walls are done with a soothing blue faux finish that explains the Soothing Ocean name. Soft music plays, and there's not a TV to be found.

What to expect: The great thing about this foot massage is the upper-body massage that precedes it. The therapist will reach down the neck of your shirt to massage your neck and shoulders—(just know that it's typical,) and the light, unscented lotion won't wreck your clothing. Some therapists use gloves, some don't. When you turn over, the therapist will cover your face with a towel while she massages your legs. At the end, per tradition, legs are bent to the chest and thrown back down, and your legs get karate-chopped, up and down.

Services offered: Foot reflexology and body massage.

Parking: Plenty in the strip mall.

Why we like it: You can easily walk in without an appointment. It's a nice place and a total bargain.

RANCHO PALOS VERDES

Han's Body & Foot Massage
29131 S. Western Ave., Rancho Palos Verdes 90275
(Western Plaza)
310.832.1888

Hours: Daily 10 a.m.–10 p.m.

Facilities: Nine chairs in the communal room, plus four private rooms with doors, although their walls don't go all the way to the ceiling.

What to expect: You must pay in advance, including the tip, and there's an extra charge if you use a credit card. The massage is very traditional, and adding the foot scrub is a good idea—they use a thick, rich scrub with large particles, and it feels absolutely wonderful. The rest of the treatment is enjoyable as well, in particular the butt massage, and it ends well with the usual back slapping and karate chopping. Remember to keep a slack jaw.

Services offered: Foot and body massage, foot scrub as an add-on, body scrub and shower and many combinations.

Parking: Plenty in Western Plaza.

Why we like it: It's pleasant and clean, and you can walk in without an appointment.

RESEDA

Reseda Foot Reflexology
7243 Reseda Blvd., Reseda 91335
(Between Sherman Way & Wyandotte)
818.996.5956 or 818.401.5562

Hours: Daily 11 a.m.–10 p.m.

Facilities: A storefront on busy Reseda Boulevard with 12 comfy and colorful (sea foam green) recliner chairs. Enter from the back or the front.

What to expect: Soak your feet, relax, have a foot massage, relax, have a body massage, relax, and the next thing you know, the hour just flies by.

Services offered: Foot soak and reflexology.

Parking: Huge public lot in back with inexpensive parking.

Why we like it: You can get an awesome Chinese foot massage, shop at a Vietnamese market next door, nibble on tasty Thai desserts made in front of the market and have a bowl of pho at one of the numerous Vietnamese noodle houses within one block. Need we say more?

While you're there: The New Bangluck Market next door (7235 Reseda Blvd.) is a great place to explore and purchase exotic spices, fresh noodles and other Thai and Vietnamese treats. Also Pho 999 (7255 Reseda Blvd.) serves tasty and cheap pho.

Shiny Foot Massage
6900-A Reseda Blvd., Reseda 91335
(At Bassett)
818.342.8880, shinyfootmassage.com

Hours: Daily 11 a.m.–10 p.m.

Facilities: This lovely little place has five fully reclining chairs and three semi-private rooms with massage tables.

What to expect: The water for the foot soak was really hot, which felt wonderful. The certified therapists make sure you're comfortable with the pressure and are enjoying your massage.

Services offered: Foot soak and foot and body massage.

Parking: Small lot, plus metered side street spots.

Why we like it: A clean, quiet spot with a concerned and attentive staff.

SAN DIMAS

Kirana Day Spa
380 S. San Dimas Ave., Ste. 101, San Dimas 91773
(One block north of Arrow Hwy.)
909.706.2955, kiranadayspa.com

Hours: Daily 10 a.m.–9 p.m.

Facilities: This is a beautiful oasis, with a bright, gracious reception area and all the rooms you'd need: two for massage, one for waxing and two for facials. Ask Paula to give you a tour.

CHINESE

What to expect: Lupe was our masseuse for the foot reflexology, which is done on a comfy massage table with an extra cushion for the small of the back—which means this is nothing like authentic Chinese reflexology. At Kirana, the foot massage is for the feet and hands only. Strip down to your underwear and slip under the sheet. The therapist will massage the pressure points in your feet and calves and use lotion to facilitate the process, making it very soothing. Ditto for the arms and hands. It's reflexology because of the focus on the pressure points, but the experience is more upscale American spa, not ethnic Chinese reflexology.

Services offered: Swedish, deep-tissue, Reiki, warm stone and pregnancy massage and other body treatments, including reflexology, as well as organic facials and waxing. Massage add-ons include herbal poultice and aromatherapy. Gift certificates available.

Parking: Easy parking directly in front.

Why we like it: If you want a welcoming, Americanized version of Chinese reflexology, this is the place. Know your experience will be nothing like this if you go to Chinatown or San Gabriel. Check out the organic Hungarian skin-care line and pick up some discount coupons for a massage or facial.

Swan Day Spa
622 W. Arrow Hwy., San Dimas 91773
(San Dimas Station Shopping Center, near Applebee's)
909.599.9888, swansspa.com

Hours: Tues.–Sat. 10 a.m.–8 p.m.; Sun.–Mon. 10 a.m.–6 p.m.

Facilities: Swan has a steam and sauna, showers, a locker room and massage rooms that double as rooms for other

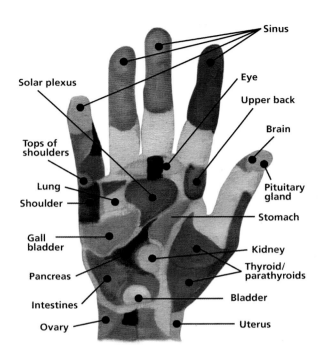

kinds of treatments. There's also a reflexology lounge for foot massages.

What to expect: Pay first, and they'll give you a robe, towels, spa sandals, disposable underwear and a locker. The space is small but clean and pleasant; the receptionist will show you around on your first visit. Body massages are given in a private room, and the foot reflexology is done in a communal lounge.

Services offered: Foot reflexology, body massage, facials, waxing and other body treatments.

Parking: Lot in front.

Why we like it: It's a pretty facility with great products for sale. It's a bit pricey, but it's often so quiet that you'll feel like you have the place to yourself, so it's worth the splurge.

SHERMAN OAKS

Super Relax Foot Massage
14449 Ventura Blvd., Sherman Oaks 91423
(Corner Van Nuys)
818.783.9999, superrelaxshop.com

Hours: Daily 10:30 a.m.–10:30 p.m.

Facilities: This strip-mall storefront has eight reclining chairs in the main room and, off to the side, two massage tables separated by large curtains.

What to expect: They'll soak your feet in warm, herb-infused water, and while you're soaking, they'll massage your head, neck and arms. After about ten minutes, they'll remove your feet from the tub and massage each one for about fifteen minutes each. After that you turn over for a back and leg massage.

Services offered: Foot and body massage.

Parking: Lot in front, which gets crowded on weekends. **Why we like it:** A traditional Chinese foot soak and massage in a clean, quiet setting.

Another location: 10160 Mason Ave., Chatsworth 91311, 818.886.8866

STUDIO CITY

Pampered Foot Spa
11384 Ventura Blvd., Studio City 91604
(1/2 block east of Tujunga)
818.763.8988, pamperedfootmassage.com

Hours: Daily 10 a.m.–9 p.m.

Facilities: In a basic strip-mall setting is a lovely little foot massage place that has eight soft reclining chairs and a private room with two chairs.

What to expect: At the entrance are heavy curtains that help block the harsh Valley sunlight. Pay for your service and enter through the curtains. It'll take a few minutes for your eyes to adjust, and once they do, you'll like what you see.

Services offered: Foot and body massage, nail services.

Parking: On the street or behind.

Why we like it: Make an appointment for a foot massage, and you won't be disappointed. The staff is courteous, and the massage is delightful. Ask for Jack.

TORRANCE

Fu Kang Health Center
22829 Hawthorne Blvd., Torrance 90505
(California Credit Union Center, between Sepulveda & 230th)
310.373.5218

Hours: Daily 11 a.m.–11 p.m.

Facilities: Past a small reception area done in soothing pastel colors are several rooms—one with two chairs for foot reflexology, and four with tables for full-body massage. We spied one lonely portable kneeling massage chair in the back; it's used for the quick (15- or 30-minute) massages.

What to expect: We tried the quick kneeling massage. After the therapist disinfected the face pad, he folded and tore a paper towel and placed it on the chair. Typically you're covered with a towel, but that didn't happen here. The beginning was the best part—standing in front of you, he uses his palms on the shoulders. It's soft on soft—no pain, no slapping. Ah, but this is Chinese, so the soft doesn't last long. When he moved to the neck, we felt like he was trying to pluck our tendons like a bass string. Normally we don't ask therapists to back off, because they're the professionals, but we had him retreat to "soft." Next comes shiatsu and deep-tissue technique down the back, and you might feel like the tissue is being separated from the spine. Also know that shirts can ride up; it's most comfortable to wear a long, loose T-shirt for this kind of treatment. Ultimately, it was an awesome massage, if a little painful. It concluded with the expected karate chops to the back, some slapping and a final pat-down.

Services offered: Foot reflexology and body massage.

Parking: In the shopping center.

Why we like it: The upper-hip massage in a kneeling chair alone is worth the price of admission. If you haven't tried one yet, it's 15 minutes you won't regret.

Torrance Massage Therapy & Foot Reflexology
1147 W. Carson St., Torrance 90502
(Cost Saver Mall)
310.320.6188

Hours: Daily 10 a.m.–10 p.m.

Facilities: A quiet place with good signage, soft lighting and a peach-colored décor, this place has a communal room with six chairs, and three private rooms, separated by real walls, and has tables for full-body massages. One room has two tables for a couples massage.

What to expect: The full-body massage we had in a private room was one of the best we've had in the area. Take off your clothes (you can leave your panties on) and get under the sheet; your body will be draped at all times except where the masseuse is working. She'll use oil to facilitate getting out the knots, but you can ask for a dry massage if you prefer. The therapists use firm pressure with their thumbs, palms and heels of their hands.

Services offered: Foot reflexology and body massage.

Parking: In the mall.

Why we like it: Good parking, easy to find, a professional vibe and, most importantly, a great authentic massage. Ask for Lee Lee.

VAN NUYS

A+ Health Center
7100 Van Nuys Blvd., #114, Van Nuys 91497
(Corner Sherman Way)
818.779.1288

Hours: Mon.–Sat. 10:30 a.m.–10 p.m.; Sun. 11 a.m.–10 p.m.

Facilities: Nine chairs arranged in three rows in a dark, soothing room with no TV. There's also an ergonomic massage chair.

What to expect: A strong reflexology session done by a staff of mostly male therapists. They accept walk-ins.

Services offered: Foot reflexology.

Parking: Lot in front.

Why we like it: The place is quiet, and the staff is professional. They provide just one service, and they do it well.

LA Natural Healing Center
6730-A White Oak Ave., Van Nuys 91406
(Corner Vanowen)
818.758.9747

Hours: Daily 10:30 a.m.–9 p.m.

Facilities: A true hole-in-the-wall with a sign outside reading "Massage Therapy & Acupuncture." Inside are four reclining chairs for foot massages and three private rooms with doors.

What to expect: A thorough and traditional acupressure/reflexology massage. The therapist knew the acupressure points and massaged them correctly, so we felt more tension relief than pain. Signs in the room remind guests that this is a professional place and not a place for prostitution.

Services offered: Foot reflexology, body massage.

Parking: Lot in front.

Why we like it: The wonderful acupressure practitioner Johnny, really knows how to unblock painful areas. He did a thorough examination first, asking where we felt pain, and he continuously evaluated the pressure, asking if we were okay. He is a true professional.

VENICE

Oceanside Health Center
1718 S. Main St., Venice 90291
(Corner Venice Way)
310.827.6797, venicehealthmassage.com

Hours: Daily 10 a.m.–9 p.m.

Facilities: This two-story building has massage rooms on both floors, and all are separated by white curtains. The overall look is light and airy.

What to expect: They'll ask you to remove your clothing, but you can keep your underwear on (we did). They'll cover you with a thin sheet, and if you're cold, they'll add a blanket. You remain covered—the therapist only removes the sheet to work on that particular part of your body. They offer oil if you like.

Services offered: Chinese acupressure, deep-tissue and sports massage.

Parking: Street or pay lot, but it's not easy to find a spot in Venice.

Why we like it: Unlike its sister operation on the boardwalk (at 517 Ocean Front Walk), this tucked-away gem is a true locals-only neighborhood Chinese massage place. Even though parking is a challenge, the casual nature and relaxed ambience make it worth the trouble.

WHITTIER

Qi Yuan Acupuncture
13211 E. Whittier Blvd., #G, Whittier 90602
(Park Plaza, between Painter & Washington)
562.907.5691

Hours: Daily 9:30 a.m.–9:30 p.m.

Facilities: This was a great little find in Whittier, with five chairs in the communal room and two tables separated by curtains.

What to expect: The reflexology foot massage we had was standard, but Jenny made it memorable because she was a little rough. Our shoulders needed it though, because we left feeling better than when we came in. Sometimes it pays to submit to the more masochistic masseuses--they are trained therapists, after all. There's a small fee for using a credit card.

Services offered: Foot reflexology, acupuncture, acupressure, cupping, stone massage and facials.

Parking: In Park Plaza.

Why we like it: A traditional Chinese massage at a bargain price.

WOODLAND HILLS

Chinese Foot Massage Happy Foot Health Center
22427 Ventura Blvd., Woodland Hills 91364
(Between Capistrano & Shoup)
818.334.7128

Hours: Daily 10 a.m.–11 p.m.

Facilities: A mini-mall joint with ten reclining chairs and one massage table, this place gets busy on the weekends, so make an appointment.

What to expect: A traditional Chinese foot soak and body massage. We added jasmine to the soak and really enjoyed it.

Services offered: Foot reflexology and foot soaks.

Parking: In a pay lot or on the street.

Why we like it: You can add jasmine, rose salt or milk to your foot soak for just a little extra. And you can get a full-body massage with your clothes on.

While you're there: Stop at Juicy Ladies next door for an organic fruit smoothie.

Island Foot Spa
22829 Ventura Blvd., Woodland Hills 91364
(Corner Fallbrook)
818.222.1388, islandfootspa.com

Hours: Daily 10 a.m.–9 p.m.

Facilities: As evidenced by the "SSSHHHH" signs posted throughout, this place promotes peace and quiet. They have ten reclining chairs and six massage beds in a room off to the side. A splashing fountain adds to the serenity.

What to expect: The foot soak and massage start with 15 minutes of a neck and shoulder massage while your feet soak in a warm (almost hot) herbal tub. Next they'll focus on your head, face, arms and hands. After they remove your feet from the herbal bath, they'll massage them, focusing on the reflexology points. The massage ends with a good back massage.

Services offered: Foot reflexology and sea salt and coconut oil exfoliation.

Parking: In back or street metered.

Why we like it: The quiet, calm experience. We added the sea salt and coconut oil exfoliation to the foot massage, and it was worth it—it really did smooth out our rough feet.

Anther location at 8640 Wilshire Blvd., Beverly Hills, 310.652.8889.

Lucky Feet
4882 Topanga Canyon Blvd., Woodland Hills 91364
(Corner Dumetz Rd.)
818.340.4088

Hours: Daily 10 a.m.–9:30 p.m.

Facilities: Eight fully reclining chairs nicely angled to give a sense of space; they also use mirrors to make the small place look larger. It's dark inside and very quiet, and there's no TV.

What to expect: A lovely foot soak and massage in a clean place. For a little extra you can add mile or rose, lavender or jasmine salts to the foot-soak tub.

Services offered: Foot soak and massage.

Parking: Lot in mall.

Why we like it: After this massage, our feet really felt lucky.

Warner Plaza Foot Spa
21793 Ventura Blvd., Woodland Hills 91364
(Warner Plaza)
818.719.8677

Hours: Daily 10 a.m.–9 p.m.

Facilities: A hole-in-the-wall in Warner Plaza, it has six chairs spread out in a communal room. They're used for both foot and full-body massages.

What to expect: Your body will be covered with a towel while your feet soak, and the therapist will drape a smaller towel over your eyes. We felt something funny in our foot bath and had to peek—it was a floating tea bag. The rest of the treatment went as expected and was great. There's a fee for using credit cards.

Services offered: Foot and body massage. Gift certificates available.

Parking: Plenty in Warner Plaza.

Why we like it: It's neat, clean and a good bargain. Ask for Nancy. And it's the first and only place we've seen that takes competitor's coupons.

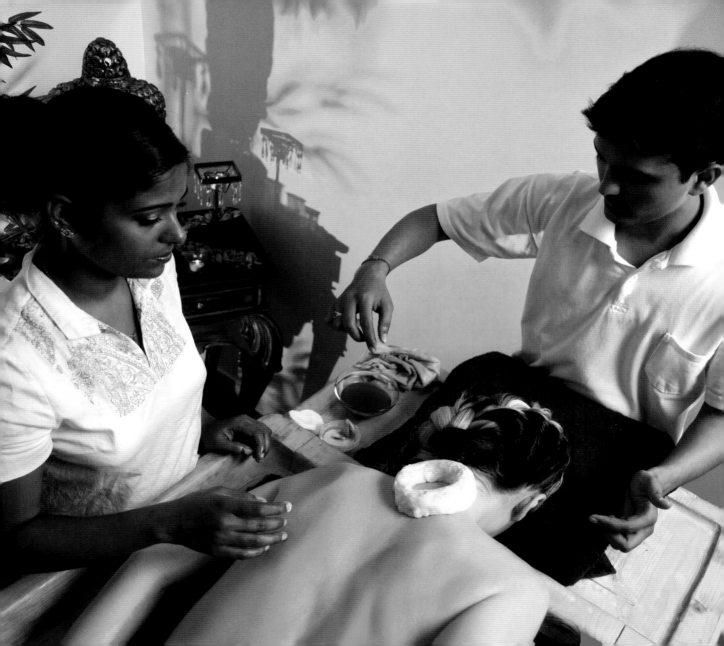

Chapter 7 –
Even More Massage Therapies

- *Indian Body Massage*

- *Indian Head Massage*

- *Lomilomi*

- *Maya Abdominal*

- *For Our Men Friends*

In our explorations across the county, we've uncovered a few treatments that are more rarely seen in L.A., but they're just as worthy of seeking out. Here are our favorites.

INDIAN MASSAGE

Indian massage, or *abhyanga*, is part of an ancient natural healing system known as *Ayurvedic*. The word *Ayurveda* comes from the combination of *ayur*, meaning "life," and *veda*, meaning "science" or "knowledge," and this "science of life" incorporates a holistic approach toward diet, meditation and yoga. Ayurveda teaches that health is the manifestation of balance between our environment, body, mind and spirit.

As with other ancient therapies, abhyanga seeks to unblock and open the channels of energy in the body. The Ayurvedic massage experience is meditative, rejuvenating and luxurious. One or two therapists can perform it in synchronicity. They use generous amounts of oil made with a blend of organic Indian herbs; as the oil is massaged into the skin, it loosens toxins. A hot towel treatment follows. This type of massage enhances the immune system, increases circulation, stimulates detoxification and creates deep relaxation in body and mind. If you have the opportunity to add steam therapy (*svedhana*) to your treatment, you'll increase the rate at which toxins are released from your body.

INDIAN HEAD MASSAGE

In this Ayurvedic bodywork treatment, also known as *champissage*, the head, neck and face are massaged with the purpose of clearing the body's energy channels. Blocked channels can contribute to illness and pain. It's a vigorous treatment that focuses on circulation to the head, neck and shoulders.

Kata basi, an Indian massage treatment

You may be fully clothed or asked to remove your top to allow access to your shoulders, where the massage typically begins. Areas worked include the upper back, shoulders, upper arms, neck and head. The movements are smooth, and the pressure to the head is quite nurturing. Be aware that they use oil liberally on your head—you will need to wash your hair afterward.

Scalp massage is good for your hair, and it's said that the stimulation also improves the brain's activity and its connection with the body. Choose this type of massage if you have insomnia or suffer from headaches, depression, eyestrain, TMJ syndrome or tightness in your neck or shoulders.

Dancing Shiva Yoga & Ayurveda Healing Spa
7466 Beverly Blvd., 2nd floor, Los Angeles 90036
(West of Martel)
323.934.8332, dancingshiva.com

Hours: Hours vary; treatments by appointment only.

Facilities: This second-floor place is primarily a yoga studio, but it also has a treatment area for massages.

What to expect: We had the abhyanga bodywork, an ancient Indian massage done with an aromatic oil made from a blend of organic herbs. We followed that treatment with *swedhana*, an herbal steam therapy.

This massage starts differently from any other we've ever had. Lying face up to start, you are asked to take three deep breaths to prepare for the anointing. The masseuse says a prayer, then pours warm oil onto your chest and limbs, massaging it in with long, gentle strokes, with the goal of opening the body's energy channels to release

toxins. The massage table is covered in plastic, which doesn't make it the most comfortable, but it's necessary because of the generous amount of oil used. The therapist pays particular attention paid to the feet, hands and heart, and oil does get rubbed into your hair, so don't arrive with freshly shampooed hair. It's a special kind of oil with a unique scent—very earthy, reminiscent of incense.

After the massage, add on the steam therapy if possible. It's done in a structure that looks like a one-man bivouac. The therapist neatly tents a sheet over your table and pumps an herbal steam into the tent. It's fabulous, and we could have stayed in there much longer.

To conclude, you can take a warm shower in the single shower in the changing room, or you can go home to shower—but you'll want to shower soon, because of the oil in your hair.

Services offered: *Shirodhara* (warm oil poured in a continuous stream over the forehead), acupressure, facials, pregnancy massage, *svedhana* (the herbal steam described above), *pinda sweda* (small bags of cooked, herb-soaked rice pressed into the body) and *kati basti*, in which the therapist creates a warm, medicated oil reservoir on your lower back with a bridge made of dough.

Parking: Two-hour spots on Gardner and Vista and two-hour street spots on Beverly, plus a small lot in back available before 9 a.m., after 5 p.m. and on weekends.

Why we like it: The anointing with oil and its spiritual symbolism are lovely.

While you're there: Grab a bite to eat afterwards at Buddha's Belly across the street (7475 Beverly Blvd.). The food is healthy and tasty, and the plates are generous enough to share.

Soul Spa & Chiropractic
341 N. Redondo Ave., Long Beach 90814
(Near Colorado)
562.438.9831, lbsoulspa.com

Hours: Tues.–Fri. 9 a.m.–9 p.m.; Sat.–Mon. 10 a.m.–6 p.m.

Facilities: Mimi is a licensed massage therapist and co-owner of this lovely little place. Two rooms in the bungalow are used for massage. She sells a skin-care line in the reception area and uses the products in the facial treatments.

What to expect: For the Indian head massage, the therapist asked us to take off only our top and bra and slip under the sheet face-up on the massage table. She began by pouring oil directly on the forehead and then massaging it into the neck, shoulders, arms and hands. She pays extra attention to the head, neck and shoulders to increase circulation and energy flow. It's a very soothing process. If you, like us, remember that blissful childhood state when your mother brushed your hair, you'll love this.

Services offered: In addition to Indian head massage, they do hot-stone, deep-tissue, sports massage, pregnancy and Swedish massage, as well as reflexology, facials, waxing and chiropractic care. Gift certificates available.

Parking: Some on Redondo, or look on the side streets.

Why we like it: Soul Spa is aptly named—we loved the homey atmosphere. Mimi is passionate about her work, and you can feel her warmth throughout. There's a real grace to this place.

LOMILOMI

In the Hawaiian language, *lomilomi* actually means massage, and this healing art comes from the ancient Polynesians. It is performed using the fingers, palms and elbows in long, continuous, sweeping strokes (think of the gracefulness of the hula). It can feel like ocean waves washing over you, particularly since different areas of your body may be massaged at the same time. This effect is magnified if you get a "four-hands" treatment—two people massaging you is a very luxurious experience.

Hawaiians believe thoughts and tension can both block the flow of energy in the body. Lomilomi unblocks energy flow, addressing not only physical pain but also mental, emotional and spiritual issues. A blessing or prayer is commonly performed before the massage begins, with the masseuse gently placing his or her hands on your back. Nut oils, such as macadamia and coconut, may be used during the treatment.

Massage Therapy Center
2130 Sawtelle Blvd., Ste. 207 (2nd floor),
Los Angeles 90025
(Sawtelle Place, between Mississippi & Olympic)
310.444.8989; massagenow.com

Hours: Mon.–Sat. 9 a.m.–10 p.m., Sun. 10 a.m.–9 p.m. Gift certificates available.

Facilities: The reception room is warm and welcoming, with a shop selling bath and beauty products. There are separate locker rooms for men and women, each with showers and a eucalyptus steam room. All the shower amenities are provided, as are plush robes, slippers and towels. All treatments entitle you to use the eucalyptus steam room and to enjoy the fruit and lemon and cucumber waters. Even if you've already showered that day, plan to shower here just before your massage. Eight rooms are used for massages, and one for facials.

What to expect: Its humble strip-mall location belies the quality of services. Once inside, you know you're in for a superior experience. From the patient history form (which you can download from the website and fill out in advance), you can tell they're all about customizing the experience for guests. Lomilomi is one of the most beautiful forms of massage in the world—it looks almost like a dance done by the practitioner, and it can take varying forms, depending on how the therapist was trained and what her family tradition is. It typically consists of graceful, sweeping arm movements and ceremonial music. Therapists use their elbows and forearms, and they usually do some fingertip shiatsu.

Services offered: Lomilomi, Swedish, deep-tissue, shiatsu, sports, Thai and couple's massage, as well as reflexology, acupressure, facials and skin care services. Follow them on Twitter or Facebook to score last-minute specials.

Parking: Two hours free parking; make sure to keep your receipt, because that serves as your validation. Be prepared for a parking challenge during peak hours.

Why we like it: First-rate massages and treatments without the snobby attitude. Within three blocks are lots of places to shop and grab a bite to eat afterward.

While you're there: Try Tofu Ya, a Korean tofu house (2021 Sawtelle); one of its rice dishes is easily shared. Favorite shops: Giant Robot Store (2015 Sawtelle), based on the successful magazine of Asian and Asian-American pop culture, where you'll find original artwork and artists, art books, notebooks, OX Uglydoll items and T-shirts;

Happy Six (2115 Sawtelle), a place for all things Angry Girl, Hello Kitty and Tokidoki (to name but a few); and Asahiya Bookstores (2130 Sawtelle, second floor) for Japanese and English books, magazines and CDs.

MAYA ABDOMINAL MASSAGE

This technique has been practiced for centuries, passed on by generations of midwives and shamans. It is a noninvasive technique performed on the abdomen and pelvis to reposition internal organs and relieve tension in the diaphragm.

The activities of daily life can cause a woman's reproductive organs to shift, which is said to obstruct blood flow, lymph vessels, nerve pathways and energy. These blockages, the theory goes, inhibit the delivery of hormones, fluids and nutrients to the organs, creating constriction in the tissues and congestion in the abdomen and pelvic areas. Maya abdominal massage puts the uterus back into place, improving both reproductive and digestive functions. This therapy is used for infertility, to lessen painful periods and to treat a displaced, fallen or prolapsed uterus.

The therapist will have you strip to your underwear and lie on a massage table. Your upper and lower body will be covered, but your stomach from just under the bust line to your pubic bone will be exposed. The therapist will use her fingertips to apply pressure vertically and diagonally, from the pelvic bone and ribs toward the belly button. It feels like your insides are being rearranged from the outside, which is an interesting sensation, to say the least. It's not painful, but you may find your stomach a little tender afterward. Maya abdominal massage should not be attempted during your period, if you wear an IUD or if you're in the first trimester of pregnancy.

Tao of Venus Wellness Center
3037 Sunset Blvd., Los Angeles 90026
(Silver Lake, near Silverlake Blvd.)
323.660.1200; taoofvenus.com

Hours: Tues.–Thurs. 9 a.m.–8 p.m., Fri. 9 a.m.–3 p.m., Sat. 11 a.m.–5 p.m.

Facilities: Beth is the kind owner of this place, moving from her previous Santa Monica location. Community acupuncture is her bread and butter, but she has a gift (and the training) to help women with fertility and other gynecological issues.

What to expect: You must fill out a health history form before your session; you can download and bring it with you or fill it out in the Inspiration Room while enjoying a cup of tea. This room doubles as a library, with books on health, fertility, cancer prevention and support. Keeping your upper body clothed, you'll strip down to your skivvies and lie on the massage table. Your legs will be covered, but your stomach will exposed from your lower ribs to the upper part of your pubic bone. This is the real estate where the work is performed. Considering all the time spent on every other area of our bodies for massage, the stomach is often left untouched. How great then, that the belly is the sole focus? The masseuse keeps her hands together, index fingers touching and thumbs tucked below, and she uses her fingertips to apply pressure as deeply into your belly as you can comfortably handle. There's no denying that the first time it's a very odd feeling. Hopefully you'll get into the groove of the deep kneading. Since this is such soft tissue, the masseuse can move her fingertips around easily, and her strokes will range from straight to spirals around the upper abdomen, rib cage, navel, lower abdomen and pelvis. Men can also benefit from the Maya abdominal, but

we haven't yet found any takers. Because the therapists believe self-care is important, they'll happily give you a lot of instruction if you have an extra 15 minutes after your massage.

Services offered: Maya abdominal massage, acupuncture, Chinese herbs, cupping and many massages, including fertility, women's, pregnancy, hot-stone, lymphatic and deep-tissue massage. Ask for Rosa or Beth.

Parking: Metered street parking in front or try a side street.

Why we like it: We think it's totally cool to have our insides repositioned—this is some serious interior decorating. If you have fertility or gynecological issues, check out Tao—and if you don't, add Maya abdominal massage to your bucket list, just for the experience. We can also recommend Rosa Rosales, a CMT in Duarte, for Maya abdominal massage. To find a certified practitioner in your area, go to arvigotherapy.com.

FOR OUR MEN FRIENDS

Dear men,

We love you and are glad to share the planet with you. This includes many of the facilities listed in this book. Unfortunately, we've observed some habits that aren't so pleasant in a spa environment. Consider these tips, which will also help if you're looking for a partner or want to keep the one you already have.

Trim your toenails. There's no apology large enough to give a masseuse for hideous-looking feet. A few well-spent minutes at home will ensure you won't have to apologize.

Stay modest. Even though you can strip down to your skivvies, it's best not to in a co-ed facility. We've been in co-ed Chinese reflexology rooms where guys have disrobed, and it was uncomfortable. It makes them look desperate for human contact, and it creeps out a lot of women. We've seen the other therapists give Underwear Guy's poor therapist a sly smile in sympathy.

Bathe before you go. Getting scented oil rubbed on your back is no substitute for a shower. You're not fooling anyone.

Tip generously. Did you know a generous man is considered more handsome? It's true!

MEN-ONLY SPAS
REVIEWED BY KEITH MALONE

GARDENA

Gardena Green Spa
1839 W. Redondo Beach Blvd., Gardena 90247
(Republic Plaza, at Western Ave.)
310.516.7892

Hours: Daily 8 a.m.–10 p.m.

Facilities: In the corner of Republic Plaza you'll see a sign that says Green Sauna. At the entrance is a small bookcase where you leave your shoes. To the right is the locker room that contains a shelf with shorts (if you want to wear them), towels and a few other amenities. Behind the locker room is a curtain that leads to the massage area, with a quiet, dark rest area on the other side. A wet area has four stand-up four sit-down showers, a large whirlpool with a skylight above it, a cold pool, a steam and dry sauna room and a table for body scrubs.

What to expect: The kind owners make you feel very welcome. They'll ask if it's your first time and show you around if you like. Take your shoes off before entering the locker room. Undress, put your clothes in the locker and head for the sauna. Large towels are not allowed in the sauna—it's pretty much a towel-less experience here, so you'd better be comfortable being naked.

Services offered: Body scrub and massage

Parking: In the mall lot and on the street.

Why we like it: The owners and staff are delightful, always making sure you are well cared for.

Seoul Health Spa
15212 S. Western Ave., Gardena 92049
(North of Redondo Beach Blvd.)
310.327.7738

   (spa only) *(services)*

Hours: Daily 9 a.m.–10 p.m.

Facilities: The unassuming strip-mall exterior belies the fairly attractive interior, which was recently renovated. The spa includes five stand-up and three sit-down Korean-style showers, a scrub table in a semi-enclosed area, dry sauna, steam room and three whirlpools: hot, warm and really cold. Beyond the locker room is a relaxation area with several recliners and a large TV, as well as a heated jade stone room laid with bamboo mats, so you can lie down and absorb the warmth.

What to expect: Pay the entry fee or treatment fee and you'll get a towel and a locker key. Take a quick shower and, if you like, make use of the sauna and steam rooms. (A rain shower sits between those rooms.) After the sauna we had a massage, which was great. They are given by sweet, very strong Korean women who walk on your back and most of your backside using the two parallel bars anchored above the massage bed.

Services offered: Body scrub, massage

Parking: In the lot or on the street.

Why we like it: Although small, the sauna is clean and quite comfortable, with plenty of amenities.

LOS ANGELES

Lions Spa
4551 W. Pico Blvd., Los Angeles 90019
(West of Crenshaw, at Muirfield)
323.931.1166

Hours: Daily 8 a.m.–9 p.m.

Facilities: This is an anonymous-looking building in a somewhat gritty neighborhood. Inside are a spacious, well-lit locker room; a resting room complete with recliners; wet and dry saunas; hot and cold tubs; a cold pool; the usual stand-up and sit-down Korean showers; a room for body scrubs; and a sleeping room with a heated onyx floor.

What to expect: Enter from the parking lot in back, pay for your entry or service fee, and get your towel and robe. If you want more towels, just ask. Take off your clothes, put them in the locker and head for the showers before you dip into any pools, go into a sauna or have a scrub.

Services offered: Body scrub, massage.

Parking: Large lot in the back.

Why we like it: The entrance fee is reasonable, as is the price for the body scrub. It was a vigorous scrub to say the

least, but well worth any discomfort. Lions may not be the most authentic in terms of the clientele, but the steam room, saunas and showers are clean and modern.

Wilshire Spa
3440 Wilshire Blvd., Los Angeles 90010
(Koreatown, at Mariposa)
213.388.4111, wilshirespa.com

   (spa only) 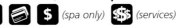 *(services)*

Hours: Daily 24 hours.

Facilities: Enter on Mariposa. Pay at the reception area and then walk downstairs to the spa, which is complete with a gym if you are want to work out. In the spa proper are hot, very hot and cold baths, a jade bath, dry and steam saunas, standing and sitting showers, scrub tables and a rest area with a heated jade floor. TVs are located throughout.

What to expect: When you check in and pay the entrance fee, you'll get an electronic locker key. Remove your shoes,

Riviera Health Spa

put them on a shelf, collect your one-size-fits-all robe and towel, and shower before you get a treatment or get into any pools. One of the hot tubs looks like a rock pool fed by a waterfall, and it's shallow enough so you can lie down in the water and rest your head on the edge.

Services offered: Acupressure, foot massage and body scrub.

Parking: Secure lot on Mariposa behind the building.

Why we like it: It's more authentic than the others. Clean, relaxed and unpretentious.

TORRANCE

The Riviera Health Spa
3601 Lomita Blvd., Torrance, 90505
(At Hawthorne)
310.375.5600; rivierahealthspa.com

    (spa only) 💲💲 *(services)*

Hours: Daily 8 a.m.–midnight.

Facilities: The men's spa area is very large and includes a steam room, elegant wet and dry saunas, seated and standing showers, a scrub table and three whirlpool tubs: hot, very hot and cold. The common area, complete with a small restaurant and juice bar, has a handsome, rustic look, with large logs serving as pillars and dividers. The floor is heated and there are plenty of mats for lying down.

What to expect: Enter, pay for your services, and get your clothing (heavy cotton shorts and a shirt) and an electronic key for your locker. There's a separate locker for your shoes. Before and/or after your treatment, allow time to cook yourself in the jade, clay and salt saunas, and then cool off in the Ice room.

Services offered: Shiatsu, Swedish and combo massages, plus body scrub.

Parking: Private lot.

Why we like it: This place is immaculate and clean, with resort-level amenities. It's family oriented but is also a great place to relax and be pampered

Index by Treatment

abhyanga, 13, 147, 148

acupressure, 13, 17, 18, 30, 46, 47, 64, 65, 67-69, 73, 75, 87, 92, 96, 97, 100, 106, 110, 115, 117, 121, 129, 135, 142, 143, 148, 150, 154

acupuncture, 13, 19, 23, 28, 41, 47, 87, 95, 96, 98, 106, 109, 110, 115, 117, 129, 142, 143, 151

aromatherapy, 13, 30, 43, 65, 84, 139

Ayurvedic, 13, 15, 23, 147, 158

banya, vi, 13, 14, 17, 81, 83, 159

body scrub, vi, 14, 15, 27, 29, 30, 31, 34, 38, 43, 44, 48, 50, 51, 59-61, 63-71, 73-78, 83, 84, 101-105, 116, 121, 138, 152-154

bulgama room, 60,69, 70, 76, 77

champissage, 15, 147

clay room, 60, 65, 68, 71, 75

coral room, 60, 75

couple's massage, 30, 32, 35, 37-39, 41, 43, 44, 50, 51, 54, 55, 77, 84, 92, 106, 108, 116, 117, 121, 122, 131, 137, 150

deep-tissue massage, 14, 17-19, 26, 27, 29-36, 38, 39, 41, 43-46, 48, 49, 51, 52, 54, 55, 64, 65, 75, 77, 83, 93, 100, 101, 106, 115, 125, 135, 139, 141, 142, 151

foot reflexology, 27, 28, 32, 39, 40, 41, 44, 56, 64, 67, 71, 95-97, 99, 102, 104-110, 112, 113, 115-117, 122-131, 133-135, 137-139, 141-144

hot-oil massage, 43, 92, 101, 106

hot-stone massage, 15, 26, 27, 30, 36, 38, 41, 44, 45, 49, 84, 92, 93, 102, 115, 121, 125, 132, 134, 149, 151

hwangto room, 60, 62, 67, 71

ice room, 60, 68, 74-76, 154

Indian head massage, vii, 15, 147, 149

jade room, 60, 62, 65, 73-75

jim jil bang, 15, 60, 61, 69, 70, 75-77

kati basti, 148, 158

Maya abdominal massage, vii, 16, 147, 150, 151

onyx room, 60, 71

pinda sweda, 148

platza, 12, 14, 17, 81-84

pregnancy massage, 16, 17, 20, 27, 28, 30, 31, 36, 39, 41, 43, 44, 49, 51, 55, 125, 139, 148, 149, 151

Reiki, 41, 93, 139

Russian Bear, 84

salt room, 60, 65, 68, 73, 74, 75

salt scrub, 73, 84, 101, 102

scraping, 98, 117, 120

shiatsu, vi, 13, 16, 17, 19, 23, 30, 36, 39, 44, 51, 64, 69, 77, 78, 87-93, 110, 111, 125, 129, 141, 150, 154

shirodhara, 148

Index

6 Star Villa Foot Spa, 127

A

A+ Health Center, 142
A&K Body Care, 30
abhyanga, 13, 147,
acupressure, 13, 17, 18, 87, 96, 97
acupuncture, 13, 19, 23, 87, 95, 96, 98
Ajenn Spa, 100
Alibaba Foot Spa, 107
Amazing Thai Swedish Massage, 49
Ancient Thai Massage, 56
Angel Thai Spa, 32
Anthony's Asian Massage Therapy, 100
Apple VIP Spa, 134
Arcadia Spa, 100
Aroma Wilshire Center, 62-63, 72-73
aromatherapy, 13
Asian Foot Reflexology, 123
Atlantic Beauty & Foot Spa, 104, 105
Aurora Foot Spa, 123
Ava Foot Massage, 132

Avant Rowland Heights Reflexology Center, 108
Ayodhya, 48
Ayurvedic, 13, 15, 23, 147, 158

B

Baipoo Thai Spa, 45
Bambu Body Works, 33
Bangkok Thai Massage, 48 51
banya, vi, 13, 14, 17, 81, 159
Bao Foot Spa, 123, 124
The Barai Day Spa, 39
A Beautiful Day Spa, 105, 106
Beauty Foot Massage, 110
Beverly Hot Springs, 58, 59, 63, 64
Body Balance Chiropractic Spa, 51
Body Healing Center, 106
body scrub, vi, 14, 15, 38, 59-61
bulgama room, 60
Burbank Spa & Garden, 124, 125
Busaba Thai Massage, 43